# THE ENJOYMENT OF THE ARTS

# THE ENJOYMENT
# OF THE ARTS

Edited by

**MAX SCHOEN**

*Essay Index Reprint Series*

 **BOOKS FOR LIBRARIES PRESS**
FREEPORT, NEW YORK

NX
165
S3

INTERNATIONAL STANDARD BOOK NUMBER:
0-8369-2173-9

LIBRARY OF CONGRESS CATALOG CARD NUMBER:
74-90678


PRINTED IN THE UNITED STATES OF AMERICA

# FOREWORD

Since the intent of this book is the subject of the introductory chapter the author wishes to utilize the space usually devoted to a preface to express his thanks to its contributors for their hearty cooperation, and to introduce them to the reader.

Thomas Munro (Painting) is Curator of Education, the Cleveland Museum of Art and Chairman, Division of Art, Western Reserve University.

Joseph Bailey Ellis (Sculpture) is Professor of Sculpture, Carnegie Institute of Technology.

Laszlo Gabor (Architecture) is Director of Display, Kaufmann's Department Store, Pittsburgh, Pennsylvania and Assistant Professor of Architecture, Carnegie Institute of Technology.

Antonin Heythum (Industrial Arts) is chairman of the faculty, Industrial Design Section, California Institute of Technology.

David Daiches (Poetry) is Assistant Professor of English, University of Chicago.

Barrett H. Clark (Drama and Theater) is Executive Director, Dramatists Play Service, New York City.

Van Meter Ames (The Novel) is Associate Professor of Philosophy, University of Cincinnati.

Milton S. Fox (The Movies) is Instructor, The Cleveland Museum of Art and The Cleveland School of Art.

Glen Haydon (Music) is Professor of Music, University of North Carolina.

George Boas (Criticism) is Professor of the History of Philosophy, John Hopkins University.

Max Schoen (The Realm, Art) is Professor of Psychology and Education, Carnegie Institute, Technology.

# TABLE OF CONTENTS

# ILLUSTRATIONS

# CHAPTER I

INTRODUCTION

THE REALM OF ART

by

MAX SCHOEN

In the Preface to *The Nigger of the Narcissus* Joseph Conrad defines art as the single-minded attempt to bring to light the very truth underlying every aspect of the visible universe by finding "in its forms, in its colours, in its light, in its shadows, in the aspects of matter and in the facts of life what of each is fundamental, what is enduring and essential— their one illuminating and convincing quality—the very truth of their existence." In his quest for the truth of nature the artist is therefore one with the scientist and thinker; but whereas the facts unearthed by the scientist, and the ideas evolved by the thinker, appeal to our common sense and our intelligence, and fit us best "for the hazardous enterprise of living," the artist "speaks to our capacity for delight and wonder," the part of our being which although less loud, less distinct, and sooner forgotten, is nevertheless more profound, more stirring and permanently enduring than the changing wisdom of successive generations. Art is "the appeal of one temperament to all other innumerable temperaments whose subtle and restless power endows passing events with their true meaning," and since an appeal to temperament can be made only through the senses, the artist struggles to blend form and substance to a perfection that may "arrest for the space of a breath, the hands busy about the work of the earth, and compel men entranced by the sight of distant goals to glance for a moment at the surrounding vision of form and colour, of sunshine and shadows; to make them pause for a look, for a sigh, for a smile . . ."

In these few insights by a supreme artist-novelist is to be found the essence of the numerous theories about art and beauty, the disagreement among which has led many persons to the conclusion that art is something that can only be felt but not explained or understood. To the serious student of the role of art in human life these contradictions are, however, more apparent than real: a difference in detail and emphasis rather than in substance. Most differences are usually readily discerned because they lie on the surface of things; and only too often a concern with them to the exclusion of their common-ground yields a superficial understanding. Intellectual strife, as Alfred North Whitehead has well said, is mainly concerned with "questions of secondary generality which conceal a general agreement upon first principles almost too obvious to need expression, and almost too general to be capable of expression." It is to these first principles of art, discovered by Conrad through his own arduous artistic labors, that the attention of the reader is here invited for his orientation in the general nature of art, before he proceeds to the study of each art in particular where differences are likely to strike him as outstanding.

## Art as Delight and Wonder

The universal identification of art with enjoyment does no more than suggest that the aesthetic interest in the world of things and events differs from that of the practical and the scientific. For both practical and scientific affairs enjoyment is of secondary importance. Food need not be flavorsome to gratify hunger or nourish the body; and an idea does not have to be palatable to possess scientific validity. But a painting, poem, or piece of music fails to fulfill its function as art unless it is a source of enjoyment to someone. The practical is a necessity, for one must act in order to live; and the scientific is an obligation, since one must inquire if he is to be intellectually honest. But the aesthetic is not a necessity, for an art object does not demand that anything be done about it, and it is not an obligation, for it raises no issue as to its truth. If it is pleasant it is both good and true; if not, it is ignored and nothing is lost. Since there is neither necessity nor obligation to enjoy there is no price to be paid for the failure to enjoy. Art is like play: one goes to it willingly and yields to it eagerly and spontaneously. He is thrilled if he plays well, while failure exacts no penalty that is not willingly paid. So, whereas the practical, scientific, and aesthetic together fulfill the call of life to act, understand, and enjoy, the last is the highest member of the trinity, for both acting and understanding are at their best when carried on the wings of joy.

The aesthetic is further distinguished from the practical and the scientific by a quality of enjoyment that is unique. The pleasure derived from a practical situation is the by-product of the elimination of a state of displeasure. We enjoy food when hungry, rest when tired, drink when thirsty, sleep when weary. Likewise it is the unpleasant awareness of ignorance or of uncertainty that compels the quest for knowledge. We are thus driven to these activities by an unbalanced state, whether of body or mind, in need of restoration to normal functioning. Such pleasures are ephemeral because the needs from which they arise keep on recurring; and moreover, these pleasures are hazardous, for the joy of today may become tomorrow's grief, and what is wisdom now may later turn out to have been but folly. Aesthetic enjoyment, on the other hand, is without any risks, encumbrances, or liabilities. No one is driven to art by any specifiable need. There is nothing particularly wrong which art sets right, for it is sought only when one is all well in mind and body. So aesthetic pleasure is not a restoration of the self to its natural condition of balance by the removal of the cause of unbalance; it is a recreation of an already wholesome self into a still higher wholesomeness by the process of transforming the focus of attention from oneself, where it usually is, to the object that is being attended to.

Under ordinary circumstances we become aware of an object only when some need compels us to pay attention to it. So the feeling that possesses us at the time is not so much a feeling for the object as for ourselves in relation to the object. But when the body is in its normal state of equilibrium, and something in the environment attracts one's attention, one is drawn out of himself by being drawn into the object. A person caught in a thunderstorm with lightning playing about him is most likely to seek refuge from the danger to himself. But it is possible that the atmospheric panorama may so engross him as to push the idea of the danger into the background of consciousness. When this happens the feeling of restlessness and anxiety is replaced by a feeling for object. An important feature of aesthetic experience is a feeling of such intensity for an object that has attracted attention to itself by virue of its own inherent qualities as to absorb the person to the exclusion of self-consciousness. Such experience is enjoyment by being experience that is entrancing, that enhances living with a moment of respite from the self that must be everlastingly preoccupied with itself in the interest of keeping alive. It is the joy that comes from a moment of life having become an eternity through the blotting out of the consciousness of time and space.

It is this unique quality of aesthetic feeling which leads us to describe its object as an object of beauty, and that makes

the experience itself a delight and a wonder. Beauty is synony-
mous with perfection, for it is only what is experienced as
fully complete, self-fulfilling and self-sufficient, to which the
term is applied. A beautiful idea differs from a good idea by
its being prized for what it is as an idea, rather than for the
consequences that may flow from it. And as an intrinsically
esteemed idea it is perfect. Likewise a deed felt to be worthy
of itself becomes a beautiful deed, versus a good deed whose
value lies in what it accomplishes. Experience that is its own
reason for being has a vitality all its own; for it is experience
in which life is attained in contrast with experience through
which life seeks attainment. Such experience is a joy that is
a delight as a respite from the life of struggle and strife; and
it is a joy that is a wonder, as an aspect of life that is encoun-
tered but rarely and quite unexpectedly. When life savors of
its own flavor, when it gains insight into itself, when it gets
to know itself for what it is by and for itself, it delights in
itself and wonders at itself. In the commonplace there is
neither wonder nor delight. But whenever in the course of
the processes of existence some fragment of life is fixed in its
course and becomes steadfast and whole, as a bit of visible
nature in a painting, a fraction of human enterprise in a drama
or novel, some one mood in a melody or poem, experience
rises to a level that is "more like life than life itself." It is
only art that ever attains such complete grasp of experience,
by inviting us to stop and look that we may truly and
for once delight in what we so intensely feel because for once
it is so wondrously clear.

## ART AS FORM AND SUBSTANCE

Art, said Conrad, is "striving for the utmost sincerity of
expression." But this dictum, like its companion that art is
enjoyment, only serves to raise the question, "Expression of

what and how?" To answer that it is expression of emotion, or even sincere expression of emotion, is not sufficient. A person in a rage expresses himself with great sincerity, yet produces anything but an aesthetic effect on an observer. Every overt act of a living body is an expression of an inner condition of the organism. Nevertheless, all expression is not art, although all expression could become artistic.

The one condition for artistic expression is that its fruit show unquestionable evidence of a sincere concern for the manner of expression. This is the basis for the popular distinction between the worker as an artist and as laborer on the ground that the artist is he who works for the sake of the work while the laborer works only for his hire. It is not so much that the artist works for the sake of the work as that he is careful of the way he is working out of a concern for the appearance, the form, of the product of his work.

The experiencer becomes an artist as soon as he begins to give thought to the most fitting way in which his experience is to be expressed; while the degree to which he succeeds in making his expression a fit record of his experience determines its aesthetic impressiveness. Thus, were the enraged person to curb the impulsive drive of his emotion by giving thought to the best way of giving utterance to it, the expression would transform the emotion from a spectacle of horror to one of beauty, as in the case of the art of acting.

Considered sincerity of expression has a significant effect both on the worker and on the product of his work. When a worker is seriously concerned with the way he is working, he is deeply engrossed in his work, lives in it, and becomes one with it. It is this living way of working that gives life to its product; that is the source of its expressive quality; and that turns the artistic way of working into the creative way of working. To create means no more than to give the old a new significance and thus regenerate it. "For don't you mark," remarks Browning's painter in *Fra Lippo Lippi,* "we're made so that we love first when we see them painted, things we have passed perhaps a hundred times nor cared to see." By investing familiar things in significant garb, in feelingful form, the artistically inclined mind brings the dead to life by compelling us to pay attention to it anew.

The substance of art is, then, feeling for form; and it is in this sense that art is expression of emotion. Feeling for object as form generates an emotion quite distinct from feeling for object as subject, and results in quite a different attitude. Where feeling is for object as subject it is feeling for oneself in relation to the object, or feeling for the object as a utility. In such feeling the object is acted upon as a means to an end. The pipe is lit to gratify the desire to smoke, otherwise it is ignored. Feeling for object as form is an interest in the object for what it is as a delight to contemplate. When the pipe is admired as a visual object the idea of its use is temporarily in abeyance. In the first instance a thing is enjoyed as subject; in the second, as object. The difference in the enjoyments is that the former is pleasure in the use of the object, while the latter is a wonderment at its beauty.

The aesthetic principle that beauty is feeling for a thing as a form, versus feeling for it as a meaningful content, does not imply however that content, or subject, is irrelevant to art. The form and content of an experience can be separated only by a deliberate act of abstraction, which is an unnatural act, and must result in an unnatural product. So art cannot ignore subject. Only for art it is the form of a subject that constitutes the substance of experience, while for workaday purposes subject is of paramount importance. Far from being exclusive of each other by being antagonistic to each other, form and content are further related by the fact that form enhances content while content enriches form. A portrait, for instance, is not a significant art work simply by virtue of resembling its subject; but neither will it be accepted as art by those who know the person if they feel that it falsifies him in physical appearance or personality, or by complete strangers who may feel that what they see contradicts their idea of a human being. The portrait must be true to life, to the idea one has of a particular acquaintance, or to that of man in general. Adherence to the truth of a thing, to the sort of thing it is, is an indispensable condition of art. But provided this condition is met, provided the beholder feels that the portrait is true to his friend, and that it is a great portrait, the quality of greatness lies in the experience that what he sees on canvas is more the true self than is the person in the flesh. The subject of the portrait has become an enhanced subject by becoming an enhanced object through the form given it by the painter.

While form enhances subject by calling attention to it through a significant presentation of it, a form in turn depends for its richness on its subject. The painter desires to paint a certain person because he is a good subject; because he offers an abundance of expressive qualities for his brush. The wealth of the whole is in proportion to the abundance of its details, and the richness of the idea the painter obtains of his subject determines the quality of the object he will produce. Herein lies another reason why form and content are inseparable. Since the artist is delineating what he observes, and only what he observes, and since the whole is the integration of its parts, and only of its parts, it is inevitable that if he paints truly what he sees the result must be a true representation of what is before him. It therefore is a foregone conclusion that if the painter knows how to draw, if he is a master of his palette, if he sees clearly, and if he is unhampered by some preconceived notions of technique or theory of art, but lets his eye guide his hand, his product will resemble his subject even more so than it does in life, for his eye catches subtleties that are missed on common occasions when they are of no importance. The artist sees his object face to face, whereas ordinarily it is seen but darkly through the glass of self-interest. It is then not a fancy but a fact, that art holds up the mirror to nature, that in art life is more like life than life itself; for by bringing form to life art also renews the life of the subject of the form.

## Two Problems in Art

The conclusion that art is a concern with the form of a subject, that the aesthetic quality of a product lies in the treatment of a certain matter in an expressive manner, finds support, at least in part, from the light it throws on the much debated issue of "art for art's sake" versus "art for man's sake," and also from the answer it gives to the equally controversial question whether art is for the many or the few.

If "art for art's sake" means that art is independent of subject, and "art for man's sake" implies that an art product is to be valued in the main for its theme, then the two are indeed exclusive; for the former would divorce art from the workaday world while the latter would make it subservient to it. The fact is, however, that life does not run away from the environment, nor does it submit to it, but uses it for the gratification of its needs. One of these needs, the need that gives rise to art and is gratified by it, is man's craving to savor the flavor of things by coming into closest possible contact with them. Such intimacy, such self-identification with things, is denied him by his practical and scientific needs, in both of which he stands over things, calculating, judging, demanding, and questioning. Art is obviously then for man's sake; but it is for man's sake only when, and in the measure to which, it is for art's sake; when the artist truly serves the function that art fulfills in human life. The man of art "lends his mind out" in the same way as the man of science and the man of practical affairs. Each of them serves man best by adhering closest to the mission for which he was designated by the special gift bestowed on him by nature.

Yet, though art does not set out to instruct man in the true or to set him on the road to the good, its salutary effect on his mind and his heart reaches even beyond its direct purpose to delight.

An art work cannot be anything but wholesome in its influence on several counts. First of all, as enjoyment of the nature of delight, it raises the self to a realm of experience cleansed of the dross and dirt, the strife and struggle, the back-biting and back-sliding, which more often than not are the sum and substance of day-to-day existence and make it a burden that must be borne with patience and fortitude. The one common thread that weaves through the historical theories of beauty is this power of art as a spiritual tonic for life. No one can leave what is to him a great performance of a great play or symphony without the feeling that for once he had been in touch with perfection; that for a moment which was also an eternity, God was truly in His heaven because all was truly right with the world. This is the good at its highest because it is life at its best.

Then again, if the right in human action is action in keeping with personal integrity, action that promotes the harmonious operation of personality, then art sets the model for right action by being an attainment in harmony. There can be no test or standard for right action other than harmonious social operation; for even the moral precepts of social convention aim at the prevention of social disintegration. It is in the art work that the highest integration is attained, for the artist at work is guided in his choice of each stroke he makes by his vision of the whole. The integrity of the whole is thus attained by the integrity, the rightness, of each of its parts. For this reason an art product is the attainment of an ideal, a realization of the ultimate. He who would apply the lesson of art to his personal life, who would guard his behavior and his thoughts as does the artist every one of his brush strokes, would be on the way of turning his personality into as shining an example of an attainment in creative living as the art work is in creative working. And a society that would set itself to the task of bringing about an integrated social body by as conscientious a choice of its individuals through its educational process as that of the artist in the selection of his material, could have the assurance that it was doing everything within its power to bring about a state of progressive social harmony through increasing social coopera- tion among its component members. The spirit of art is the spirit of wholesomeness, and the emulation of this spirit by human beings in their daily contacts and ordinary daily affairs would assure the creation of what would be truly an artistic social body.

Finally, where the spirit of art rules evil is inevitably outlawed. The evil is the ugly, the repulsive, while the repul- sive is the distorted, the unwholesome, which is abhorrent to art. By stressing the beautiful, art sensitizes us to the ugly and creates the will for its elimination. Art is witness to the fact that there is nothing ugly in life which does not arise from a distortion of the true. It is for this reason, as is witnessed by the subject-matter of some of the greatest masterpieces of fiction, drama, and painting, that the dross of common life is transformed into purest gold by the alchemy of art, and it may even be, as has often been proclaimed, that the thirst for beauty arises precisely out of the desire to escape from the ugliness generated, in the words of Romain Rolland, by "the common horse-pond, where, as they drink, men stir up the mud with their feet, . . ." "What a comment on life is the least strain of music!" exclaimed Thoreau. "It lifts me above the mire and dust of the universe . . . Suppose I try to describe faithfully the prospect which a strain of music exhibits to me. The field of my life becomes a boundless plain, glorious to tread, with no death or disappointment at the end of it. All meanness or trivialness disappears." Here is a purifying agent, a spiritually unlifting influence, which does not require any sense of duty or social threat for its compulsive power. Art is an influence which by its spontaneity, its intensity and its joy, teaches man that the life of virtue is not something that must be paid for by the denial of life, but something that is rather rewarded with the attainment of life.

The problem of "art for the many or the few" arises from the failure to recognize the psychological fact that whereas the need for art experiences is present in all human beings, all are not susceptible to it in equal measure. These differences in the degree of aesthetic susceptibility between individuals correspond to the differences in the degree of aesthetic quality possessed by different art works. There is art wherever there is considered expression; nevertheless considered expression ranges from the verses of Edgar Guest to those of Keats and from a popular tune to the melodic achievements of a Beethoven or a Brahms. Pope touched the heart of the matter when he wrote that

> "Tis with our judgments as our watches, none
> Go just alike, yet each believes his own.
> .. .. .. .. .. .. .. .. .. .. .. ..
> Yet if we look more closely, we shall find
> Most have the seeds of judgment in their mind;
> Nature affords at least a glimmering light;
> The lines, tho' touched but faintly, are drawn right."

# THE REALM OF ART

Good art is like good food. Food is good if it nourishes the body. Yet the same article of food does not provide equal amounts of nourishment for all bodies. So food is not for the few, nor for the many, but for all in accordance with the sort of food each needs and the amount of it he needs. Likewise good art for any person is the art that meets his need for aesthetic experience. It is the art at the level of considered expression he can absorb. The composer of a popular tune strives as much for utmost sincerity of expression as does the creator of a musical work destined for the ages. The distinction lies not so much in the earnestness of the striving as in the depth of the attaining. Both have their wagon hitched to a star; only their stars are not equi-distant from the earth. And whereas it is true that one's reach should exceed one's grasp, it is equally true that one can reach only for what is within his potential grasp, unless he is to reach for a phantom. But the reach that is within one person's grasp is as valid a grasp for him as is a higher grasp for another. Higher and lower do not designate superiority and inferiority; they do no more than point out differences and the need for their recognition. Pope recognized this when he wrote further that

> But as the slightest sketch, if justly trac'd
> Is by ill-coloring but the more disgrac'd
> So by false learning is good sense defac'd
> Some are bewilder'd in the maze of schools,
> And some made coxcombs Nature meant but fools.

There is no need for anyone to be bewildered by the maze of schools in art any more so than by the varieties of views in politics, religion, and even science and philosophy. Mazes of schools are not necessarily indications of confusion among their makers. They are different approaches to the same truth, some of which undoubtedly lead into blind alleys. He who is bewildered by the schools is responsible for his own bewilderment through his failure to recognize that schools only provide him with the opportunity to chart his own way on the sea of thought. He need not unbutton his mind for all the winds of doctrines to raise a storm in it; he need only open it to them to stir it into activity. The intelligent person uses these conflicting views to arrive at a view of his own; to discover the ground on which he stands, and to realize that it is not the only ground that is firm. So the fool in the realm of art, as the fool in any other sphere of thought, is not born but made. Let him be natural by being true to himself and he ceases to be a fool. The truth about art is that there is art for everyone in keeping with the measure of his craving for aesthetic experience. No one has an intellectual obligation beyond knowing his own taste, which will prevent him from suspecting the soundness of a taste other than his own.

## THE REQUISITES FOR AESTHETIC ENJOYMENT

The preceding examination of the nature of art and the service it renders life points to the fact that he who would receive in full measure what an art work has to offer him must come to it with a state of mind that is well disciplined along two lines.

One discipline is a clear understanding of the relationship that exists between the creative worker and the fruit of his work. What the relationship is has been well described by W. Somerset Maugham. "It is not for nothing," he wrote from his own personal experience, "that artists have called their works the children of their brains and likened the pains of production to the pains of childbirth. It is something like an organic thing that develops, not of course only in their brains, but in their heart, their nerves and their viscera, something that their creative instinct evolves out of the experience of their brain and their body and that at last becomes so oppressive that they must rid themselves of it." If this is a true account of the creative process, and if the fruit of the process is in truth what Milton called it, "the precious lifeblood of a master-spirit," it must be granted that the person who would judge the value of such a manifestation of the human spirit entirely by its effect on himself is doing a grave injustice to its creator. The art product is a reflection of its maker. It is more than a part of him. It is himself at his best; and whereas all those who are not pleased with his best are entitled to ignore him, they have no right to judge him. All that is to be expected of a human being is that he do his utmost to be honest with himself. This is a virtue in which the creative worker is supreme; and it is a virtue that is easily recognizable in his work. The first requisite for the aesthetic enjoyment of an art work is, then, a proper respect for it, which is cultivated by an honest effort to understand its significance as a striving for the utmost sincerity of expression.

The habit of judging art works instead of trying to understand them also renders the judge a great disservice by erecting a wall between him and the object judged. It does this in more than one way. Even good habits become liabilities when permitted to control instead of being controlled. Many art critics are a case in point. They follow the easy path of fault-finding to the point when they become blinded to all merit. One can always find what he is looking for if he looks only for what he is out to find. This is one reason why the layman in art should be wary of professional critics. But the layman himself can become a victim of his own critical tendencies. The number of persons is legion who are attracted to the concert hall, theatre, or art exhibition mainly by the opportunity it affords them to judge the merits of what they see and hear and thus make a display of their superior tastes or knowledge. Their pitiful condition is so much the greater, that they are unaware of their blindness; that instead of yielding themselves freely, eagerly, and hopefully to the delights that may be in store for them, they enclose themselves in a wall of self-complacency and a smugness that even the brightest of aesthetic lights may not be able to penetrate.

The condition of the person who would reject a work of art after a single unfavorable contact with it is no happier than is that of the habitual critic. First impressions are not to be trusted for they are superficial. It is a fact of everyday observation that a person one dislikes after a single encounter often becomes one's cherished life-long friend as a result of further acquaintance. It is only the superficial that can be superficially grasped. The simple, the easy to comprehend, has no lasting qualities, having no depth, no promise for the future. Popular art owes its vogue to its obviousness, and for that reason it is here today and gone tomorrow. A rich idea comes from a rich mind; and spiritual wealth never comes all of a sudden, as material wealth sometimes does. The seed is planted in the soul where, if it takes root at all, it grows slowly by imperceptible steps into the fullness of its powers, but only with careful and patient cultivation. The case is indeed as Plato described it, that "after long intercourse with the thing itself, and after it has been lived with, suddenly, as when the fire leaps up and the light kindles, it is found in the soul and feeds itself there." So out of fairness to the creative idea, as well as for one's own sake, it is best to cling to the initially elusive, for its very elusiveness may contain the promise of its worthiness, and therefore how can one know but that his reward for persistence may not be out of all proportion to the effort expended in vistas of hitherto unsuspected depths of experience. And if the hoped for reward does not come there is still satisfaction in knowing that the failure to receive was not due to the unwillingness to give.

What leads a person to mistake his response to an art work for a judgment of its worth as art is not only his failure to respect it for its expressive significance to its maker, but also his neglect to ascertain his own aesthetic needs. The virtue of self-knowledge is equally effective on all fronts of human experience, for wherever it operates there it introduces order and harmony by outlawing misunderstanding. One cannot have traveled far along the road to self-knowledge without having discovered the fundamental principle, already spoken of in a previous connection, that whereas all human beings are motivated by the same needs, the motivation for any one need is not equally strong in everyone. In what they need, men are alike; in how much they need there are differences from person to person. So it happens that what is but a convenience to one, is a necessity for another. Beethoven lived in his music, as did Keats in his poetry; which is the reason why they were creative in their respective fields. For many persons music, poetry, or any other art, is, in the main, an occasional source of recreation. To such persons it is but to be expected that neither the music of Beethoven nor the poetry of Keats is likely to appeal, since they have no need for aesthetic products of that level of vitality. This is nothing to be deplored. It is but a law of human nature that must be recognized in order to avoid pretense, confusion, and distortion of personality. The application of this principle of individuality in art would have two salutary effects. It would lead to the conviction that the question, What is good art? is to be answered realistically only by another question, Good for whom? And once this question is injected into any disputation about tastes the light of reason introduces sanity into the heat of emotion. It would also prevent anyone from mistaking his feeling for an art object for a judgment of its artistic value. Instead of condemning that which failed to "take him in" the person would conclude either the possibility that it is beyond his reach, or the probablity that the first impression is not to be trusted. His self-knowledge, coupled with his knowledge of the nature of art, would do justice both to himself and to the artist, by granting to each the inherent right to selfhood.

The self-knowledge needed for the right estimation of an art product is of two sorts. One of them concerns one's temperamental nature, the other one's sensory equipment.

Temperament is the quality of emotion which provides each personality with its unique color. Now whereas it cannot be said that any one color is, in itself, better than another, there are nevertheless color preferences among human beings. And so it is with human temperaments. One temperament is as good as another; but in the interaction of temperaments it is but natural that any one temperament should respond most favorably to one of its own sort.

The bearing of these considerations about personality preferences on art appreciation is that since art is an expression of feeling, the creative output of an artist is necessarily a reflection of his temperament. The art product is the personality of its maker, and though the brain children of the creator are not duplicates of each other, each of them bears the stamp of its begetter. Together they constitute one family, the members of which are quite distinct from each other, yet sufficiently like each other to indicate a common origin. These variations in temperaments of the creators of art products correspond to the temperamental differences among those who come in touch with them; so that a show of favoritism is but to be expected. Every individual contemplates an art work through the colored glass of natural prejudice. This is inevitable. What is not inevitable is that a natural prejudice should produce the unnatural result of condemning whatever does not fit into its own framework. Once the naturalness of individual temperament of both artist and spectator becomes recognized and cherished, and once the spectator looks upon his contact with art works as an adventure in self-discovery and self-fulfillment, quarrels about differences in taste will be replaced by reports of joyful adventures in the gratification of taste.

The need to get acquainted with one's sensory equipment is prompted by the consideration that just as there are variations in temperament, so individuals differ in the way their sense organs function. All eyes and ears are not equally keen; and since each art has its own sensory material, it follows that an art can appeal to one only in proportion to his sensitivity to its medium. This is but another form of the general rule that one receives in the measure to which one gives. And one cannot give what he does not possess, or any more than he possesses. In many cases the failure to be impressed is due not so much to the spectator's inattention as to hazy perception traceable to sensory inefficiency. The profoundest of ideas is bound to be lost on him who is a stranger to its language. The most delicate of rhythms is wasted on one who does not possess a delicate sense of rhythm. This means that the person who is unaware of the state of his sensory equipment is likely to conclude that "there is nothing" to that which he has seen or heard instead of placing the blame where it truly belongs. Again, this is not something to be deplored; it is rather a fact to be recognized and to act upon.

The action called for is the discovery by each person of the art to which he is most responsive and from which he is therefore most likely to receive the highest aesthetic pleasure most frequently. No one is equally sensitive to the different artistic materials. A keen and discriminative visual sense, for instance, which makes one highly susceptible to pictorial impressions, may exist side by side with an auditory equipment so dull that to listen to music that is not of the most obviously tuneful sort becomes a torture. A master of literature like Charles Lamb, in writing of his musical adventures, reported that

"Above all, those insufferable concertos, and pieces of music, as they are called, do plague and embitter my apprehension. Words are something, but to be exposed to an endless battery of mere sounds; to be long adying; to lie stretched upon a rack of roses; to keep up languor by unintermitted effort; to pile honey upon sugar, and sugar upon honey, to an interminable tedious sweetness; to fill up sound with feeling, and strain ideas to keep pace with it; to gaze on empty frames, and be forced to make the pictures for yourself; to read a book, *all stops,* and be obliged to supply the verbal matter; to invent extempore tragedies to answer to the vague gestures of an inexplicable rambling mine —these are faint shadows of what I have undergone from a series of the ablest executed pieces of this empty *instrumental music.*

For the same person one art can be meat and another poison. Nature is but rarely lavish with all-round endowments, and even to the few she favors most highly, she distributes her gifts unevenly. So be the case what it may, it is best to know one's best avenue to aesthetic enjoyment in order that one may make the most of it.

This book offers the reader the means for attaining his orientation in the realm of art by a careful study of what those who have a right to speak have to say about the art which is their main interest because it is the art to which they are most highly responsive. The reader should be on guard against overstressing disagreement among writers on art to the neglect of agreement. Scientists may not agree on the scientific worth of a certain piece of research, but on the nature and value of the scientific outlook and scientific procedure they are of one mind. Likewise, disagreement among art authorities often occurs as to the artistic worth of individual art products, and only rarely in their conception of the intent of the artist and the role of art in human life. So whereas the reader of this volume is likely to encounter clashes among its contributors, let him make sure that he does not fail to discern the forest because of the trees.

Chapter II

# THE ENJOYMENT OF PAINTING

by

Thomas Munro

Painting as an art is usually understood to mean the painting of pictures. In a broad sense painting can be used, not to make pictures, but to cover a house or a chair with a uniform coat. On the other hand, a picture is not necessarily a painting; it can be made by drawing, etching, photography, or even mosaic or tapestry. It is called a painting when made with oils, tempera, water-colors, or some other type of paints. These are spread with brushes or other instruments on a surface, which is usually flat, rectangular, and definitely marked off, as by a frame. Canvas, plaster, wood, paper, and silk are the commonest types of surface.

A painting is usually a picture of something; it represents some object, scene or person. This is called the "subject" of the picture. A picture represents a subject by arranging lines and color areas so as to resemble it, and thus call it to the observer's mind. He may then (if he is willing to yield to the illusion) be able to imagine for a moment that he is looking at the "real" scene itself, and not at mere paint. This is especially easy when the picture is comparatively realistic, looking very much as the scene would look from a certain viewpoint under certain conditions of light and atmosphere.

But pictures, and the art of painting, are not restricted to realistic representation. Often the resemblance to any natural object is slight or absent, as when the painter is interested only in the decorative or expressive effects of lines and colors in themselves—e.g., to make a design, or express joy or agitation. Then the painting is said to be "abstract," since it leaves out most of the details which a concrete object shows. Abstract paintings are also called pictures, even though they are not pictures of anything in particular. They have, in common with representative pictures, at least the basic aim of interesting the observer through an arrangement of differently colored streaks of paint.

(*Courtesy Freer Gallery of Art, Wash., D. C.*)

**Fig. I**

**Chinese (Sung Dynasty): Emperor and Sage**

From the standpoint of technique and physical form, paintings are divided into several main classes. The commonest are "easel" paintings, of a size which is capable of being made on an easel and hung in a frame on the wall of a room. "Mural" paintings are usually larger, and made directly on a large wall, or on canvas applied so as to be hardly distinguishable from the wall. They are sometimes made in "fresco"— that is to say, with paint applied to the plaster while it is still moist so that it penetrates a little way and is fairly durable. Mural paintings were popular in medieval and Renaissance churches, and have once more come into favor, especially in Mexico and in American government art projects. At the other extreme of size are "miniature" paintings, such as those made to embellish the pages of medieval manuscripts. Slightly larger are album or portfolio paintings, especially water colors on paper, which may be framed and hung if one wishes.

As compared with drawing and etching, oil painting is like a full orchestra in comparison with a solo violin or string quartet. It is capable of great variety, richness and intensity of color effects, and of realistic textures and atmospheres. It can yield the finest of delicate line drawing or coarse, thick slabs of paint applied with a palette knife. Pencil drawing, etching, engraving, black-and-white photography, and similar mediums have a narrower range of effects. But this does not mean that their products are necessarily inferior. A simple melody for violin alone, written by a master, may be greater than a symphony by a mediocre composer. Many artists who use oil paint are not capable of bringing out its possibilities, and their work seems crude beside a simple sketch by Michelangelo or Rembrandt.

Each medium, each type of paint, has qualities of its own. It can yield certain kinds of effect more easily than others can. Water colors, for example, tend to produce a rather dry, powdery surface. They easily yield a thin, delicate brushstroke, with luminous glimpses of white paper showing through, which is well suited to a sketchy, abbreviated mode of painting. Pictures which emphasize the effects most natural to a certain medium are said to "express" that medium, and to achieve consistency between medium and form. They are often praised by critics for that reason, in preference to those which could be done equally well in some other medium. For example, critics sometimes condemn a watercolor which displays a thick, rich, glossy surface, more natural to oils. A

Fig. 2
Giorgione: A Concert in the Open Air (Paris)

versatile artist tends to choose different kinds of paint for different kinds of picture. One whose skill is more specialized may prefer to stick to his favorite medium, and try to make it produce a wide range of effects. In the hands of a gifted artist, any medium can disclose new possibilities, and one is not necessarily bound to do only the conventional sort of thing with it.

The subjects represented in painting, since its origin in the caves of Ice-Age France, range through all the world of man's visual experience and imagination. They include not only the fellow-humans, animals, plants, and landscapes, the stars and lightning, the man-made towns and utensils which he can see, but hosts of things of which he can only dream— the gods and demons, fairies, imps and monsters with which his imagination has peopled the unseen world.

The greatest paintings of the ancient empires were mostly portrayals of gods and minor spirits, or of earthly kings and nobles, shown in an austere, godlike way, often in triumph over their enemies. But, not infrequently, the ancient painter found an excuse to express his love of humbler creatures, such as the animals of the chase and farm, the servants of the royal house, the trees, flowers, and food that exemplified the master's wealth.

Humanistic movements in Graeco-Roman and oriental culture, and again in the European Renaissance, turned the painter's eyes away from visions of deities to human beings of all sorts: noble and commoner, rustic and city-dweller, abstract types and peculiar individuals, nude and clothed, adults and children. As a transition, the divinities of Greek and Christian religion were represented in a fleshly, naturalistic way, from human models. People were shown in every conceivable situation and activity of life: in war and peace, work and play, love and commerce, feasting and mourning, dancing and worshipping, until the art of painting became a detailed, vivid record of human life in all its aspects, during all the main periods of civilization.

Landscape appeared at first only as a subordinate background for these figures, but later grew in importance to be a subject of patient and admiring contemplation in itself.

There were grand vistas of parks and mountains, then humbler scenes of ordinary fields and farms. Still life objects—flowers, fruit and other foods, dishes and utensils—attracted the painter, not only for their human associations, but also for

Fig. 3

El Greco: Burial of the Count of Orgaz (Toledo)

their variety of shapes and colors, their easy arrangement into compositional groups. Many of these shifts of interest in subject matter have occurred several times in the history of painting. For example, there was a rise of humanistic and everyday subjects in late Greece and Rome, and again in the late Renaissance, after the medieval return to otherworldly religious art.

Even in representing the common sights of the world, the painter has done so in ways which express his age and his individual personality. For art is always selective; it is impossible for an artist ever to set down every visible detail of a scene or object, even if it were desirable. Inevitably and more or less unconsciously, he sets down those aspects which seem to him especially important, memorable and significant, typical or unique, beautiful or ugly, good or evil. Even when he includes many details of what he sees, he tends to emphasize certain ones, through giving them a central position, large size, bright light or rich coloring. To be sure, artists differ in their powers of selection, and the result is apparent in their work. Some select comparatively little, trying to set down everything they see. Some select, in a hackneyed, conventional way, aspects of nature which have been pointed out by many artists before them. Some select the trivial and some the important aspects—but it is hard indeed to tell which is which, for apparently trivial details can be profoundly significant and moving.

When the artist sees and selects in a fresh, original way, and sets down his choice for us to see, the result is to open our eyes to something we had never noticed before, and could not have noticed without his help. Visual and other phenomena crowd so swiftly before us all the way through life, and we have so many distracting problems, that we seldom stop to look at any one thing closely. The painter says to us, "Wait a moment! Stop and see just how a wild goose looks when flying, silhouetted against the sky at dusk. Notice the different reddish-brown textures of a copper pot, a carrot and a crust of bread, by candle-light. Compare the jagged branches of a weathered pine-tree with the graceful lines of a weeping willow. See how a wounded soldier falls, clutching the arrow in his throat. See how an old woman bends under a heavy burden." Each time we accept his invitation, we receive a visual experience that is clearer and sharper than the ordinary. We remember it, and notice that sort of thing in nature and life more clearly, when next we encounter it. The result of looking at many pictures in this way is to develop our whole mechanism of visual perception; to give it powers of sharper

Fig. 4
Brueghel: The Return of the Hunters (Vienna)

focus, wider range, and more complex organization. Wherever we go, even among scenes that ordinary people consider ugly and boring, even in filth and desolation, we see visible forms that excite our interest.

The artist's more imaginative flights also reveal his basic thoughts, fears, and aspirations, as when he depicts his conception of a god, of heaven and hell, or of the long-lost Golden Age on earth. This is one source of the endless fascination which painting holds for those who have studied it in the light of psychology and cultural history. It is one of the most revealing types of human expression. It is almost universal, occurring in every important culture. As compared with literature, it is more readily understood by the foreigner, more concrete and tangible.

Through pictorial representation, human eyes and hands are able to save for a time a few cherished images from the eternal process of change and decay, which destroys all beautiful as well as ugly things. There is much justice in the artist's claim that he can "immortalize" the subject of his portrait. But, with cynical humor, he sometimes chooses to immortalize qualities other than those of which the subject is proud—his pompous hypocrisy, perhaps, or a cruel line about the mouth. Thus painters such as Rembrandt and Goya often present us with vivid psychological data. They are interested in preserving, as long as paint and canvas last, not only human nature but revealing glimpses of all types of phenomena, from the most enduring rock to the momentary sheen of sunlight on a butterfly's wing. Unlike the motion picture, which usually changes faster than the world itself, static pictures give us time for leisurely, renewed observation, so that we can return again and again to savor the full quality of a particular visual experience. Since the picture endures for careful scrutiny, it can be packed with intricate detail, as in some of Brueghel's canvases, enough to hold the attention for many hours of study.

It was mentioned above that some pictures are realistic, while others sacrifice realism to design or expression. One of the commonest mistaken assumptions of the layman in regard to painting is that all pictures are trying to do the same sort of thing—that is, trying to give an accurate representation of some person or scene in nature. Accordingly, he judges a picture by two criteria: is the subject interesting, beautiful, amusing, etc., and is it accurate lifelike, true to nature? He tends to like and enjoy it only if the answer is "yes" to both

Fig. 5
Rembrandt: Artist's Mother (Vienna)

questions. Now there is nothing wrong in liking a picture for these characteristics. Let us add, there is nothing wrong in enjoying pictures for any reason whatever, or in any way one chooses. Any way that yields harmless enjoyment is to that extent a good way, and no connoisseur has a right to condemn it. As a matter of fact, many of the paintings recognized as great by connoisseurs are true to life and interesting for the subject represented. But there are also other great pictures which lack one or both of these characteristics. When the layman closes his eyes to them, he is depriving himself of a rich additional source of interest and pleasure. Perhaps he is so constituted as to be unable to enjoy them; but many others, once similarly blind to non-realistic art, have learned to do so. There is no reason to argue here about which kind of art is best; the fact is that many kinds exist, and a person who can enjoy them is well off in the same way as one who can enjoy many kinds of food, amusement, place, and people. The world possesses fewer dull spots for him; his enjoyment is less dependent on any one sort of thing.

Non-realistic painting has been common in other periods than ours. In Persia or Byzantium there would have been no need to defend it. But in Europe and America during recent centuries, the trend was strongly toward realism, and frequently toward the neglect of other elements in art. In the work of great European masters, these other elements were present along with realism; but the public has often failed to notice or appreciate them. Toward the end of the nineteenth century, there came a revival of interest in decorative painting, partly through the influence of Japanese prints, Persian miniatures, and other exotic styles. An interest in pictorial form for its own sake, aside from subject-matter, was fostered by critics and theorists. This has flourished ever since.

It has been carried to an extreme of specialization by some "post-impressionist" painters, and combined by others with a moderate realism. Picasso, for example, has specialized at various stages of his career on different components in pictorial form. Sometimes his pictures bring out the linear contour of objects in wiry sharpness, devoid of shadows. Some of his pictures emphasize solid masses, and the bulging of giant muscles. Others, on the contrary, flatten out everything, until a still-life composition becomes a patch-work design of light and dark, vari-colored areas. He has painted faces as if they were weirdly stylized African masks, and again with nightmarish expressions of war's pain and terror. The styles of

Fig. 6
Le Nain: Peasant Family (Paris)

painting thus produced differ radically from each other, so as to be hardly recognizable as the work of the same man. Each gives a distinctive and powerful visual and emotional effect, whether or not one considers them beautiful. Indeed, post-impressionist art has been little interested in conventional types of beauty—the pretty girls of magazine covers, the appealing children, lovely flowers and sunsets of popular art. It prefers new, striking effects of shape and color, and adaptations of exotic, unfamiliar styles. These often seem ugly to the public, though advance-guard enthusiasts discover new kinds of beauty in them.

Few modern artists have specialized along so many different lines as Picasso. But many artists have chosen to specialize on some particular aspect of visible form, such as geometric shape or sunlight reflection. Whatever they choose, they tend to emphasize it in a way which seems exaggerated at first sight; also, they tend to leave out some of the features which delight us in the old masters. An old-master painting, by Titian or Vermeer for example, is usually an all-round, many-sided picture, capable of interesting all sorts of people in different ways. It has subject and story interest, and usually the charm of showing beautiful people in a beautiful setting. In adopting a more coldly analytical viewpoint and pursuing specialized experiments, recent art has been somewhat analogous to modern science, with its minutely subdivided researches. Perhaps a new period of synthesis will come after the war. But there is still much to be done in assimilating the newly discovered exotic styles, and in trying out new technical methods and materials.

Meanwhile, it is not surprising that the layman is puzzled and often offended by the bizarre effects of modern art. Where there is a recognizable subject, altered so as to heighten design or expression, he is apt to feel an ugly or freakish quality of "distortion." Natural proportions of limbs and features, for example, may be altered so as to produce a design through the repetition of certain curves or angles. The layman sees only the distortion, the failure to be true to life; he misses the design, because his eyes have not been trained to perceive it. Those who learn to perceive design tend to be interested more in the positive aspects of such a picture. The differences from nature cease, as a rule, to annoy them.

It is sometimes asked, "Why cannot the artist leave out representation entirely, and give us pure design, instead of distorting nature?" He can, and sometimes does; but then he loses the important source of interest which images from nature give to art. A musician may start with some natural

Fig. 7
Chardin: Still Life (The Hague)

sound, such as a bird-song or a waterfall, and turn it into a piano composition. It will be altered or "distorted" by comparison with the original sound; but this is not found unpleasant, even when the general resemblance is noted. "Why not the same mode of treatment in painting?" asks the post-impressionist.

There is no settling the issue by argument, as to whether he has a "right" to do so, and whether the result will be pleasing or not. Some observers will remain stubbornly opposed, and there is no logical way of proving them wrong. But several facts are relevant. In the first place, the "distortion" which post-impressionism practices is nothing new, but much older and more common in the history of art than strict visual realism. Countless millions of people have enjoyed that sort of art. Secondly, a great many people in recent years, through learning to look at paintings in terms of pictorial form, have come to enjoy it intensely, both in post-impressionism and in older art. If the stubborn conservative refuses to like it, he is injuring nobody but himself—except when, through some influential position in schools or elsewhere, he deprives his students also.

A third fact is that nearly everyone, conservative realists included, likes "distortion" when it is frankly caricature, and done for comic or controversial reasons. What most people need to learn is only that non-realistic pictures are not necessarily funny; that they can be enjoyed for serious reasons also: for the decorative beauty of patterns and color-relations, or for expression of moods and abstract qualities as in music. The value of such reasons cannot be verbally proved, but it is a common fact of experience that repeated study of non-realistic art (the best of it; some has no justification at all) often leads people to like it more and more without the need of argument.

Like other arts, painting contains several factors besides representation. It contains a decorative factor whenever lines and colors are arranged so as to repeat certain themes—e.g., red and blue areas, angles and curves. When such thematic relations are fairly complex and unified, we have a visual design. The appearance of unity, coherence, or integration is produced in various ways: especially by similarity of parts, and by subordinating details to some underlying general pattern. Extreme similarity and unity tend to make a picture

Fig. 8
Hiroshige: Taiko Bridge (Cleveland)

monotonously simple and static; it ceases to hold the attention. Contrast and irregularity make for surprise and dynamic tension; carried to extremes, they become chaotic. Romantic tendencies in art favor a comparatively high degree of irregularity; classical and austerely formal tendencies favor unity, balance, and symmetry. As a rule, styles in painting fluctuate somewhere between the two extremes, trying to achieve a design that is almost but not quite regular, combining some unity with some variety. Both romantic and classic movements have occurred many times throughout the history of art.

There is a slight amount of decorative, thematic development in most pictures. It can exist along with realistic representation, or take the place of it to any desired degree. A favorite game of the painter is to conceal his design in an apparently realistic picture, by slightly emphasizing and developing the thematic relations which occur naturally in any scene. For example, in portraying a child in a garden, he can intensify a little the redness of her mouth and hair-ribbon; of roses and a painted watering-can in the background; thus bringing out a thematic series of bright red areas. If distributed through the picture, these tend to hold it together as well as to contribute an effect of decorative pattern. Painters like to stress the contrast of flowing curves in the human figure, and in clouds, trees and vines, with the rigid straight lines and angles of architecture, furniture, floor tiles, books and boxes. In the works of Titian, Veronese, Rubens and Vermeer, a strong design is achieved by such means, with little distortion. But in such post-impressionists as Cézanne, Matisse, Picasso, and Braque, design tends to become more abstract and dominant, with greater departure from nature.

In noticing the decorative aspects of painting, the observer is paying attention to what is directly visible; to what is directly presented to his eyes, rather than what is suggested to his imagination. The layman tends to miss these directly visible qualities in thinking too much about what the picture represents; about the people or places depicted, and how he might deal with them in real life. For that reason, great emphasis is now laid, in teaching the appreciation of painting, on learning to perceive lines, colors, light and dark areas,

Fig. 9
Cézanne: Peasant (Water-color, The Hague)

textures, masses and spaces, without regard to what they mean or represent. There is no need to ignore these associated meanings indefinitely; they are all parts of pictorial form as a whole. But it is worth while practicing it at times to avoid overlooking them. One useful device is to turn a picture upside down for a while to obscure some of the representative meaning.

When one has gained facility in noticing subtle details and complex patterns in visible form, it can become an intense and never-ending source of pleasure. There is no end to the variety and richness of the feasts which modern painting has provided for our eyes. Those who can enjoy them feel much the same pity for others as those with good eyes feel for the blind, or those who can enjoy music feel for the deaf. Yet people who never notice the visual aspects of pictures are often quite confident that they are seeing all there is to see.

Another factor in pictorial form is exposition: the expression of abstract ideas such as those of religion, philosophy, and ethics. This is common in oriental and medieval art, which is more devoted to religious ends than is modern western art. It involves symbolism and allegory, which are sometimes developed into very complex forms. Thus some Tibetan paintings set forth a vast conception of the universe according to the Buddhist belief, with its many heavens and hells and its eternal chain of rebirths. To understand this factor in art requires historical and philosophical knowledge, so that one can interpret symbolic images.

More familiar to the western world is the utilitarian, functional element in art. In pictures, this appears as the attempt to guide or influence people's attitudes and conduct, as in advertising and propaganda. It usually involves representation also, but not necessarily in a manner true to life. People and things are made to look attractive or repulsive, as in political cartoons, so as to influence the observer's attitude toward them. The use of art for social, economic, and military ends, as an instrument for controlling public opinion, has come into the spotlight in recent years. But it is as old as the Egyptian kings who employed it to glorify themselves and demean their enemies.

These four modes of composition, or factors in art, constantly recur in pictures of different periods. Sometimes representation dominates, sometimes design, sometimes exposition, and sometimes utility. Usually two or more are present in

Fig. 10
Rousseau, H.: Rain in the Jungle (New York)

some degree. The varying emphasis and combination of them, made in different styles of painting, is one source of the endless novelty which pictures present to those who understand them. One who notices these different factors in painting finds infinitely more to interest him than one who merely looks in a superficial way. To the great majority of museum visitors, most pictures are closed books, which merely look "queer" and "crude." A little study of the reasons behind their apparent strangeness is amply rewarding.

Histories of art, written a few decades ago, expressed the common belief that painting as an art began with Cimabue and Giotto, in Italy, at the close of the middle ages. The progress of art was conceived in terms of increasing realism of anatomy, three-dimensional modeling with light and shadow, and perspective into deep space. As such, it was thought to have reached perfection in Raphael, and the art of earlier ages was regarded somewhat condescendingly as the quaint, outlandish product of benighted heathens, or as immature groping toward the perfection of the Renaissance. Now, we still admire the Renaissance for its great achievements, but we see that ancient Egyptian, Chinese and Japanese, Carolingian, and many other styles of painting had distinctive values of their own, some of which were lost in the Italian Renaissance. When we learn to enjoy Egyptian painting for its firm, clear-cut outlines, its hieratic dignity, its vivid portrayal of ancient life, and its many other values, its lack of deep perspective no longer bothers us, and even comes to seem an attractive feature of the Egyptian style. Its flatness is positively decorative, producing a kind of picture which stays right on the picture plane; accepting and emphasizing the wall-surface instead of trying to destroy it with illusions of distance. Its rigid arcs and angles take on a charm of their own, which is pleasant to view after an excessive diet of late Greek, flowing curves.

The late Renaissance masters were intensely preoccupied with a certain kind of visual realism: that is, with showing how a certain scene or vista in space would actually look from a certain viewpoint at a certain moment. To have achieved this was a major contribution to art; but it forced the abandonment of many other interesting kinds of picture.

It tended to restrict the imagination, in that different episodes in a story, different aspects of a scene, could no longer be shown in the same picture. Furthermore the tendency was to rule out mystic visions and religious conceptions of the unseen world, as well as expressive personal interpretations of reality.

Seurat: The Circus (Paris)

It tended to make painting a copy of external appearances, instead of a vehicle for thought and fancy. It was never merely this in the works of first-rate European masters, but the common run of paintings did over-specialize along this line.

The recent rediscovery of exotic, archaic and primitive

styles has been an invigorating but unsettling influence. It has shown modern artists how much there is and can be in painting besides the main European tradition. But it will take years of peaceful work to adapt these diverse materials to the needs of contemporary expression. Fortunately, the appreciator does not need to grapple with the artist's problem of how much to follow old traditions, and how much to throw them aside in exploring new paths. He can enjoy each style for what it is, without trying to find any use for it.

The reader may ask, is it necessary to study all these kinds of picture in order to enjoy the art of painting? Is it necessary to analyze them intellectually, into factors in form and so on? The answer to both questions is "no." Painting is a world in which anyone may enter and wander as he sees fit, finding enjoyment in his own way. The foregoing paragraphs have merely given a general sketch of the whole terrain. They have used a few technical words as the shortest way to distinguish certain main types. The intellectual, scientific student of pictures will want more technical analysis, and will raise theoretical problems. The more sensory, concrete-minded person will find such analysis boresome, and will revel in the pictures themselves without wanting to theorize about them. The historian will see in each picture a historical document, significant for an understanding of its age. The artist will be impatient at much looking, and will want to get his own hands at work with brushes and paints. The collector will delight in acquiring and owning pictures, and perhaps in arranging and caring for them. Some people are interested in the painter as well as in his product; they like to know about his life, and how he came to paint as he did. For others, such ideas are irrelevant, merely serving to confuse the study of the pictures themselves. The versatile person can take different attitudes at different times.

Individual differences in personality profoundly affect our likes and dislikes, in art as elsewhere. Some people are more auditory than visual by innate endowment, and will naturally enjoy music more than painting. All of us have had individual experiences which condition us favorably toward certain

Fig. 12
Picasso: Acrobat (Paris)

types of image, unfavorably toward others. For example, we dislike a certain artist or type of art because a person we dislike is annoyingly enthusiastic about it. We publicly express dislike of some kind of art, and pride restrains us from chang-

55

ing our minds later on. Psychological factors such as these can be very obstructive to enjoyment, and it is often worthwhile to analyze and correct them, as far as possible. In other words, the enjoyment of painting or of any other art can be increased by attention to the psychology of liking and disliking, as well as to the art itself.

In dealing with younger children, we must be especially careful not to impose adult, sophisticated attitudes toward art. Intelligent teachers have learned to avoid prematurely imposing adult techniques on children's own art work, and the same caution should be followed in teaching art appreciation. The fact that some new kind of art is in vogue among advanced adult circles is no reason for us to expect children to accept it with equal enthusiasm. It was mentioned above that much adult painting, especially during the last fifty years, has been highly specialized on some one type of pictorial form. For the child, much of this is apt to be confusing and incomprehensible. He may assent politely if asked to admire, but can not genuinely grasp it. He prefers a story picture, or at least a picture of some interesting subject, to any amount of abstract pictorial form.

Children's ways of appreciating pictures change with their age, and differ somewhat according to sex and individual personality. But certain general characteristics apply to most of them. Children tend to look at a picture mainly for what it represents. They prefer as a rule to look at realistic pictures by modern adults, rather than pictures by other children, or primitive pictures resembling those of children. When they become interested in primitive art, it is usually for the associations of primitive life. To them, as for adults untrained in art, a picture is an occasion for imaginary projection of oneself into the pictured scene, and perhaps for self-identification with one of the characters. A boy looking at a picture of cowboys and Indians likes to imagine himself in the fight. A girl sees a picture of a scene at court, and imagines herself as the princess. This is one pleasant way of looking at pictures, which lasts with minor changes all through life.

Few adults, and still fewer children, are naturally interested in visual form, design, or technique for its own sake, or in any specialized, aesthetic approach to art. Older boys tend to regard decoration in itself as rather effeminate. Younger boys, as well as girls, often love bright colors and patterns; but this tends to decline among older boys in favor of accurate linear or photographic portrayals of reality. The taste for fantasy in art—for scenes of magic, fairy-tales and weird improbabilities—tends also to decline in favor of realism and practicality. We do not know as yet how much of this tendency is due to the present American environment, and how much to basic trends in mental development.

Nor do we know exactly what education can and should do to oppose them. Our environment, in school and out, has on the whole been extremely discouraging to the taste for fantasy and decoration, especially for the older boy and man. Girls are subject to similar influences, but are apt to see more practical value in a decorative approach to personal and home adornment. Here and there, one finds an exceptional child, boy or girl, who can take at an early age the viewpoint of an adult artist or connoisseur. But the vast majority see little in pictures but subject-matter, and lose in later childhood whatever small taste for other values they may have acquired in the lower grades. Art teachers who believe in the educational value of a more thorough kind of art appreciation deplore this tendency, and hope to oppose it through more emphasis on cultural and aesthetic values in the school curriculum. But they face tremendous obstacles.

It is interesting to watch the kinds of art which children

naturally like—the comic newspaper strips and booklets which they devour; the illustrations they pin up in their rooms and preserve in scrapbooks. Their choices express their present interests and desires at each age-level. Pictures to them serve a valuable psychological function in giving conscious clarity to their mental and volitional life, thus aiding normal development. Methods of teaching art appreciation to children should be based on observation of their spontaneous interests in art, and should attempt to lead these gradually into mature understanding and discrimination.

Can the enjoyment of painting, or of any art, be taught or explained in words? Only to a limited extent: in so far as it depends on an understanding of the nature of the art, and a development of certain specific abilities, such as that of visual perception. But one may have this understanding and ability to a high degree, and still not enjoy painting or anything else; perhaps because of physical illness or emotional depression. To such a person, one may explain art indefinitely, and he will still say, "What of it?" All one's reasons for liking this or that leave him cold.

Some people, on the other hand, seem able to enjoy art and almost everything else in life with little urging. Quickly and easily, they find something interesting and delightful in whatever confronts them—pictures, music, gardens, or people. Books and lectures about art may seem to them unnecessary, as a mass of words coming between them and art itself. Sometimes this easy enthusiasm seems a little shallow and undiscriminating, but on the whole it is an enviable trait, born of a general vitality and exuberant, affirmative character.

A third type of person has learned in youth, while still flexible, to like a few restricted kinds of thing. Since then, he has lost the ability and the desire to form new tastes, and now glories in his prejudices. In art as elsewhere, he resents the strange and unfamiliar. He has no desire to be shown how to like or enjoy anything new. He wants rather to be confirmed in his present likes and aversions.

Books on art appreciation are written for people who do not fall into any of these categories: for people who can still learn to like new things, and want to do so in a reasonable, discriminating way. They have learned that understanding an unfamiliar thing often helps us to enjoy it, and that a word of explanation from someone who has studied the subject often saves much time in understanding. They can also profit by hearing of other people's enthusiasms and aversions. Without necessarily imitating these, they look for suggestions as to what might be worth while exploring for themselves. The discriminating layman, facing a new field of experience, does not want to be told exactly what to like and dislike; any such dogmatism is a challenge to his right of individual choice. Nor does he want to be told to like everything; he feels sure that in art as elsewhere there are good, bad, and indifferent examples. He cherishes the right to praise and condemn as he goes along.

Until recent years there were comparatively few books on art appreciation. Art was assumed to be easy to understand; all one had to do was to look at pictures. If their meaning was not obvious, they were bad. In any case, art was a rather trivial matter, a leisure amusement at best, especially for the young lady. Why study it seriously?

Much has happened in the last generation or two to change this attitude. For one thing, we have discovered how many different styles of art have flourished in past centuries. Museums have become bewildering in the variety of their collections. Meanwhile, modern artists make matters harder for the layman by acrimonious disputes and a constant succession of radically different styles and movements. Small wonder that looking at pictures, which used to be a simple amusement, has become a formidable task. Enjoying them is no longer easy and natural, for so much of what one sees is confusing or repellent at first sight.

It is aided, for many observers, by an understanding of what each artist is trying to do. If one realizes that a certain artist is trying to make a decorative panel, a political satire, or a weird fantasy, one can more easily forgive him for not giving an accurate representation of nature. Sometimes the artist's own explanation of his purpose is enlightening, and sometimes not. He is apt to talk in high-sounding generalities, or to mislead the public with some mischievous, cryptic title. Rare indeed is the artist who will frankly admit indebtedness to previous artists; each likes to claim complete originality. Yet one of the best ways of finding out an artist's aims and methods, his place in the whole scheme of things, is to compare him with other artists, past and present. One will often find that he is trying to adapt some old, exotic style of art—e.g., Coptic textiles or African Negro sculture—to modern techniques and subjects. Perhaps he is trying to make a new synthesis of elements from several older styles. Knowing this, one knows at least that he is not completely insane and aimless; that there is method in his madness.

To be sure, after finding out the artist's aim, one may still feel that it was not worth while, or at any rate not agreeable. But in practice, the onlooker often finds that understanding breeds interest and enjoyment. Just as cricket or football becomes more interesting to watch after one understands the game, so does painting. Painting has no single set of rules; each artist can think up a new game of his own.

At the same time, the main objectives in painting of all styles and periods are few in number. They can be understood in a way that will include even the most radical new departures.

When one has grasped them, the profusion of styles has a tendency to become less confusing and irritating. One can enjoy the contrasting spectacle in a general way, and pick out for closer acquaintance what seems most congenial.

This is a great age to live in for the person of diversified

Fig. 13
Picasso: Still Life (Paris)

tastes and broad tolerance in art; less so for one who is intensely devoted to some particular set of values. It is an age when previously unfamiliar styles of art are pouring in upon us in overwhelming quantity, through excavation, exploration, photographs and traveling exhibits. Even scholars are having a hard time to assimilate and interpret it; to weigh its relative values. Much less can the layman do so with any thorough understanding or assurance. To enjoy it keenly, he must be a person of wide and plastic tastes, who can exult in the profusion of newly-found cultural riches, and in the welter of modern eclecticism and experimentation. Perhaps such a person, like the age itself, suffers in comparison with those in which the standard of value is more simple, clear and fixed. The other alternative, and one which many will prefer, is to select some particular style, old or new, live with it closely and ignore the rest so far as possible.

This is not the place for a detailed account of individual artists and their styles. These are available elsewhere, and it need only be said that reading a few such accounts is indispensable to an informed enjoyment of art. So far as possible, one should select those which comment on specific pictures, and read them in the presence of the pictures themselves. This will gradually open one's eyes to the great and varied world of pictorial form. Eventually, one may acquire, not merely book knowledge about art and artists, but a background of mental images of pictures seen and specific qualities in each. As a result, when encountering unfamiliar examples of old or modern art, one can interpret them in relation to this background. One can say, "Here the artist followed a tradition, or the influence of this and that painter. Here he said something new and original, which makes this picture unique." To be able to do this, and to keep one's bearings in any art exhibit, is a fairly good guarantee of lasting enjoyment.

One may not like all the pictures equally well—far from it—but one likes the general process of looking at them. And there can be real enjoyment in studying a picture which one considers to be ugly, clumsy, unoriginal, or bad in certain ways. One enjoys the picture, perhaps not as the artist would have wished, but as material for critical thinking of one's own.

Few indeed are the pictures which do not present something to be enjoyed for its own sake, apart from criticism. It is hard to play an ugly note on a well-tuned grand piano; and it is hard to lay colored paints on a canvas in a way which will not present at least the charm of crude color. Those who profess to be pained by some picture are pained because it fails to do some particular thing which they expect of pictures, or because it suggests some unpleasant idea. If one wants to be pained, one can always concentrate attention on such faults, as one can on the faults of a human being. On the other hand, one can look for good qualities, and be pretty sure of finding some in the clumsiest student's work. The one attitude results in a sharper critical sense; the other in a happier feeling toward the world. Much so-called pain in looking at art is not really very painful, but a strong way of expressing disapproval. And it is often due to a narrow insistence on some particular criterion of merit in art. Why grade all pictures by the same criterion, any more than one grades all people? We can like different ones for different values, and cease blaming them for what they don't possess. But this, in turn, requires acquaintance with different kinds of value in art.

In adopting this relativistic attitude toward art, we do not need to abandon our scale of values, or to like the inferior work as much as the masterpiece. It is always possible to say, of the former, "This has only one poor, trivial little virtue, to which (for my own enjoyment) I shall pay most attention at present." Of the latter, one can say, "This is great, because it has many important virtues; few and slight defects. The enjoyment it yields is profound, many-sided, and far-reaching."

We must not assume, however, that an attitude of Olympian tolerance and fairness is necessary for the enjoyment of art. People with a well-developed instinct of pugnacity get more fun and excitement from a good fight about the respective merits of two rival painters than from any amount of peaceful aesthetic contemplation. A bland disposition to see something good in everything irritates them as neutrals always irritate belligerents. Some of the giants of the history of painting, such as Michelangelo, have been violent partisans in their day, and unable to appreciate the merits of their rivals. Critics and connoisseurs with some discernment in a limited field (Ruskin for example) are often blind to worthy innovations in their own day. The world of art has its feuds and perennial controversies like those of politics and economics, which flare to new intensity when each succeeding group of young radicals stands up to denounce the stuffy traditionalism of the previous group. Thus, by heated affirmation and denial, selection and synthesis, art moves on to new developments. Meanwhile, it provides a lively show for the bystanders and referees, as well as for the combatants.

CHAPTER III

## THE WHY AND WHEREFORE OF SCULPTURE

by

JOSEPH BAILEY ELLIS

Gentle reader and fellow mud-pie maker: for, if I may have my way, I have high hopes that you may find the urge to not only read the following lines as to the "Why and Wherefor of Sculpture" but feel a further urge to actually make some mud-pies of your own!

Unless I am greatly mistaken—and quite a few years of practicing and preaching along this line give me a fair degree of certainty that I am not—you, if only you will try, can look forward to a deal of fun and constructive pleasure by "digging in" on your own account in this, the simplest yet the most subtle of the fine arts.

As a starting point, a spring-board, so to speak, from which to take our plunge into the waters of sculptural discernment, allow me to start you forth with two pertinent statements:

SCULPTURE IS FORM—completely felt and fixed for present and future enjoyment.

SCULPTURE IS FUN—worth knowing how to appreciate and how to create.

After your first plunge in these perchance unknown waters of sculptural discernment you will, I trust, gain a courage and a determination to follow through to the achievement of a full measure of fun of your own in this search for a feeling for form and what it can amount to in the way of quickened appreciation and the joy of true creating.

Good sculpture, irrespective of the age in which it was made; the land that fostered it; or the hand that fashioned its creation: Good sculpture holds enduring and basic qualities of *form* and *fun*.

Whether your interest at this particular moment be that of a weary doubter or a care-free doer, let me mention one simple fact: Anyone can learn to model, carve, or appreciate sculpture! That is, anyone who has the capacity to figure out that two and two make four, and four and four add up to eight. That person, through a simple and logical use of his sense of

Fig. 14
Integration Potentials "What-Where-Which-Why"

sight and sense of touch—motivated by real desire and determination—can learn how to appreciate and record Form.

This does not mean, however, that everyone can become a second Phidias, a Michelangelo, or a double for Rodin, nor should we want to if we could. Technically, many a man has modeled or carved as well as have the three shining performers just mentioned. Technical skill and acumen can

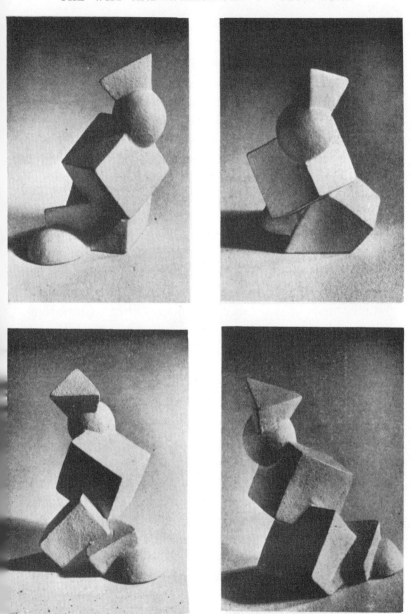

**Fig. 15**
A student's "building block" arrangement as asked for in problem one

be acquired by the many, as well as a rudimentary appreciation of sculptured form.

Let us take two contrasting examples by way of illustrating a subtle point that so frequently makes the telling difference as to the why and wherefore of aesthetic quality. Here is a piece of scultpure. It looks like a man, a general type or maybe a specific individual. It has man's articulations, sinews, and muscles presented with accurate and painstaking fidelity. All of its details have been meticulously portrayed. Anatomical knowledge and modeling skill or carving dexterity are manifest. Yet it is not a work of art. Aesthetically its perfections leave us cold.

Here is another sculptural work which looks like nothing we have ever seen before; it is neither bird, beast or fish, nor man or his mate by any stretch of our wildest imagination, yet it intrigues us by the sheer presentation of its intrinsic form. It can and does arouse our curiosity. It is vibrantly alive. It expresses living form to a greater degree than does all of the anatomical accuracy or modeled excellence of the other example!

These sharp comparisons may lead you to believe that I have little use for accurate anatomical knowledge as it applies to sculpture; that modeling skill and technical perfection are to be given no account in the making or the evaluation of a masterpiece. You may even presume that I have gone "all-out" in favor of the abstract and am now bent on urging you to do the same. Such is not the case; rather am I trying to point out that sculpture, in its aesthetic oneness, must possess many well considered attributes or ingredients properly fused and functioning. And certain of these essentials must be felt and catalogued as factors of prime importance with others playing their lesser role.

To further press my point allow me to state that a working

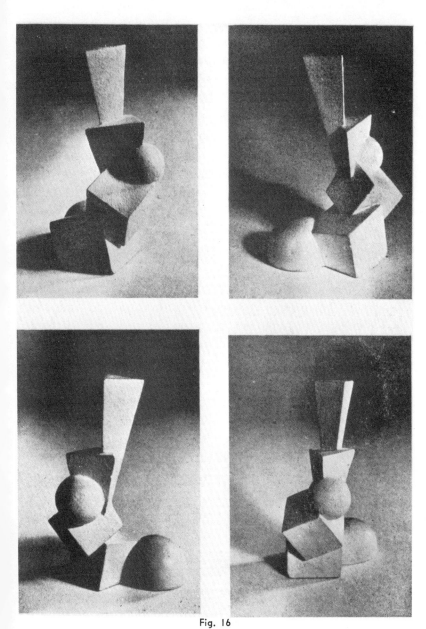

Fig. 16

Visual evidence as to what can come from a solution of problem two

knowledge of design, with all its implications and ramifications, just about tops the list of essential ingredients which make the producing of outstanding sculpture possible and which, in turn, will give one the wherewithal to truly evaluate and enjoy such works of art.

And, may I add that this ingredient of Design is the "ne plus ultra" yardstick of measurement for sculpture and all other art manifestations as well, be they in the fields of painting, music, architecture, drama, or the dance.

You can see with what importance stands Design on my list of " Measured Musts" for critical evaluation. What then is Design? Simply and precisely Design is arrangement—planned arrangement. In sculpture it is a planned and developed arrangement of volumes integrated for basic qualities of mass, contour, flow, and the carrying attributes of sequence and light and shade.

I believe we are now in a position to formulate a statement that will give us a workable definition of Design, one that can apply not only to sculpture but to all other fine arts fields. Here is that statement:

*Design* is *planned arrangement* of *spot* and *space* to make, in combination, *a satisfying whole.*

If you will take time out to make the significance of this statement your very own, you will readily see how its implications apply to painting—the arranged pattern of light and shade, the spotting of the color areas, the development of positive *forms,* which may turn out to be men or mermaids, machines or marsh marigolds, their placement on the canvas with relation one to another and to the pauses known as "background space."

In the field of music, the composer, the creating arranger, gives us a tonal masterpiece through his planned arrangement of vibrant notes put together in chord combinations built upon a sustained or changing tempo, with a spacing known as beats and rests.

The architect in his particular field follows a like procedure;

**Fig. 17**
Here integration takes on bird-like attributes

**Fig. 18**
Here integration plus imagination becomes a dog

**Fig. 19**
Here integration becomes a fish

**Fig. 20**
Three-dimensional development as integrated man

planning the arrangement of his component parts and areas from esquisse to blueprint stage for the final three-dimensional fabricated development that must stand the strain of rampant elements and, in addition, the strain or test of qualifying as a masterpiece of functional form, of aesthetic excellence, in the majesty of its visioning.

Space not permitting, I shall have to leave to you the further categorical application of *design significance* through *planned arrangement* to the field of drama and the dance, or to poetry, literature, or the all-embracing art of living life.

The point I wish to emphasize is that "The finest of the fine," be it in the fields of art or the adjacent, verdant pastures of high thinking, or the triumphant facing of life's realities, can become pregnant with aesthetic meaning.

To attain to a personal understanding and enjoyment of the why and wherefore of sculpture one must first acquire this feeling for *pure form,* and strive to gain experience in its use and development.

What I am now about to ask you to do may seem the equivalent of sending you back to kindergarten. If this be your reaction please be fortified from what The Good Book says— "Unless ye become as little children ye cannot expect to enter the Kingdom of Heaven." Such celestial aspirations may seem far fetched, but I would testify to a whole-hearted belief that the possession of a love and understanding of the arts, that really stirs from within, brings to its possessor a real corner of a heaven here on earth.

If you are still of a mind to carry on with this "search of the significant," if you are willing to hark back to childhood days to play for a moment or two with some geometric building blocks, here are a few symbols of pure form to play with three-dimensionally.

A glance at Fig. 14 will show you two cubes, two spheres and two tetrahedrons. We could as well say three pairs of three dimensional *spots.*

For design experience and a furthering of our efforts in true "mud-pie" making, our problem is to see now just what we can produce in the way of our own spot and space arrangement through this process of intergrating one block in to another and still another and yet another until we have brought

(Photo. New York Graphic Society. Stoedtner)
**Fig. 21**
**King Khaf-Ra: Cairo: Musée dés antiques Egyptiennes**

into full play and use the entire six elements. This will not prove as easy as it sounds, for we have a real problem on our hands to gain the most in the way of full cooperation and contribution from the merging of these six solids to just the

73

right depth and degree that will give, in combination, a new entity.

Fig. 15 will show you what may come from an honest effort in the limited arrangement of these six solids. The illustration shows an integration of the elements involved as seen from four different positions.

Should your curiosity, and my verbosity, now succeed in changing you from one who only wants to look to one desiring to do, then, by all means, get yourself some plasterline and integrate to your heart's content. Control of contours, a balancing and counter-balancing of thrusts and turns will lead to experience and confidence in this manipulation and arranging of pure form. How much of this—how little of that— an adjustment here—a change of position there—and you will be well on your way towards making sense and gaining sensitivity in this designed arranging—so simple, yet subtle beyond belief.

With your courage and your curiosity still holding, I would have you move on to a second experiment. And I believe I can assure you that in this effort you may look forward to much more fun and to the producing of an arranged integration which will prove more stimulating, and develop results giving far greater satisfaction, because of your heightened experience and because of a greater latitude now at your disposal. The forms for use in our second integration are these—two cubes, two spheres, and two trylons—but not three pairs. For here we come to our new latitude, not so much a difference of *shapes* as a difference in *size*. One cube is to remain constant to the size selected for our first effort, but the other may be of greater or lesser volume according to your choice. The new latitude also applies to the spheres—one to remain at the same diameter as in effort 1, the other, according to your choice, to be given more or less in the way of a new diameter.

Our tetrahedrons from effort 1, now become trylons, and the only element that needs to remain the same, as in our first effort, is that *one* face of *one* trylon shall be an equilateral triangle of the same proportions as were given the faces of the tetrahedrons in our first integration. With this lone limiting factor you may make your trylons as long and as large as you find it convenient or desirable. Now proceed with your second effort in the integrated arrangement of *pure form*.

Fig. 16 will give you visual evidence of how this second effort many develop. Here again, as the illustration can only give evidence in two dimensions, our three dimensional result is shown as it carries from several positions.

Through your efforts and accrued experience at this point you should now begin to realize what further range of varying potentials lie within your grasp—variety of shapes, the inclusion or substitution of other geometric solids, variety of size, applied to any of these basic solids, and variety of placement or position one to another, and variety of integration, or the degree of fusing of one form into another and another. If you have begun to glean the wherewithal of arranging possibilities now awaiting your command, we are ready to move on to effort 3. This should give you more confidence, more experience, and much more in the way of satisfaction through an ever-widening sensing of the possibilities now and forever after to be at your command.

Suppose we state that you are now to be given more latitude—in fact with effort 3 you are now "on your own" with full power and permission to make your own choice as to what geometric solids you wish to use—where you propose to place them with reference and relation one to another: which are to be made large and which small and which shall be given the leading role. We might call effort 3 a problem play to bear the title "My Arrangement of Spot and Space in a Three Dimensional Way" to suggest or symbolize a bird, beast or fish, man or maid. Please note that I stress a symbolization of your subject and ask you to ponder long and well with the directives *what, where, which,* and *why!* The *why* brings us back to the title of this chapter and to the statement in Dr. Schoen's preamble. "There are at least three requisites for aesthetic enjoyment:

(1) an intelligent conception of the nature of art in general and of each art in particular;

(2) a sensitivity for the material of an art which varies in degree from person to person;

(3) a knowledge of one's own taste or capacity in any one art.

Specifically am I interested in having you apply this third requisite—a knowledge of your own capacity and taste—to this third effort for the acquiring of further sculptural sensitivity and acumen. A glance at Fig. 17 will help in presenting tangible evidence as to what may lie ahead in a continuing projection of your skill in selection and arrangement or the perception of these qualities in the arrangements of others. Here then in Fig. 17 is a planned arrangement of *spot* and *space*—geometric solids integrated for *mass, movement,* and *contour*—the *flow* of *form* and the carrying attributes of *sequence* and *light* and *shade.* Here is variety within unity and the unity of this greater whole works out as the symbolization of a *bird.*

Now glance carefully at Fig. 18 and you will see how *spot* and *space* integration has been developed to give us, through a different arrangement, a symbolization based on pure geometric form which adds up to a design presentation of an *animal.*

For our basic sculptural approach what has here been achieved is of far greater importance in the way of gleaning sculpture's aesthetic essentials than any amount of accurate animal anatomy or a wealth of realistic surface modeling.

All or any of these attributes may be added and worked out later with minute perfection as contributing factors of preferment. Without this control and understanding in the

(Paris: Louvre, Photo. Alinari)
**Fig. 22**
**Babylonian-Arryrian Relief: Camp Scene**

setting up of design essentials there is every reason to believe that what could result would prove to be an exposition of only the "letter of the law" rather than the richer, truer exposition of the "law's" motivating spirit. To put it another way, the sculptor, whose approach to his work is that of the true

77

Fig. 23
Gold Cups from Vaphio

artist, a planner of the whole, must be cognizant of the entire range of all factors at his command with their relative import- ance and build accordingly—firm foundation to structural frame work, to under surface adjustments, to the final exterior degree of surface finish.

Too frequently has the significance of such procedure been inadequately felt, and a work brought into being that misses the full measure of its aesthetic potentialities because of the lack of this fuller range of discernment which men of genius in sculpture's field or stream have somehow seen, sensed and seized upon in their arrangings. It has been well said that one must learn to see life whole, and this as surely applies to sculpture and to the advantage of our learning how to enjoy, evaluate or execute tellingly.

May I, therefore, again refer you to this volume's preamble and specifically to Dr. Schoen's closing sentence—"So whereas the reader of this volume is bound to encounter clashes among its contributors let him make sure that he does not fail to discern the forest because of the trees."

Now many a sculptor has failed to discern the beauty of the whole forest of sculptural fineness because of his complete absorption or interest in the tree of surface sufficiency; the tree of copied realism or the tree of stilted imagination. Many a would-be appreciator of sculpture's telling qualities fails to glimpse the complete, satisfying, serenity of the forest's verdant depths because, with the first tree or two he perceives, and his interest in beholding qualities more or less akin to the realism of his own little orbit, he is satisfied to remain beneath the shade of this first admired tree which, no matter what its fine limited qualities may be, is still only one member in this enduring growth of sculptural timber.

What I am trying to stress is the extreme desirability of learning how to put first things first and thereby be in a position to move on to other qualities and relationships, the further "raison d'être," for fuller satisfaction.

Now just what are some of the reasons for man's absorbing interest in sculpture's stream? First of all we must admit that man is interested primarily in *man* and man's possessions, including "his purloined rib." Such has been man's state of being and interest from antideluvian Adam to Alexander

Fig. 24
Parthenon Horsemen (Athens: Acropolis Museum. Photo Alinari)

the Great, and on through to our own Great Gildersleeve: the urge of self-preservation, passion, pride of possession and hoped for perpetuity. Call it instinct, call it desire, or herald it as instinctive desire and you will still have, I believe, the leavening factor of life and a terse compendium as to the reasons for most of the created whys and wherefores of sculpture; whys and wherefores stemming from man's desire to make lasting records of his prowess as a mighty hunter, to flaunt the grandeurs of a conqueror or ruler of his fellowmen, to glorify civic pride or secular ostentation, to serve as enduring visual evidence for national commemoration, religious fervor, or man's aspirations toward the better life.

To get back to the task at hand after this digressive journey to some of the specific trees in sculpture's forest or motivating evidence along sculpture's stream, let us glance at Figures 19 and 20. Here lies further visual evidence as to what may be done with our delvings into pure form and the variety of planned arrangements at our disposal.

*What, where, which,* and *why* should now take on new significance if you are still to follow the forest trail. Unfortunately, you are again at an extreme disadvantage in having to draw your three dimensional conclusions from evidence submitted in only two. You are further penalized in not having the advantage of backing up your sense of sight with that of touch, as would be the case if you were about to reconsider an integration of your own. This last statement should be taken for its full worth, which means that I am still trying to get you to become that *doer* we have been making mention of and not to remain satisfied with a "Stop-Look-Listen" approach.

To get back to Figs. 19 and 20 and the significance of their presentation:

Note in Fig. 19 the piscatorial attributes culminating from the judicious use of selected, integrated volumes. Note also the flowing transitions from sphere to ovoid to curved column. This is something more than just another "fish story."

Fig. 20 shows how man-made man can materialize from the interplay of geometric form arranged and adapted to our bidding.

Coincidental to the approach here offered, I would refer

81

you, at your leisure, to the perusal of a most interesting book titled SCULPTURE, by A. M. Rindge, and specifically to this

Fig. 25
Roman Head: Caracalla (Naples: National Museum)

quotation: "Until we have learned a Vocabulary of Form we may be wrong to expect ideas too." I would further give whole hearted reutterance to another statement from this same pertinent source, "As a rule, the most successful teaching is visual, seeing is believing, men want to see their ideas in concrete objects"—Form—"in order to believe them more."

It has been aptly stated that variety is the spice of life. Varied interests, various experiences, variations in moods and methods, all make for a richness of living. Variety within unity may as truly sum up the prime condiments for art's enrichment. No two of us talk, walk, or think in terms of equivalent ditto-marks, yet all are "brothers under the skin" and tend to stand or fall on the accumulation of wisdom and experience handed on from father to son in true tribal fashion. We also gain or lose, agree or disagree, from the present and personal testings of the values of this and that in terms of pleasure, soul satisfaction or reward. My likes or dislikes are my own and have meaning to me. Yours should bear a sacred significance to you. Most of us resent vehemently the slightest suggestion that we are not free agents in full control of our own volitions or vicissitudes.

Yet we stand to gain definitely, and perhaps with real distinction, if we will but learn the value and desirability of stressing the letter "T" as it applies to growth in the acquiring of *taste, tenacity,* and *tolerance.*

What I have been trying to express and convey, these many pages, is the belief that surely, in the art of sculpture as well as in the art of really living life, we can benefit from a knowledge and appreciation as to what has gone before, as to what others have thought, done, and sometimes died for, with an evaluation as to their motives for so doing. We stand to gain by further reserving the right to draw our own conclusions, revaluations, and a clearer visioning of what the future may unfold in the light of the past and present, and our own personal appraisement.

The "stream of sculpture" has been flowing for many and many a year. In fact, to reach back to its beginnings, we must retrace our sculptural steps some seven thousand years back to a time when man was little better than a tailless ancestor, yet intent on "the telling of a tale" that might set forth a lasting record of his deeds and desires.

So came into being the scratchings and paintings on the cave walls found in that part of terra firma now called Spain and Southern France. Bits of carving there are too, cunningly worked out on the horn of some antlered victim of the chase. The directness and distinction of these prehistoric pieces; the simple statement of essential form here shines forth in challenge to many a sculptural superfluidity of later evolving. "Except as ye become as little children" is tellingly expressive to the evidence portrayed in such examples.

For the next recording down sculpture's stream we must submerge with the stream until it reaches the delta country of the Egyptian Nile with some 4000 years having intervened. Here in the land of the papyrus, the lotus, and the asp, with stone abounding, we find Egyptian carvers who worked so tellingly for the cause of sculpture and the recording of man's becoming of age.

Simplicity and the carved directness of portrayal here develop subtle form to a degree that only long and careful study will assure of complete appreciation. The telling qualities of this subtle directness are given in Fig. 21 but one must hope for a face to face meeting with the gentleman in question, one King Khaf-Ra, for a truly satisfactory beholding of his majestic countenance and heroic contours in all their monolithic grandness.

Here in civilization's cradle the stream of sculpture takes on new force and meaning with its overflowings in this fertile delta and the give and take of form-felt activation and appreciation. Would that we might pause for further soundings in these Egyptian eddies but the limitation of this streamlined presentation of our stream will not allow. So on we move, as the stream takes course, toward another section of this fertile

Fig. 26
Apocalypse Tympanum (Vision of Christ on Judgment Day. Moissac. St. Pierre Abbey Church)

crescent. Here along Babylonian banks, where stone was scarce but clay abundant, and Hanging Gardens, known in later times as one of the Wonders of the World, called for walls which in turn gave reason and urge for sculptural enrichment and produced, along with other fine reliefs, the masterpiece presented in Fig. 22. Note with what a minimum volume and apparent effort the fine felt pattern of selected essentials has been achieved. Here is tangible evidence of the gain accruing to any sculptor's work through not only knowing what to develop and include but what to leave out as elements of inconsequential value. You would do well to bear this admonition in mind as you proceed on your journey of evaluation.

Our next stopping place along the stream finds us on the shores of the Island of Crete at a period now dated as around 1300 B.C. Here flourished a highly developed civilization sometimes called Minoan, from their great King Minos, and numbering many a skilled carver and craftsman who knew how to work exceedingly well. While many of their objects of art and the crafts show strong influence of the sealane's contact with the Land of Egypt, these master craftsmen of Crete should be given credit for having used such influencing factors and examples of Egypt's art as mere stepping stones to a rich harvesting of truly magnificent Cretan arrangings which qualify for marveled consideration in the light of today's standards of taste and tempo.

I think that you will agree with me as to these qualities as exemplified in Fig. 23. Please note the variety of spot and space planning, the flow of form and pleasing pattern, the richness and verve of this impelling bit of repousse design, and realize that this excellent cup of sculptural fineness was made not yesterday nor yester-year but some fifteen hundred years before the beginning of our Christian era.

On moves our stream of sculpture, and so must we, from Cretan shores to a nearby mainland where amid "Greek Gorges" came into being some of sculpture's most magnificent manifestations. Would that we might tarry for more than a passing glance at the work of such greatness as was that of the Greeks. Here, however, we can only present a fragment from that processional masterpiece known as the Parthenon Frieze. Would that you could look upon the original marble, now a priceless part of the fine collection treasured in the

Athens Museum, rather than having to be satisfied with glancing at Fig. 24. Nevertheless some of the priceless ingredients inherent in the carved Greek original may carry through in our reproduction. What spirit, style and the essence of sculp-

Fig. 27
Claus Sluter: Moses (Dijon: Chartreuse de Champnol)

tural selection, emphasis and handling make this an enduring legacy of the highest order for all time! Surely the Greeks had a way with their carvings as well as a "word."

As waned the power and glory that was Greece's, not only does our mythical stream move on to Roman shores but so did many an actual Greek statue and also some of their makers; treasure trove of conquest to add to Roman luster. It is interesting here to note that the hustling and bustling Romans still had an eye to the recording of the actual features of their men of power and prowess, and not forgetting the ladies. From such motivation we have for the record many a well-limned face of character or cunning now preserved in chiseled and polished stone to augment any present day inference as to the implied qualities of craft, statesmanship or moral turpitude possessed by those who once were part and parcel of Rome's Empire.

Such an effigy awaits you and your skill or intuition as a reader of character or the thoughts and inclinations which once motivated the individual presented in Fig. 25.

With Rome's decline and eventual overrunning our stream moves on, as did one Constantine, to the shores of the Bosporus where this emperor built a new capitol on the site of the old Greek town of Byzantium and called it Constantinople. Now Constantine and our stream of sculpture have a certain significance the one to the other, for Constantine, by embracing Christianity and as ruler of Rome's remnant of glory and titular champion of this then stripling faith, paved the way for the subsequent building of Santa Sophia, that great "Monument to Faith" by one Justinian and added a supporting element of Christian color to the stream's turbulent waters.

For a truly great depicting of this Christian coloring of sculpture's stream I would have you move on to a "Romanesque Rising" of our waters and to Fig. 26.

Here showing is the Apocalypse Typanum over the main entrance to the Romanesque Church of St. Pierre at Moissac. Evidence indeed as to Christianity's motivating urge and coloring propensities—a fine example of sculpturesque form and pattern that makes use of a spot and space arrangement of religious and sculptural significance; that carries a message in terms of design, architectural and sculptural merit; story-telling elucidation and Christian symbolism; variety within unity

Fig. 28
Michelangelo: Moses (Rome: S. Pietro Vincoli)

developed into a super-satisfying whole.

Christianity's further influencings now give rise in our stream to a whole series of progressing monuments, to the outpourings of spiritual faith and the enrichment of the Here in terms of the Hereafter; Gothic Gorges for sculpture's stream producing stone sermons of fine portrayal in France, Germany, the Netherlands and Merrie England.

As one such bit of carved inspiration we are selecting for

Fig. 29
Constantin Meunier: Dock Hand (Paris: Luxembourg)

our record, with Fig. 27, a Gothic interpretation of Moses by one Claus Sluter as typical of a multitude of sculptured saints and prophets brought into being for the significant enrichment of many a Gothic niche and columned fluting.

As our stream now continues in ever-increasing form and fullness, we reach that period of art's rebirth called the Renaissance. Here, I believe, we cannot do better than present for visual evidence the sculptural work of a rare personage whose contributions to this Renaissance have not only increased the wealth and true significance of sculpture's stream but have, furthermore, added to the enriching of "The Painting Record" in like full measure. I give you Michelangelo Buonarroti— and for reasons of comparative analysis in Fig. 27, my selection of a sculptural masterpiece from the hand of this master of the glyptic art is confined to his own majestic "Moses."

Look well at Fig. 28 for a summation of heroic import and true importance, and take resolution that, at a not too distant date you will make it a point to see for yourself more reproductions of equal masterpieces created and carved by this indefatigable genius.

You will find a wealth of such reproductions between the covers of a printing by Oxford University Press on "The Sculptures of Michelangelo." If, as, and when you take this suggested opportunity, remember that I ask you to pay particular attention to the many plates that show detailed parts of the several well-presented masterpieces. By your doing just this and, at the same time thinking back to our presentation of sculpture's spot-and-space relationships in terms of arranged and integrated volumes for qualities of mass, contour flow and the carrying attributes of sequence and light and shade, you will, I feel certain, find yourself gaining added pleasure and a deeper understanding as to that part played by pure form and the transitions and designed arrangings that must be felt and presented in any true aesthetic expression of sculptural significance.

From Michelangelo to Meunier, from the days of the

91

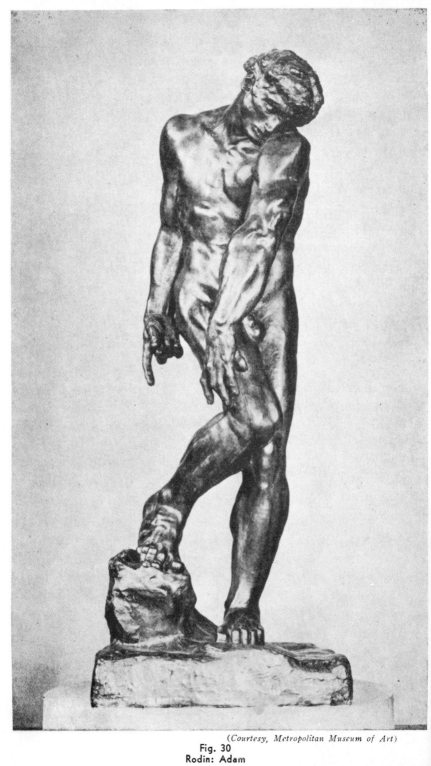

**Fig. 30**
**Rodin: Adam**

de' Medici to the dating of the nineteenth century, moves sculpture's stream with many a maker of statues having produced much in the way of evidence more or less significant all along the way. Also, along with the good, there was produced much that for its lack of aesthetic worthwhileness could just as well lie buried on the bottom of our stream without being missed at all.

In Constantin Meunier, whose "Dock Hand" is reproduced in Fig. 29, we have a sculptor who, in spite of privations galore and with many a necessitous detour thrown in, somehow managed to find the courage, understanding and clarity of sensitive visioning which enabled him to create this telling masterpiece of sculptured form with a simple, wholehearted directness that puts to shame many a preceding and subsequent work of ostentatious display and well modeled inconsequence.

We can state with certainty, I believe, that men of true aesthetic might are ever worthy of our praise and admiration.

Along with Meunier we must give more than passing recognition to a "Stormy Petrel" in sculpture's stream, one who had the strength and courage of strong convictions and seemed more than willing to stand or fall on his own findings. I refer to August Rodin whose works of sculpture have perhaps caused more quickening heart throbs of commendation as well as headaches of severe denouncement than falls to the lot of most men of sculpture. An innovator of power and persuasion to his generation, his influence has been, and still is, provocative and far reaching. In Fig. 30 you will see his strong delineation of "Adam." Here stands not only Adam, but Rodin his maker in so far as preference of posture and the surfaced amplification of form and its resultant effects of light and shade are concerned.

You would do well to compare this "Adam" with his "Eve"

and the two against—as far as Rodin's making goes—an earlier "St. John the Baptist," or his more publicized "Penseur." Should you wish to test your growing powers of perception and that personal ability to evaluate, it might be well to suggest your gaining such ends by referring you to another

(*Courtesy, Ewing Galloway, New York*)

Fig. 31
St. Gaudens: Contemplation

publication from the Oxford University Press on "The Sculptures of Rodin."

Suppose we now follow the flow of the stream to our own American shore and present evidence through Fig. 31 to a statue considered by many as the finest creation of Augustus St. Gaudens who worked so well and so willingly for the advancement of the finest of the fine not only in his own creations but toward the encouraging and developing of these qualities in others who here and now carry on.

(*Courtesy Museum of Modern Art*)

**Fig. 32**
Brancusi: Mlle. Pogany (Photo.
Soichi Sunami)

**Fig. 33**
Gargola: Picasso

Before we continue with a further word or two regarding St. Gaudens the man and the fine creation of his shown in our present plate I wish to clear the record as to my reasons for jumping from nineteenth century evidence as presented in France to the American equivalent without making mention of our own earlier exponents in sculpture's stream. This will have to be excused not as a desire to slight in any way the men who have stood out as significant forerunners, but rather that space will not allow for such recording.

With so many of our earlier works and their makers having

95

stemmed so completely from the stream's continental channels and the echoings of Parisian or Roman ateliers, we can well concentrate on St. Gaudens before moving on to present day waters. Now to Fig. 31 and "Contemplation." Note the quiet, brooding repose and the simplicity of modeled means

Fig. 34
Mestrovic: Moses (London: Tate Gallery)

by which this has been achieved. There are soul stirring qualities permeating this grand presenting that give faith and courage to a better doing of our daily tasks. Look well and be assured! And for further stimulated viewing make it your "must" to know this man's "Lincoln," his "Shaw Memorial" and his fine equestrian statue of "General Sherman," for here are works of enduring fineness and fame for all time.

We come, at long last, to the present currents, eddies and back washes of sculpture's stream. With this journey of

Fig. 35
Archipenko: Sitting Mother

discernment so nearly completed, or at least having reached to the mid-stream of today, it behooves us to pause for an evaluation of works by sculptors now in the mid-stream of their own creating, both here and abroad, or who have so recently laid down their earthly tools to answer a carver's call to the great beyond.

Before we continue on you are urged to hark back to that bit of friendly advice regarding our stressing of the T's of *taste, tenacity* and *tolerance.* And to the further recalling of

97

an introductory statement, "Sculpture is *form*—completely felt and fixed for present and future enjoyment." If you now find that some of the examples fail to produce present enjoyment, as far as your taste is concerned, be tolerant and hold to a future when you may come to fuller understanding. You will note that some of our present day mud pie makers prefer to hold close to the symbolized or abstract statement while others carry through to the presentation of a more naturalistic and anatomical development.

All, I believe, in the plates selected for presentation, give evidence of a consideration of the aesthetic essence; of a sure knowledge of what to emphasize and what to let go by the board.

Our choice in the works here included has of necessity been limited. This, however, should not deter you from the fun and values to be gained by carrying on to additional selection of your own—your nominations to a growing "Hall of Fame" for sculpture of designed sensitivity. And who knows but that some fine day we may here find works of your own!

Now a searching glance for the Figures about to be presented. These are numbered 32, 33, and 34, and give comparative evidence as to three ways that modern men have chosen to make record interpretation of another's physiognomy. It is evident in the extreme as to where, or in what range, Brancusi has elected to arrange Mlle. Pogany, presented in Fig. 32. Here is designed simplification carried to the "steenth" degree.

This may or may not be a telling likeness; your guess is as good as mine; but at least we shall have to admit that it seems the essence of studied simplification.

In Fig. 33 we find two dimensional evidence as to the way Pablo Gargola chose to record a portrait likeness of his friend Picasso; strong character presented to the point of driving caricature.

Fig. 36
Lachaise: Bronze Nude

Let me suggest that you would do well to make further visual inquiry as to other Gargola arrangements; for here is a sculptor who handles his arrangings in a variety of materials and moods, all stressing the basic qualities of designed approach.

With Fig. 34 we find ourselves again in the presence of that man of biblical might—"Moses"—this time the interpretation of Ivan Mestrovic, himself a man of might in sculpture. Mestrovic's likeness of the Man Moses bears striking reminder of another carving of this same patriarch by an earlier master of the glyptic art.

I refer you back to Fig. 28 and to Michelangelo Buonarroti of whose genius we have already made mention. Now note well the play of light as it ripples over Mestrovic's compelling integration; pure form personified and vibrant with qualities of designed arrangement. And this is just a sample, so to speak, of carvings by one who is well worth knowing as an outstanding exponent of the handling of pure form in a way that vitalizes his presentations as figured works of art that adhere to human anatomical fidelity, yet, at the same time, gain that extra essential ingredient of controlled emphasis in the choice of giving dominant "right of way" to underlying design principles.

Next on our honor roll for presentation as exemplars of form essentials, whether used in extreme abstract or augmenting a more naturalistic surface development, come Figs. 35, 36, and 37 showing how three more sculptors of today's stream have ˉhosen to carry through in their development of spot and space relationships as applied to the human figure.

In Fig. 35 we present "Sitting Mother" by Alexander Archipenko. Here is pure form only once removed from complete abstraction. Human attributes, yes, but with the predominant emphasis that of integrated abstract form.

100

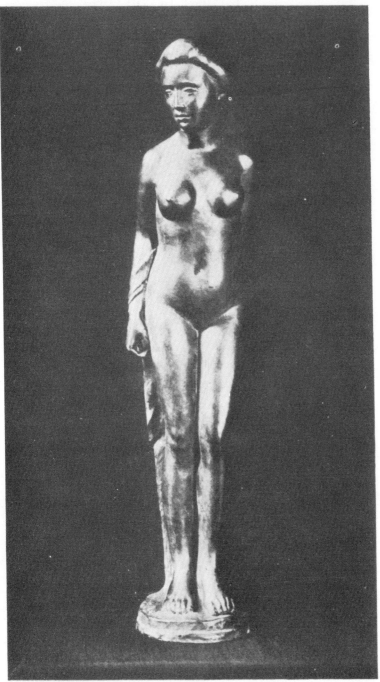

Fig. 37
Maillol: Bronze Nude

With Fig. 36 comes a differing interpretation entitled "Bronze Nude" and produced by Gaston Lachaise. My wish is that you might now be viewing the actual life-size bronze rather than this two dimensional reproduction, for thus you would stand to gain that fuller experience of a personal evaluation of the rich qualities this work so outstandingly possesses.

(*Courtesy Carl Milles*)

**Fig. 38**
**Milles: Dancing Group**

The same wish applies for your viewing of "Bronze Nude" by Aristide Maillol, here presented in Fig. 37, and to the viewing and evaluating of any or all three-dimensional works as has been rather definitely suggested in the course of this chapter. I trust, however, that, even from our necessitous two-dimension evidence, you may still find it possible to grasp the many fine qualities this statue possesses as part and parcel

*(Courtesy Lu Duble)*

Fig. 39
Duble: Dance Congo

of the current of Sculpture's Stream. Maillol should be on your "must list" for further critical appreciation and knowing, and especially does this apply to your learning to know his superb "Femme Accroupie."

Now to introduce you, through Figs. 38, 39 and 40 to

103

the works of three more sculptors of today; all three possessing qualities stemming from the past but pressed into a moulding of the present and pointing to the continuing of sculpture's stream of tomorrow. All are now working on the stream's American shore and we can, I believe, look forward with forecasting interest to what future forms they may choose for their arrangings.

Even though we will have reached the end of this Little Journey of Discernment with our presenting of these three, I can assure you that sculpture's stream will continue on, and in that bright current of tomorrow will be found satisfying sculpture of aesthetic eminence forthcoming from the understanding and well-grounded fledglings of today!

In Fig. 38 you will see the "Dancing Group" of Carl Milles. While this is not one of his latest creations, I desire to include it as being concerned with the handling of a two-figured composition, as are the works of both other sculptors here included. Note the rhythm of this flowing bronze baccanal; the transitions of grace and lilting movement; the fullness of form and the unity achieved. And compare this dancing group with the group shown in Fig. 39.

Here is again a dancing composition, yet a dance of quite different tempo and temperament. Lu Duble, its creator, possesses that rare ability of seizing upon the dynamic forces that underlie each projected composition, and has found her own inimitable way of dealing with such forms. Whatever her chosen subject, one feels that nothing has been left to chance for its recording nor has a work been pushed through to completion without due thought and deliberate experiment having been given to see that each and every quality and attribute had proved sufficient for the need and the desired control.

And now, with Fig. 40, we come to the work of Janet

(*Courtesy, Janet de Coux*)

Fig. 40

DeCoux: Annunciation

de Coux and the last presentation in our series. It almost goes without saying that Janet de Coux is definitely of today and tomorrow, yet there are strong ties with the past specifically as regards her heartfelt interest in terms of sculpture's contributions to religious aspirations and religion's reciprocity as it has given urge and meaning to the many sculptured works of worth along the stream. Her sincerity and her willingness to thoroughly explore each well considered step in the working out of her designed arrangings are strongly evident in "Annunciation to Sarah and Abraham" and can be traced with equal sincerity in her "Savonarola" and her sensitively carved "Deborah's Song." May she continue to move forward in the enriching of sculpture's stream!

Thus, having attempted to somewhat, somehow, cover the WHY AND WHEREFORE OF SCULPTURE, I would proffer sincere hope that you may find continuing fun and a high degree of personal satisfaction and pleasure in a growing understanding and appreciation for this simple, subtle, yet all satisfying Art of Making Mud Pies!

CHAPTER IV

AESTHETICS IN ARCHITECTURE

by

LASZLO GABOR

It is a long way from primitive dugouts, stone caves, and pile dwellings to the temples of the Greeks which western civilization considers the most significant period of pure architectural expression. Unquestionably the first stage in the development of architecture was dominated by practical needs. In the course of further development practical considerations continued to prevail, giving architecture a unique position among the arts. It is important to stress as a fundamental fact this distinguishing and intrinsic element of architecture because it enables us to follow its development more easily through the ages, a development marked by a struggle, often tragic, between the earthbound, material facts and the fantasy of the creative mind. In all parts of the world where man attempted the erection of dwellings, he had to cope first with structural problems, which dictated the psychological approach. This restriction differentiated architecture from the other arts which could strive more freely toward an aesthetic objective. We will notice throughout our investigation how influential in the development of architecture structural shapes and ,constructional details were, and how mechanical inventions played an intrinsic role in the growth of architectural style through the ages.

The three-dimensional structure designed to shelter human beings must not only grow out of the soil but also be well anchored to it. It must be built to withstand all the hazards of strain, stress, and the vicissitudes of the elements, all of

107

which require skill and technical knowledge of a special kind to cope with. This means that problems of a clearly practical material nature must enter into the thinking of the builder. Even the planning of the structure cannot be done without consulting its prospective occupants, so that the desires and practical considerations of people with set ideas must definitely influence the spiritual approach to the problem of the architect. All these limitations put architecture into a unique category among the arts, since artistic expression here is not only a happy combination of intuition and intellect but also the result of a practical understanding of the limitations of material and people. Based on this understanding, the artist in the builder has to overcome the difficulties of the materials, has to rise above banalities of the client, and must be able to erect a structure of an order freed from the foregoing obstructions.

There are exceptional works of architecture where the artist has been able to rise above the prevailing structural limitations with a design that demanded the hitherto impossible, and thereby compelling his helpers to discover the means for turning his dream into a reality. The craftsman and the engineer have usually been able to meet the demands of a man of genius, not, of course, without the reluctance of their conservative minds. The age-old struggle between the static mind of the craftsman and the far-flung imagination of the creative artist is apparent nowhere so clearly as in architecture, Poetry, music, painting, and sculpture can grow in an abstract domain. No outside help or subordinate cooperation is necessary to them, and the result can be, at its best, entirely unaffected by the outside world. When architectural expression is able to rise to the same height it becomes true art.

There are a great many definitions of art. Almost all art historians and theorists devote much time to the clarification of the source of art and its fruits, finding a great many philosophical and aesthetic rules to rationalize their conclusions. Some of them base their principles on the classic ideals of beauty; others approach the analysis with Teutonic dynamic exuberance and deny that the classic order is a final unchangeable law for the arts. Other more conciliatory scholars hold that a proper maintenance of balance between the two ideals is the true expression of art.

Applied to architecture, no definitions of art in general are able to cover or explain fittingly the characteristics which

(*Courtesy Philip Grendreau, N. Y.*)

Fig. 41

The Parthenon floor plan and elevation. Solemn dignity is here expressed by perfect co-ordination of artistic idea with building construction.

Fig. 42

The Mellon Institute, Pittsburgh, Pennsylvania. A masque of a Greek temple hiding a chemical laboratory. There is no relation between the idea and the function of the building.

make an architectural structure so outstanding that it becomes a work of art. Architecture is primarily order. This order which becomes the outstanding symbol of every good work in this discipline never changes as a principle but its interpretation varies greatly through the ages. For example, the most outstanding symbol of classical order is the Parthenon in Athens. The planning of the Greek structure is an amazingly finished coordination of the exploitation of the given terrain or site, the prevailing engineering capacity, the expressiveness of the fundamental artistic beliefs of the time, and the fitting solution of all the materials as well as the people, their cultural behavior and their spiritual high standing. Today, when the grandeur and finality of this ancient building are no longer as apparent as at the time of its completeness, humble and simple people who approach it nevertheless feel the solemn dignity of it and are touched with unprecedented awe. Professional cynics and revolutionaries by principle who try to banalize and criticize it, do not succeed in their purpose because it expresses the true order of the period so profoundly and convincingly that it becomes, in a true sense of the word, "finality."

What criteria were applied to the Parthenon which make it fit into the landscape so perfectly that no one has the desire to change or improve it? Are architectural principles alone able to achieve such results? Of course not. Behind this marble structure is discerned the classical Greek approach in its clarity, with its advanced humanitarian, philosophical thinking and its crystal-clear mathematical precision.

The spiritual and bodily value of the human being was greatly emphasized by the Greeks. The body as such was the principal measure for the architectural plan of a structure. The golden section, a simple but ingenious device for the guidance of builders, was developed in relation to the human body and was applied always as a measure of restraint and respect when imagination and invention tended to overbalance the intrinsic harmony. Every trait of the body helped to complete this measuring stick: the distance of the reach of the hand, the length of the foot, the pacing of the step. These measurements were the implements of an age when the dignity of the human being was held to be of utmost importance. The mathematics and philosophy of the Greeks are preserved more completely than the weatherbeaten ruins of Greek structures; but the mathematics and philosophy do not reveal the cultural level of the people in as definite and convincing a way as does the architecture.

Architecture is the clearest measure of the cultural standing of races, ages, and classes of people. On the basis of the surviving structures of the Greeks we are able to evaluate their level of civilization. Architecture is a symbol of culture

The most primitive impulse of those simple-minded people who are not able to apprehend the deep roots and fundamental principles in a work of art which belongs to a civilization different from their own is to copy it. Professional architects of today are among the most undiscriminating persons in the world. Were this not true, it would not have been possible that in a so-called modern era of civilization thousands of edifices could have mushroomed out of the earth, grinning at us with Greek masques, which they call facades, in front of a skeleton which has not the faintest resemblance to the principles of construction and order as the Greek architects would have known them.

It is not the purpose of this essay to prove by examples from the principal epochs of western civilization that throughout history the creative talents of the builders were always able to realize in full their original thinking. History records the important breaks with tradition by calling certain epochs Classic, Romanesque, Gothic, etc. How did these periods come to be? They were certainly not just the independent expressions of creative artists who decided from one day to the other to produce a new style; because, as we emphasized before, architecture is not independent of the contemporary

111

developments in engineering, of new natural or synthetic materials, or of any other major discoveries that may have some bearing upon it. Technical inventions do not dictate a new style but make already latent dreams feasible.

An artist is an outstanding example of his time, and is in this sense the truest of modern beings. The artists of the various historical periods welcomed progress eagerly, encouraged inventions in their field, and used every advanced tool at their disposal to elaborate their ideas. If materials or construction tools became antiquated by better and newer ones they were ready to discard them overnight. The most striking evidences of this fact are the ancient cathedrals of the continent, where, in many cases, the foundations and supporting columns were begun in Romanesque style, were continued by the daring and capricious engineering of the Gothic architects, and had the interior finished in the manner of the Renaissance or late Baroque. This did not happen because the builders failed to appreciate the achievements of a past generation, or because they were convinced they could not attempt a continuation of the building in the spirit of its originator; they worked in their own way because they realized that architecture is a symbol of all the achievements of the time in which it is created, and they followed proudly this conviction.

What are the ideas of the men who have busied themselves with architecture since the beginning of the 19th century? Until that time a strong resentment still existed against superficial applications of forms and symbols belonging to the past. With this breaking point, which sigfinificantly coincides with the so-called industrial revolution and with the arrival to power of the bourgeoisie or middle class, all boundaries or dams of order and decency seemed to break. Architecture ceased to be the symbol of a culture and became the servant of a power-drunk new class. The dignity of the artist which, curiously, was upheld in times of absolutism throughout the ages, started to disintegrate in a more democratic liberal era at a frightening tempo. As true servants, the architects had to fulfill the wishes of the masters who knew no restraint, and who had the money and the knowledge of the past. Humanistic education was no longer the domain and privilege of the few. Historical knowledge was broadcast by all the means of communication: by books, pictures, photographs, and travel. To justify the imitations by the 19th century architects, it could be said that it must have been easier for the builders of earlier periods, who did not know much of the world, to follow their own ideas and thus be original and creative than it was for the 19th century architects who had the resources to make copying a comfortable task.

But a certain knowledge of the rest of the world had not been denied to the people before the 19th century. The difference lay rather in the complexity of knowledge and the easy approach to the sources of origin. It is fitting, when we condemn a development, to explain the influences that brought it about in order to profit by its mistakes. The great temptation to imitate that confronted the 19th century architects came about by an amazing series of mechanical inventions which enabled them to produce and reproduce things more easily and quickly than ever before. Whereas the improvements of tools and a certain simplification of handiwork had been achieved over a period of 2000 years, the invention of the steam engine made it possible for a rationalistically thinking generation, with a great sense of its own importance, to multiply its efforts without scruple or critical analysis of aesthetic value.

It was an amazing feat when the new machines could be put to work and results appeared almost overnight. What was once the work of sweat and tears, of slowly advanced handicraft, suddenly became possible by the turn of a switch. Decency of construction, which until the era of mass production, was clearly an important and visible part of the aesthetics of architecture, was thrown overboard. The great achievements in building construction which were significant for this era were not exposed as proudly as they would have been in former times, but were hidden by false fronts and excessive ornamentation. Cast iron and reinforced concrete which came to the forefront and revolutionized building possibilities on an unprecedented scale were materials which should have found their expression in any society proud of its spirit. We can find them accidently unmasked in structures of the 19th century, but only when the builders thought it would not be worthwhile to hide them. For example, cast iron and reinforced concrete could be seen in all their uncovered strength in such utilitarian buildings as temporary exhibition halls, markets, railroad shelters. But the great majority of architects remained unmoved by the new possibilities. A group of them, still dreaming of a classical rebirth, was wrapped in a meaningless academism; another group was willing to rehash 2000 years of western architectural developments in the new, fast-growing towns of a hectic period.

For about 50 years it seemed that the machine controlled the man. Since it was quickly discovered that the machine could turn out almost any type of object, and since the products were not controlled by a superior creative spirit, aesthetically devastating results were inevitable. No appreciation of the fundamental principles such as clarity and proportion remained as a controlling force. Planning of towns, streets, recreation areas, green reservoirs, was not taken into consideration. The geometrical forms of the noble masses of the past had been forgotten. The three-dimensional thinking disappeared. One structure overpowered another in uncontrolled monumentality.

A stupid symmetry replaced true order. Light and air became secondary elements in the huge tenements which grew up. The future slums reared their ugly heads. This happened in the face of the fact that this was a period when engineering science advanced in an amazingly revolutionary spirit, when bridges spanned the big rivers in a few months, when discoveries in the field of hygiene were cutting down the death rate at an unprecedented rate. All these advances could have been coordinated into a new approach to living as far as architecture was concerned, and should have been received with enthusiasm,

*(Courtesy Ewing Galloway, New York)*
**Fig. 43**
**The Brooklyn Bridge. Excellent example of an engineering feat.**

were it not for the fact that they were accepted by a spiritually and artistically unprepared generation. The few exceptional minds who tried to fight against the stream were not able to change the picture, or did not have the courage of their convictions.

Of course it can be said that amazing things came out of this period of chaotic grandeur. Did not proud cities emerge out of sleepy villages? Were not bastions razed to erect boastful boulevards? Was not the island of Manhattan turned almost overnight into the metropolis of a great land? Yes, all these marvels did occur; only the principles of architecture were ignored—the human scale without which all these efforts had to become meaningless and worthless as the expression of art. Such attainments are worse than emergency structures which come and disappear, because, in spite of their impressive facades, in no case do they fulfill their true function. Their planning had very little to do with their usefulness. Room sizes were dictated by the facade, and since the facade was a pseudo-replica of something formerly great, it pressed everything into a scheme that disregarded actual necessities. Small inside courts where building speculation dictated their size left barely enough light to make a great portion of the space usable without artificial illumination. Compare these conditions with those in the buildings of the past which were taken as examples. A Renaissance structure in Florence or Genoa, where the courtyard was spacious and flooded with sun, cannot be compared with the ugly light shafts of the 19th century buildings of the style supposedly inspiring them. Lack of the most primitive understanding of the long-cherished principles of architecture was only exceeded by lack of a social consciousness. Speculation in real estate dictated the layout of cities, the buildings of which had to provide living quarters for the flood of clerks and industrial workers created by the machine.

The utter unpreparedness and lack of understanding on the part of architects in the face of a great problem was never before known to this extent in history. No one was willing to search deeply into the problem which was so excitingly new, if we consider the scale of the undertaking and the variety of new materials available for use. One small fact may be cited to exemplify the difference in outlook between a medieval architect and the so-called architect of the new machine age. Glass, which was used first to any extent in the Middle Ages to provide protection against the weather and to bring light into the house, was a truly great invention. It was one of the first synthetic products to revolutionize our dwellings. From the moment of its first usage, a concentrated effort was made to improve its quality and also to make as big a pane as possible. We can follow the development of glass in all its revealing stages, and we find that each success in the field of manufacture was succeeded immediately by the application of it in buildings. The bigger the glass became the less support or frame it needed to hold it together in the window. Surely, the dream of the Renaissance architect was to have a single pane between his rooms and the outside world. He was a true modern man of his time. The 19th century was able to do this, but it did not show any pride in the achievement; on the contrary, it cut beautiful large panes of glass into small pieces to put them into small prefabricated frames, thinking of some famous structure of times past and forgetting the almost limitless possibilities of the materials now at hand.

This example could be multiplied by many others, and just as convincingly. The other arts, not as closely connected with the behavior of a generation as architecture, fared somewhat better. We know that painting strove to break with the academic tradition of reviving on sweet canvases the mythological subjects of the classics, by searching for a new, living expression. This movement produced Impressionism, not only in protest, which would have been negative only, but with a deep conviction that it was necessary to find a new outlook to correspond with the great steps taken in other cultural fields in that century. From then on the painter proceeded courageously, experimenting in the realm of the visual arts, always a step ahead of architecture. We can justly blame the architect for not being the leader when he was needed most. We can also find the psychological reason why a generation which had just come to power acted as it did and persistently demanded that its wishes be fulfilled.

The grain merchant who had divorced himself from antiquated wind or water mills by applying electric power, the wool manufacturer with his newly developed mechanical looms, the steel, oil, gas, and coal men with new industrial production methods, had quickly achieved such wealth as was known only by a few rulers of the ancient Silk Road or the nobility of the past, and their primitive reaction was to give due expression to their accumulated possessions by absorbing everything at their disposal. So we cannot blame them if they went through the catalogues of ancient culture and made bold and quick decisions by asking for reproductions. They wanted to experience the sensations which had been until then the privilege of the few aristocrats. Furthermore, they wanted to challenge this prerogative by displaying their own power. As architecture has always been a true symbol of the times, it was only logical that this new class, in its naiveté, should imagine itself in a position of importance which empowered it to rule and to display itself. If the architects would not have failed, if they would have shown some courage, they would have been able to meet the onrush of demands by ingenuous planning and thinking in accordance with the new tools at their disposal, thus giving a new era its fitting expression.

Such expression is possible only if architects are able to mould actively the face of a living and everchanging organism called architecture, leaving nothing untried which might enable them to advance toward true artistic form. Ibsen once said that it must be a very good truth to be a truth after twenty-five years. Facetious as this may sound, when applied to architecture in an everchanging period such as ours, it becomes pertinent in view of the new tools, discoveries, and widened knowledge at the disposal of architects with which they can face an old problem in a new light and follow it through to its final presentation.

The bewildered 19th century was not quite sure how to meet the impact of engineering and industrialization. Very able men, seeing the massacre of everything for which culture and civilization stood, condemned the machines, curiously enough, instead of the men directing them. The oustanding example of this reaction was William Morris. He based his philosophy on the ideal of craftsmanship. He believed in trying to bring about a happy combination of the qualities of the material used and the skill of the workman in putting it into final shape. This demanded a spiritual understanding of the limitations of the materials as well as a clear judgment of how and where to apply the skill. Since he confined his purifying enthusiasm to ennoble handiwork alone, taking in, of course, established mechanical devices like printing, the beneficiaries of the new movement were those who devoted their skill to handicraft alone. This small portion of an ever-expanding civilization could not satisfy the demands of the many and thus remained in a restricted exclusive state.

This shocking contrast of simple, refined shapes against the overloaded decoration of the Victorian age, in spite of its limitations in extent and appeal, had a sobering effect upon fellow artists and the public. The movement created an enthusiastic response among partisans. Morris had instituted a new craft-art movement which spread from England over the continent, with its principles broadening as the importance of its achievements increased. It ultimately reached into the field of architecture. So, surprising as it may appear, a movement which began with the cry of "back to handiwork" in protest against the machine, became influential in awakening architects and industrialists to the possibilities of the machines at their disposal. The philosophy of being true to the materials, applying them properly, keeping the shape simple, and giving genuine expression to inherent characteristics in the treatment, was accepted as an aesthetic ideal and became the slogan of a group of architects who assumed a leading role in the profession, promulgating a broader understanding of the new outlook.

At the beginning there were only a few scattered partisans of William Morris' conception, with their humble establishments, trying to compete against the work of famous exponents of the taste of the public. Pioneers like Richardson and Sullivan in the United States were fortunate in finding a few enlightened clients who were willing to put their advanced ideas into stone and concrete, thereby enabling future generations to draw their own conclusions as to their worth. What were these ideas and in what respects were they so necessary and different from the old as to direct us toward entirely new conclusions regarding the architecture of our time?

We can conclude from our present knowledge that in spite of an occasional shockingly different physical appearance, the new ideas were based on principles of sound and established thinking. In spite of slogans like "the machine dictates the style" or "function before beauty" or "a dwelling should exist like a well-oiled machine," we find that the exponents of the new approach in architecture followed the unchanging fundamentals of architectural expression of coordinating utilitarian needs with the well-balanced play of the masses of the structure, using the greatest amount of intuition and imagination, and thus achieving a result which satisfies completely our aesthetic sense as well as intended function.

There are no new architectural aesthetic principles which do not have their roots well grounded in the old, as no art can develop out of a vacuum. The basic ideas are in a daring sense traditional. Those who resent our so-called new approach do so only because they do not recognize that the organic, and

(*Courtesy The Museum of Modern Art, New York*)
**Fig. 44**
Sullivan skyscraper. Example of structural features of a skyscraper as an intrinsic part of the facade.

hence unchanging, principles were held in abeyance during the 19th century and are now being rediscovered and reused in all their functional vitality.

The problems of organized planning which involved many important factors have remained unchanged since Phidias built the Parthenon and Michelangelo created St. Peter's Cathedral, to cite two of the most remarkable examples of final fulfillment in architecture many centuries apart. Both are examples of organization and construction brought to perfection, coordinating the proportions and leaving no aesthetic desire unfulfilled. These qualities make them true attainments of great art. The same ideals of beauty apply to present architecture. Their fulfillment is what we also strive to attain. Complete fulfillment is not a matter of aim but of a condition in which all values are happily coordinated. A few geniuses have achieved this extraordinary combination not only in architecture but also in other arts.

To plan efficiently, in our own day, we must take into consideration the intricate problems which have arisen with the increase in population, with the new standards set by engineering and hygiene, and with the changed economic and social set-ups. The town which was created originally as a bastion of concentrated defense in case of outside attack, apparently and justly received physical expression in keeping with this function. It had a center with several approaches to it which could be easily controlled at strategic points. It controlled the width of the streets, the height of the houses, so that the ultimate development was according to a set plan, excluding a growth beyond the city limits. With the introduction of modern warfare, the security behind walls dwindled and the original purpose of a fortified city vanished. Logically, the planning of new towns should have been approached from the point of view of their changed function. A town of today is a concentration of culture, trade, industry, and of the people involved in these pursuits.

There is no need for overconcentration since the development of modern transportation. The cultural centers of a town, like libraries, art galleries, concert halls, theatres, and government buildings, can be approached easily enough from all directions if built in the heart of the city. Other educational and cultural buildings should be located in such strategic points as the distribution of population dictates. This distribution should be true for shopping centers, assembly halls, libraries, schools of any nature, which would eliminate the present over-congestion of a proportionately small part of the town with trading centers, head offices of industry, all

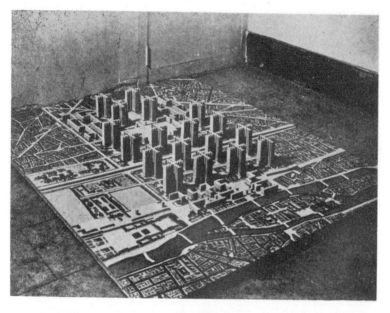

**Fig. 45**
Model of skyscraper city by Corbusier. An attempt to solve the big town problem by skyscraper tenements easily accessible and which make possible concentration of large groups at needed points.

sorts of amusement places, plus the living quarters of a great number of people. There is no justification for this congested condition today, since none of the factors exist which once dictated a concentration inside the limits of a city wall. A modern city can put the living quarters of its population well outside the section where centralization would be undesirable.

The first attempt at reorganization to solve the problems of an expanding city was made under the third Napoleon by Haussmann in his plan for Paris, which was carried out in a relatively short space of time. This proves that with the right approach, tremendous changes can be undertaken leading toward the betterment of the physical situation of a city and at the same time giving it great aesthetic value.

Up to the present day the reorganization of the crowded city of Paris by Haussmann is the greatest single attempt at putting a clear principle into effect without regard for the existing physical setup, razing hundreds of still well-preserved houses in order to solve problems of traffic, sanitation, communication, and the like. Even then, Haussmann envisioned an elaborate green belt around the heart of the city to serve as a fresh air reservoir and a recreation area for the population. The suburbs were to form a chain around this belt with the main arteries of traffic leading from them into the town proper. Even the oversized width of the boulevards in the partly executed schemes of Haussmann, the original idea of which was to reflect the splendor of the Emperor, came in very handy with the increase in population and the advent of mechanized traffic. Haussmann was not an architect but a first-rate organizer, a man of extraordinary vision, proud of his time and the engineering possibilities which were at his disposal.

We have come to realize that the problem of modern planning which we call "regional" is too complex for architects who have had no more than the customary training. The financial involvements, the social set-up, the engineering diffisulties, and the psychological approach, are major elements in the situation, each of which calls for special study, and all of which no one person can grasp. To try to coordinate all these disciplines into one mind is to invite dilletantism in one or more of them.

There have been some interesting attempts at town planning by architects in our time. Some advocate huge skyscraper blocks for the concentration of the population for easy access to work, surrounded by green belts for recreation.

**Fig. 46**
Country house at Bear Run, Pennsylvania. Nature, and natural as well as synthetic materials well coordinated, pointing to a true human modern architecture (by Frank Lloyd Wright).

Others are just as insistent in demanding decentralization into small dwelling units. Still others want to abandon the idea of large cities entirely and would put the population of large cities on a self-sufficiency basis in urban areas, limited to 100,000 inhabitants each. As stimulating as these ideas are,

125

they are not born out of a thorough knowledge of the present and anticipated future set-up of economic or social conditions. The problem is approached from a limited point of view. The ideas are proclaimed with much intensity and conviction, each of which seems to be foolproof if approached from the point of view of its advocate. But modern life undergoes very rapid changes and is influenced by far more factors than the architects know about from casual study. Very few of the schemes have been workable. The outstanding fault is the absence of a psychological approach to the people as a whole who are unprepared to receive the radical proposals and products of the architect's imagination with a favorable frame of mind. This is especially true in connection with a movement in modern architecture which overemphasizes the symbols of the industrial nature of building construction. The idea that a house has to function like a factory used to be a slogan with some people. In spite of the great publicity and emphasis with which it was proclaimed, it was a false slogan. On the contrary, a modern house, as any other house, should look entirely different from a factory since it serves a purpose which is diametrically in contrast to a factory. As a matter of fact, it would be stupid to try to convince a factory worker who has to spend eight hours a day in a factory to live the other sixteen hours in a factory-like structure.

Much harm has been done by this mechanical system for reforming the character of our houses and cities, as it invited reaction and criticism and led to unwarranted setbacks. A recent example on a large scale is the Russian venture into modern architecture of the radical type. The Union of Socialist Republics, after it had been convinced by a young and enthusiastic group of leading architects, went into modern building design and town planning for the first time on a large scale. They plunged into the project enthusiastically but without having first scrutinized the pitfalls for their advanced ideas in a country which was then at the beginning of its industrialization. Perfection, one of the main elements in architecture, could not be attained because, for one thing, steel and concrete construction was in a feeble state of development. The supply of plate glass was ample, only it was of a very faulty nature and was also applied on a tremendous scale. The workers had not been schooled in mixing concrete for huge blocks. The result was, as everyone should have known, a setback for the whole movement with one very sad result: the official Soviet architecture went reactionary. The same people, who only a few years before were enthusiastic supporters of the new style, declared officially that what the modernists had been doing was a bourgeois attempt at individualism, and they changed to a neo-classicistic style as the only satisfactory expression for the Soviet proletariat. The architects, not realizing their limitations at the time, invited this sad reaction, with their oversimplification of the problems they faced. With due consideration for the technical difficulties, for the psychological effect on an unprepared population, this reaction could have been avoided. In the case of Soviet Russia, new towns had to be planned for a new ruling class which had just overwhelmed the group which, until then, had been in power. To them, the symbol of their new might was something very tangible. They wanted to occupy the palaces of their vanquished oppressors. Of course, they never could have achieved this satisfaction by moving into dwellings which looked like factories. There is no reason for childishly overemphasizing implements of modern construction in homes, creating a barrenness and forced unity without compensating for the implements of a past era. A string of windows on a facade, uninterrupted by vertical supports, is, unquestionably, a modern technical achievement. It has its place on wall areas of utilitarian structures, but to apply it to living quarters only because of pride in a new technique is an oversimplification of the housing problem. A valuable unity which should not be underestimated becomes apparent with this use of glass; but it is problematic if it can compensate for the disadvantage of too much light, too much heat, or too much cold.

The business of the architect is not to oversimplify the problems that confront him but to find a satisfactory solution for them. A modern dwelling should develop organically from the interior, of which the exterior is an aesthetically fitting expression.

The principle which is novel with us developed as a new realization of modern architecture, and gives us possibilities unknown before. It allows a handling of the plan for a house in accordance with the exact needs of its occupants. It frees us from any stiff or tight principle of symmetry. It gives us the possibility of putting living quarters into the most favorable climatic exposure, and allows for flexibility to an extent hitherto undreamed of. Modern building materials helped the ideas of building a house from the interior outward. This idea is revolutionary because it brought an unknown new comfort into the house and changed the living habits for the better. For instance, it is possible today to handle any facade as a shield without using is as a supporting wall, enabling us to put the openings where they are needed, in an irregular manner if necessary.

It is possible also to put a dwelling on a concrete slab, getting rid of the antiquated foundations called cellars. It also enables us to span horizontal beams of considerable length unsupported by verticals over the roof, eliminating the disturbing romanticism of pitched or tilted roofing. These straightforward principles of new engineering applied to modern architecture can bring desired order into our dwellings and cities. These buildings will, of course, look different from the customary ones. But it is the architects' purpose to fit all the elements into an organic unity, which will prove satisfactory to the practical purposes as well as the aesthetic requirements of our time. His superior ability should enable him to create as gratifying edifices as those of past generations.

(*Courtesy The Museum of Modern Art, N. Y.*)

Fig. 47

Miss van der Rohe's Villa Tugendhat. A modern structure combining, with final satisfaction, advanced engineering and a clear modern creative approach.

All the tools are at his disposal, good, modern tools. His possibilities are far greater than ever before. He can truly demand the hitherto impossible. He is able to have his building transparent, if needed. His flexibility of planning is almost unrestricted by constructional limitations. Modern science has given him building materials as light and movable as the bamboo partitions of the Japanese. Technicians have developed insulation against heat and cold, enabling him to reduce the width of the wall to that of sheets. He is able to keep out noises without increasing the allowed wall size. He is able to light his rooms at any point to the fullest satisfaction without having to use heavy and disturbing fixtures. He can regulate sunlight. All in all, he can synchronize a vast technical field into a harmonizing unity.

To coordinate all the new implements with intelligence and ingenuity is the architects' main task. We know that the vast technical achievements of our day are a source of general public satisfaction. It becomes the task of the architect to bring all these developments into an order worthy of our time. When this is achieved, no one will have the desire to go back to the plaster paris columns and hollow decorations of a past era.

# CHAPTER V

# THE INDUSTRIAL ARTS

by

ANTONIN AND CHARLOTTA HEYTHUM

## INDUSTRIAL ARTS AND FINE ARTS COMPARED

There is an essential distinction between the fine and decorative arts on the one hand and the industrial arts on the other which makes the appreciation of their products a matter of quite different emphasis. The questions of usefulness, of adequacy, of fitness to a practical purpose, which are paramount in judging the qualities of the industrial arts, have less weight in the appreciation of the primarily spiritual values of the fine and decorative arts. In an object of fine or decorative art a judgment of fitness of form, expression, and material to a spiritual concept or message, cannot be made in terms of practical utility—a factor so decisive in the evaluation of industrial art objects—although even here unfitness can become ethically and materially very substantial, as in the case of a chocolate image of Abraham Lincoln.

In one respect, however, the useful and the fine arts are alike; namely, in the *principles of perfection* defined in terms of achieved form, of synthesis, unity, completeness, proficiency, honesty of expression, of integrity and harmony between inner and outer values. Yet products of the useful arts are not as those of the fine arts self-sufficient expressions of more or less immaterial dreams and concepts. They are implements and instruments of primarily material and practical value, means which serve tangible ends. And whereas the fine and the decorative arts thrive best in an imaginary sphere in which—detached from everyday reality and limitations, mind and sentiment may give symbolic expression to concepts of fancy and dreams—the creations and forms of the industrial arts reach their highest perfection only when they develop organically, or according to intelligent plan and design, on the basis of biological and physical laws, as these are operative in the everyday life of the average human being.

In works of the fine and the decorative arts we look for and find satisfaction in individualized expression of abstract ideas and ideals which lead us out of and lift us above everyday reality. In products of the industrial arts we expect to find standardized forms of useful up-to-date means which will answer our daily practical needs and desires.

## Ornament, Decoration, "Applied" Art

It is important to consider whether, and to what degree, it is justifiable to adapt to the utilitarian arts one of the strongest means of expression in the fine arts; namely, symbolic, pictorially or plastically figurative, interpretation and illustration. And if we accept the possibility, we should define how far we may go and where we ought to stop, although it must be granted that opinions in this matter may differ widely without necessarily being wrong even when extreme. Since there has been much said, and much more written, in favor of decoration and ornament than against it, the attitude: *the less ornament and decoration, the better*—must be understood and evaluated as a sound reaction against *too much of something a little of which goes a long way.*

Ornament and decoration may be justified if they add to the aesthetic values of pure form or texture by the appropriateness of their forms and motives to the function of the adorned object, and if a balanced relationship is achieved between size, shape, material, and texture, on the one hand, and pattern on the other. Here, as in everything else that aspires to perfection

132

of form, the guiding principle must be restraint and economy, even though the springs of action and source of inspiration, as in all creation, lie in wealth of imagination. What we must beware of is ornament, decoration, or pattern which does not grow organically nor according to intelligent as well as imaginative planning, but which is put on senselessly, without feeling and understanding for relationships, without respect for the beauty of plain form, or original material, of natural texture and color.

Superficial ornament and decoration diminish rather than enhance such original qualities. Think only of the irritating, unpleasant tricks certain patterns in wallpapers and poorly designed carpets play with our eyes and compare them with the charm of shadows of branches moved by a breeze dancing on a white wall or curtain, the enchanting, ever-changing patterns that the reflections of sunlight paint on plain surfaces, of which, it seems, the inventors of wallpaper and carpet ornaments have never dreamed. Or think of the serenity of a beautifully shaped unadorned vase, the enjoyment to be derived from plain colored china, from the texture of textiles or the richness of natural decorative effects of the grain in wood which has not been spoiled by illogical treatment or artificial varnish.

Once we start to think of the wealth of aesthetic pleasure which unspoiled materials and simplicity of form hold in store for everyone who has eyes to see and hands to feel, we will develop a more refined sense for ornament and decorative effects and will learn to appreciate restraint. We will see that we have overburdened our homes, our cars, our gardens, our dresses, and our minds with meaningless ornament; that we have cheapened our sense of values without realizing it and have thus come to deprive ourselves of the enjoyment and appreciation of real beauty.

In many instances it would be more civilized if we would satisfy our needs for pictorial expression through forms completely detached from things of use. Does it not seem slightly barbarian to eat roast beef from a plate covered with sweet little roses, or to step with dirty shoes on pictures and dry our hands with the cute image of a little girl or kitten adorning our mothers' guest towels?

This implies furthermore that we must train our aesthetic sense to distinguish true from false effects. Our feeling for quality must not fall victim to dishonest make-up and eye-catching superficial styling and decorative effects. We must reject disguises of every kind: the modern, over-streamlined variety as well as the antiquated but still flourishing types of period style-imitation and machine made handicraft. A radio set in the form of a tear-drop or a streamlined teapot is as misconceived, and therefore as unacceptable, as an "Early Colonial" cabinet disguise of a phonograph, a machine-stamped wood carving imitation in iron, or a synthetic material imitating the grain of wood.

## The Growth of Form

When forms which are logical and characteristic in airplane or speedboat design are transferred to radio cabinets, ashtrays, toasters, teapots, some people are annoyed, but many accept it for what it is advertised, the "style" of the day. When the outlines of a teapot or a radio set would be adapted to beautify an airplane, nobody would like it and many people would protest.

We must develop a sense of critical discrimination to protect us against falling victims to high-pressure advertising. The main reason for ill-logic in design lies perhaps in the lack of understanding and appreciation for true aesthetic values on the part of both the misguided public and the men who are responsible for this confusion.

There is a natural and logical relationship between inner and outer values. Beauty in the truest sense is not at all a superficial element which could be merely "applied" and be stressed or suppressed at will without influence upon efficiency. Quite the contrary. It is an essential factor in the achievement

Fig. 48

A form, logical and beautiful in airplane design, but utterly out of place when applied to static objects. (Northrop model 1943).

of complete functional efficiency and reaches perfection only where it appears as the logical result of organic growth, as we find it most ideally expressed in nature and in such man-made objects which are the results of slow growth and of the cooperative efforts of many generations and many minds.

Let us borrow an example from nature of the interdependence of beauty and completeness in the development of form with which Karel Honzik illustrates his study on Biomechanics. Visualize a mountain slope upon which snow is falling. A particle of snow starts rolling down-hill. Under ideal conditions, if no obstacle comes in its way, it rotates into a perfect snowball. But if the process is stopped before it is completed, the result will be an irregular *accidental shape*. If the rolling snowball hits a stone, the result will be a *deformation*. The uninterrupted and undisturbed action of the rotating momentum leads to an exactly definable modification of matter, to a form which represents and expresses a perfect equilibrium of forces present in the matter. This exceptional stage of completion, achieved under ideal conditions, results in a *perfectly balanced form* which fascinates us in a peculiar way. Our snowball represents not a sensational accidental shape, but a basic (standardized) form, and the complete perfection of this form, with its harmony of balanced strength and proportions, fills us with satisfaction.

Agreeable in a similar sense is the sight of man-made things, as certain implements, or aircraft, boats, and pure engineering constructions, such as bridges, highways, industrial machines and mechanical instruments, the shapes of which are developed in a logical process comparable to the one through which nature creates snowballs, drops, and crystals.

In examining our reactions to such forms the principal characteristics which give us aesthetic satisfaction are *formal unity, balanced strength, and apparent efficiency*. This means, first, that a form which is complete or perfect will be destroyed when we either take something from it or add something to it; second, that a perfect balance of strength is a product of either nature or of man's intelligence, which will be necessarily distorted through any interference by wilful fancy; and third,

that efficiency is apparent where form follows function but
will be lost for the eye, if not in fact, where the logical form
elements of one thing are misused as superficial *make-up*
elements for another.

In a development without preconceived ideas the form
evolves as if nature created it for us, as if our form were to
be born, not made. Such organic growth of forms we find

HONZIK'S PHYSIOPLASTIC
GROWTH OF FORM (1938)
SNOWBALL DIAGRAM OF
ACCIDENTAL SHAPE DEFORMATION
IDEAL CONDITIONS ► PERFECT FORM
DRAWING 2756 14 HEYTHUM 1943

Fig. 49
Snowball diagram of accidental shape

in the products of industries with long traditions, as in tool,
textile, pottery, glass, and silverware manufacture, in such
basic objects which have been in human use for centuries and
are the result of a slow development through the contributions
of generations of craftsmen, designers, and users. These
standard forms we find particularly in things whose function
and manner of handling have remained constant because of

the dictates of the form and mechanics of the human body. The way hands grasp and fingers manipulate, the way our lips function when liquids or half-liquids are introduced into our mouth with the help of spoons or cups, the basic ways and means of human action and reaction in certain situations and under certain circumstances remain more or less the same throughout the ages, regardless of the changes in manners in which such objects are manufactured.

Cups, spoons, knives, forks, all kinds of drinking and pouring vessels, bottles, pitchers, dishes, pots, and utensils in general are the classical examples of such standard design and function. Any attempts to improve their form, which through centuries of refinement in design has already reached a high degree of perfection, perhaps, in some instances, even final perfection, would have to be undertaken with a great degree of personal modesty. It would be a shortsighted ambition for any designer to nourish the illusion of creating essentially new forms for these objects playing with T-square and compass. When a novelty-hunting industry offers us spoons, cups, and teapots which look radically different from any we have ever seen, it will be advisable to test these products with particular care. We may discover that any changes in basic proportions and lines are harmful distortions rather than improvements of the familiar standardized shapes.

In the case of a spoon, for example, our means of judging and checking are to hold and handle it and try it with our lips if our eyes do not meet with shapes which we know by experience to give us satisfactory service. Decoration and lines "charming to the eyes" are of secondary concern. We may, if we wish, disregard them when they are harmless. But we must beware of rigid forms and sharp corners or edges and serrated or sculptured decorations which offend the sensitiveness of our palm and do not fit our fingers, nor which can be at all excused in terms of incomplete stages in the development of forms adapted to machine manufacture. The machine tries to make handmade products. The modern craftsman, meanwhile, produces with his hands forms that are ideally suited for machine and mass-production. It is obvious that the process should be reversed.

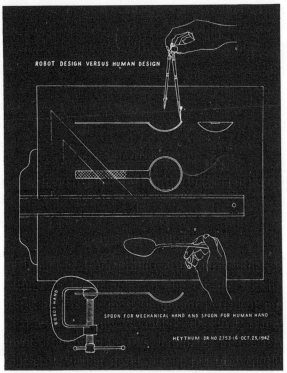

ROBOT DESIGN VERSUS HUMAN DESIGN

SPOON FOR MECHANICAL HAND AND SPOON FOR HUMAN HAND

HEYTHUM · DR. NO. 2753-16 · OCT. 25, 1942

**Fig. 50**
Robot design versus human design

We ought to dislike the type of decorative effects which make upkeep and cleaning a timeconsuming effort, an important consideration for any modern housewife, though not a decisive factor for the original sponsors of such unsocial fashions, namely, royal and other feudal households, relying on slave labor. In a radically opposite direction, cups, saucers, teapots, and all kinds of furnishings and static equipment, and even buildings, have suffered great harm lately from perverted attempts at streamlining to make them fly or swim. And there is a tendency towards overdesigning in certain industries, which, in a strangely distorted endeavor toward sound economic planning, create artificial markets through artificial obsoleteness, without much concern for the consequences which such a system produces in the economy of the nation at large.

## PREJUDICES TO BE OVERCOME

We will have to clear our minds of the confusion of aesthetic and social prejudices of our own time and making, but above all we must discard the bad habit of looking too much backward and too little forward; of too much adherence to the outlived ideals and expressions of bygone ages and cultures, and too little confidence and pride in the capacities of our own time. Modern civilization has shown a tendency to spread rather than to destroy the germ of prejudice and emotional confusion, and has made poor use, so far, of the rich knowledge and possibilities that the development of science and technology have provided. Hardly ever before has any generation had such rich store of knowledge and so large a choice of tools and means to plan and start the building of a sounder and more beautiful environment than we have today. But man is still suffering rather than profiting from his ingenuity. He is the slave, not the master, of the intricate machinery he has developed. While scientific discoveries, new tools, new materials, new social needs, call for a revaluation of concepts and ideologies, we try to fit old—and more often the bad old than the good old—habits to new problems and situations.

"We cannot intelligently accept the practical benefits of the machine," wrote Lewis Mumford, "without accepting its moral imperatives and its aesthetic forms. Otherwise both ourselves and our society will be the victims of a shattering disunity, and one set of purposes, that which created the order of the machine, will be constantly at war with trivial and inferior personal impulses. Lacking on the whole this rational acceptance, we have lost a good part of the practical benefits of the machine and have achieved aesthetic expression only in a spotty, indecisive way."

The question of social prestige and purely aesthetic or pecuniary considerations are poor counselors in judging the qualities of things of use. Our attitude would reflect little foresight and insight if we called only on our eyes and pride or sentimental impulses when we build and furnish our houses, buy a car or radio set, admire an airplane or ocean liner. Nor can we rely solely on the methods of evaluation which we used in our childhood when we examined things not merely visually, but by touching, tasting, biting, tearing, and other primitive means of testing. In earlier stages of civilization man's sensory equipment and his instincts may have served him well enough as a reliable guide, but in our day of innumerable temptations in wrong directions we must sharpen the critical faculties of our mind. Our evaluations and choices must be based on rational considerations. Our reactions must be intelligent, not emotional, because thereupon depend not only our own, but our children's and fellowmen's health, safety and happiness, our and their physical and spiritual well-being and sound development.

### ADEQUACY OF MATERIALS AND FORMS IN TERMS OF FUNCTION

It has been pointed out innumerable times, in every analysis and evaluation of the industrial arts, that forms and materials must express efficiency and logical adequacy. They must be honest. This still needs repetition and emphasis. It has been slightly less stressed that, above and before all, the purpose of utilitarian objects is to serve human beings in the most humane and up-to-date way, to make living more enjoyable, not merely more complicated.

Before the days of mechanized manufacturing methods which made possible mass production, and thereby changed not only the appearance of man's surroundings but his whole life and attitude toward life, creative imagination, skill, and the knowledge of a few basic materials and tools brought forth the individualized charm of the products of the artist-craftsman or builder. Today engineers and designers plan the appearance of things. To plan well they need more than creative imagination, skill, and knowledge of a few basic materials and simple tools. For in addition to nature's basic materials, science provides them with an ever-growing number of synthetic materials and adds to the simple tools of the craftsmen an infinite variety of the most intricate machinery.

New materials, especially the great variety of synthetic plastics and laminated materials, create new aesthetic effects, but they will rarely justify radical changes in forms which are determined by such unchangeable factors as the human body and its physical and mental mechanics. Our houses, beds, tables, chairs, and our household appliances in general, may be made in prefabricated parts or as complete objects out of newly developed synthetics and alloys, but their basic forms will, or ought to be, only then influenced by these new materials when a change of form is justifiable in terms of greater efficiency and comfort. We must beware of the attitude which has sometimes been taken: to adapt ourselves to the machine and its products instead of planning techniques and materials always with the one paramount aim in view that they will serve us better than what we had before.

Good modern design is the result of intelligent integration

of many intricate factors and it must be judged as such. Aesthetic considerations play merely a part, and in no case a paramount role, wherever questions of practical use are involved. Besides, they generally take care of themselves. Because of the confusion of terms and issues in the various fields and domains of the arts it has proven helpful to speak of industrial design rather than of industrial art whenever we deal with forms and products whose function and purpose is primarily material, and whose perfection, if it is achieved, is the result of the cooperative effort of generations or of carefully integrated planning in which the contributions of science, technology, and art can hardly be measured separately. Therefore, in the following we prefer to speak of design when dealing with the values and qualities of things of practical use. For it is more in the clear terminologies of rational design and of technology than in the problematic considerations of largely speculative aesthetic and philosophic disputes that we must look for assistance in the attempt to school our senses for critical evaluation and intelligent judgment of the true qualities and beauty of the useful.

A car or an airplane is not good and admirable unless in its design there have been incorporated above and before all such features of safety and efficient functioning as science and technology can provide at a given time, and with due regard to a maximum of comfort, ease and pleasure of manipulation and use.

To be efficient as well as pleasing, aesthetic features such as colors and surface treatment must be psychologically sound. Streamlining has to be technically justified. We must ask ourselves whether an interesting color scheme or rich-looking equipment has intelligent as well as striking qualities: whether the reflections from the shiny, senseless decorations of the control panel in our car will not hurt and tire our eyes and the dazzling armor of our bumpers irritate those of other drivers on the road, thus impairing directly or indirectly our mutual safety and comfort. Materials and color schemes, always and everywhere, but particularly in the interiors of cars, airplanes, and ocean steamers, must be chosen and judged psychologically as well as aesthetically. Some materials—as for example velvets—and certain color combinations are apt to increase the tendency to seasickness. Tests can ascertain the means which might diminish it. If all psychological and physiological human factors were taken into account in everything which is designed for human use, a natural variety of forms and materials would result without arbitrary introduction of artificial decorative features.

## DESIGN FOR LIVING

To bring light and air into our houses, as much or as little of it as is desirable under given circumstances, to establish contact between the indoor and outdoor, to frame the sight of a beautiful view, of a tree, of a flowergarden: these are the main functions of our windows, if our houses are planned the way they ought to be. This may mean glazing, curtains and sunshades of different degrees of transparency and translucency, of different texture and coloring, window-construction, proportions, and sizes of various kinds, depending on light and wind conditions, on climate and physical surroundings in general, and on the function of a particular part of the indoors.

When questions of function and efficiency and of adequate forms and materials to answer them have been intelligently determined, then our sentimental preferences may be taken into consideration. But even these we should check as to their psychological and organic justification. With a view of green foliage we will use a different color scheme in our interiors than when our windows face a row of dull houses in a street without any vegetation. Every single decision should be based on logical reasoning rather than on purely sentimental preferences or prejudices.

Arbitrary rules and generalizations may spoil the solution. The question of types of textiles for hangings and covers, of surface treatment of walls and furniture, of construction and sizes, of proportions and of planning in space, is to a large degree to be determined by regard for efficient functioning and sensible balancing of interdependent factors in given situations under given circumstances. Nor are there set laws as to the right color, texture and material combinations. There is only the steadily developed sense and knowledge of the most adequate solution in each particular case. After considering all physical and psychological relations, it is not too difficult to arrive at the right results. They offer themselves almost automatically, and we are reaching them through a sound and intelligent approach free from any traditional or modern style prejudices, because we are deciding about our furnishings with sole regard for our way of living which has to fit our personal needs, and not those of an "interior decorator" selling us ideas of the days of our grandmother or Louis XV.

The kinds and types of furnishings in our homes as well as working places must be considered, first, in terms of how well they serve us, and second, how gracefully they do it or could do it. Tables, chairs, cupboards, beds, lighting fixtures, door handles, radio sets, chinaware, silverware, all household appliances and gadgets, things which are primarily utilitarian, must serve us, not we them.

To mention particularly one of the most intricate and important pieces of furniture: chairs should be intelligently planned for various ways and purposes of sitting, with particular regard to the body's habits and needs. A perfectly fitting plaster-cast will become as uncomfortable, considering the length of time we are forced into one position in it, as the too flexible or too soft support which fails to deserve its name. The plaster-cast type of chair may appear to our eyes an interesting answer to the chair problem, efficient and functional looking, particularly if we are without prejudices against modern design; but unless we like to sit very still, we find it uncomfortable. However, for limited use, for sitting at a dinner table, for example, a certain stiffness of support may be desirable. The degree of flexibility in chair construction as well as in upholstering, choice of material, finish, form and proportions of parts, are to be determined by the type of sitting for which the chair is intended. Different rules and laws apply, depending on whether a chair is intended to serve for work at a desk, at the dining table, in connection with high or low desks, or free-standing for relaxation, reading, and conversation. The shape of seats and backs, their hardness, softness, height, depth, and width, the form and finish of side supports, proportions of parts in relation to one another: all these factors are more important than appearance. Our eyes will never sit in a chair, and before we allow them to influence our judgment, our body must taste its functional qualities. We must sit and move in a chair, handle it, carry it and push it, and think of the upkeep of its good looks before we can accept its make-up features as harmless or truly enhancing. Covers and upholstering of all seating furniture should preferably be removable and exchangeable.

We must be skeptical about fancy reinforcement structures connecting chair legs, which often are a style-element of some past period, without real technical justification, serving merely as dust catchers. Naturally, construction must be safe; chair legs have to stand a great amount of strain. In modern, not yet completely developed, models it is important to watch out for balance. Some streamlined plywood seats tend to fall over if one does not hit the right spot in sitting down. Experimental forms need encouragement, but the public should not be confronted with too early stages of development.

Radically new construction methods and materials in any field of industrial products should be allowed a longer and more thorough laboratory development than is usually possible under present manufacturing methods. Designers must be given the same chance and means as scientists to work for years, if the subject calls for it, on the development of a new idea.

As far as purely aesthetic appeal is concerned, we must judge new as well as familiar forms equally critically. But it is our duty and responsibility as living in an age full of never-tried possibilities, that we encourage experiments with new forms and synthetic materials by not buying and not asking for copies of forms dictated by the restrictions of the times of handwork, of limited choice of material, and of a different social structure.

The inconveniences of sitting in plaster-cast chairs brings a problem to mind which illustrates the dangers of the opposite extreme, namely, too unsubstantial support. In this connection our beds deserve special attention. For the outward appearance and trimmings we take over the dated features of other times and cultures which we ought to discard for contemporary forms. However, this masquerade, though unfitting, may be considered harmless as far as our physical health is concerned. But, although our ways of sleeping, our skeleton construction and our bodily mechanics have hardly changed through centuries, we use, inside this antiquated outfit, the radically newest and latest models of cloudy mattresses with complicated intestines of spring construction. The much-advertised softness resulting from the hard competition of dealers who have to trump up one another with more softness and bulkiness brings doctors in the house, who may find out that the doubtful progressive design of mattresses has caused our and our children's backaches and other troubles.

It would, of course, lead us too far afield to analyze each product of old or new design that an all too versatile modern house-furnishing industry offers us. We point out only a few most obviously misconceived designs as illustrations of what to watch out for.

There are certainly, on the other hand, many examples which could illustrate the very excellent contributions which the industries of our time have made to greater comfort and bodily hygiene and well being. But there is no lack of emphasis on such cases, while the mistakes which are naturally made are understressed and therefore survive longer than is often necessary.

The most intelligent planning and designing for our homes has so far been done in kitchen and bathroom equipment and in the field of household appliances. But even here there is still ample opportunity for improvements and simplifications. Sometimes things are overplanned, and particularly overstreamlined, if we use this expression in the wider sense of unjustified smoothening, unifying, and straightening of surfaces and shapes. Greater variety in the surface treatment of our kitchen cupboard and drawer sets, for example, might save us the trouble of opening a dozen doors to find the glass, pot, or gadget we are looking for.

An example of overstraightened design is the bathtub. The old-fashioned type, which we certainly do not with to revive, had one decisive advantage over the modern one. You could stand firmly and straightly with ample space for your feet when washing your children or cleaning the inside of the tub. The correct profile of the bathtub, and for that matter of any piece of furniture or equipment which calls for standing close to it for some reason or other, should be shaped with regard to this toe space. In the case of furniture which reaches down to the floor, the height and depth of this space is not only determined by the feet, but must also be considered in relation to cleaning facility. Whatever it may be that we design or look for, only after all the requirements in regard to human safety, comfort, and ease of upkeep and maintenance are fulfilled satisfactorily, can we consider details of form, color, material, and surface treatment.

Let us appreciate a few further relationships. Are all gadgets with which we surround ourselves really time and labor saving, considering everything? Are we sure that all of the strikingly designed modern appliances which are offered to us are really good for us, and necessary for our comfort and well being? The popular, inexpensive, unventilated gas heaters, for example, which are still allowed to be manufactured and sold in some parts of the country, though forbidden in others, are they good for our health? If not, even the most fascinating streamlined make-up cannot protect us from possible gas poisoning. An attractively disguised poisonous instrument is more dangerous than one that would warn through ugliness.

And do we really have to have those pompous refrigerator animals which appeal to our low possessive instincts through their gorgeousness? Should we not rather plead for smaller units which would be fitted unobtrusively into the rest of our kitchen equipment and would still suffice for the preservation of our perishable food. And are all the helps for food preparation which we use really necessary and good for us? May not some of the overprocessing and grinding of our food to mush or liquid have some, so far not yet scientifically analyzed, evil effects? Think only of the teeth which are intended by nature for chewing, not for letting machine-chewed food pass by untouched. If we cannot be given completely satisfactory answers to the question of principal rightness, the shape and color of objects of doubtful basic value and usefulness need be of no concern to us. They can never be beautiful or good unless they are helpful and not detrimental to our health or comfort.

Still another important factor deserving our critical attention is the *interdependence* of the things with which we surround ourselves.

It will be good for ourselves, and of immeasurable benefit to progress, if we think more in terms of relationships than of rugged individualism and isolationism. This sounds like some sort of doctrine, but here is how it applies to our daily living:

Mr. Jones wishes to surprise Mrs. Jones with a streamlined, beautiful, shiny vacuum cleaner. A high-pressure salesman makes the cleaner swallow fine dust and rough dust, demonstrates all its miraculous faculties, and elaborates on its superior qualities as compared to obsolete, or cheaper, or merely generally inferior products. Mr. Jones buys "the best vacuum cleaner in the world" because he wanted Mrs. Jones to have the very best. He drives home with his precious gift and tells Mrs. Jones: "No more slavery, dear—no more getting down on your knees to clean under cupboards and beds," and the 20th Century theme song of electrified progress rings out. "Let's get the dust from under the sofa." But alas, the sofa was not designed by a vacuum cleaner mannfacturing concern, nor by a designer who had thought of something as intangible as dust. VAC's nose is put under the sofa. Hitting his shiny back, he refuses to go further. He is not an ordinary broom. He is a mechanical broom—an electric vacuum cleaner. Have these people never heard of class distinction? Mechanical gadgets are the children of intellect and they like intellectual companionship.

The moral of the story? The same spirit that created the

house and furnishings in which it is called on for service must plan the vacuum cleaner. Otherwise they will not cooperate.

There are two ways out of this dilemma. One practical and rational, the other impractical and irrational.

We may decide to submit to and accept the logic of the

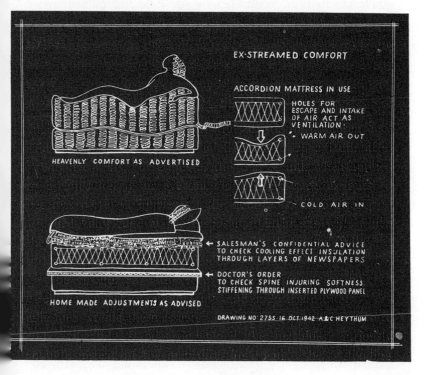

**Fig. 51**
Ex-streamed comfort

spirit that creates the vacuum cleaner, mechanized manufacture, time-saving and labor-saving devices, but which, it must not be forgotten, causes also intricate relationships and fateful interdependence. And when we accept this challenge we must be willing to plan our whole life and surroundings, including vacuum cleaner and sofa, accordingly. The alternative is to deny this spirit, to go on making and buying sofas on one hand and vacuum cleaners on the other with no concern for their interdependence. Then of course we will have to re-introduce slave labor or become ourselves slaves because of our ignorance and negligence.

Design must be controlled by scientific and humanitarian considerations, not by the doubtful economics of an antiquated profiteering system. Only thus is constant improvement and correction of mistakes assured. The human body will not change; and, although the human organism is as capable of adapting itself to changing surroundings and living conditions as of influencing them, there are a number of basic laws of nature which cannot be disregarded without the danger of injuring health of body and mind of individuals and whole nations. The fact that the human being easily succumbs to irrational influences should not be misused. The natural confusion of mind should not be artificially increased. It must be clarified by all means.

As long as bad things are allowed to be advertised, bad inside with an attractive makeup outside, quality which is necessarily inside, has no sales appeal. Nowadays, even people, unless they use the standard make-up, are overlooked. There is such loss of feeling for quality that only the well-packed, well-groomed, well-painted merchandise and people are considered worth money or attention. This is not only sad, bu' it holds a great danger for any civilization that carries a surface idolization to the extreme. People lose not only their faces under the mask, but also their souls and miss all that is really worthwhile in life.

We live in our houses with our whole body and mind, not merely with our eyes. And we should be willing to admit also that a good original piece of old furniture or a beautiful

152

Chinese vase we cherish cannot possibly provide us with an intelligent excuse for turning our whole home into an antique shop and for calling in, when we wish to build our house, a versatile stylist to design us one that will match our old chairs and silverware or Chinese vase. Nor, as we know, should we rely on the commercially-minded advice of sales catalogs as to which unauthentic copies of bygone periods are most in vogue and most fitting, because we may get the least service for the most money.

**Fig. 52**

In this studio interior the furniture is of 20th century design, and so are the Textiles and P. Pfisterer's desk-lamp. The intricacy of an ancient Chinese sculpture and of the pattern of an American Indian basket stand out to full advantage against the simplicity of the surroundings. (Designed by A. & C. Heythum. Photo O. K. Harter.)

Unless we support the attempts towards up-to-date solutions and answers to our needs and desires we slow down progress. The modern designer and manufacturer need our willingness to test their products in order that they may benefit from our

153

criticism and advice. If we discarded our often completely unjustified prejudices we would find that the beauty we have seen in copies of something old that perhaps never was really beautiful is much less real and stimulating than the up-to-date, young, original products of sound engineering and design. Sometimes the new form may seem crude—it often is crude. But only when through using and buying and criticizing it we furnish the means for its further development can refinement be achieved.

When we plan our homes let us beware of the expression "interior decorating." It would be a great step towards more honest, more real, and in the end more comfortable and enjoyable living if we could clear our minds of the prejudices of false ideals and pretensions. We would do wisely to give 80 per cent of our antiques, if they are authentic, to our local museum, and keep only 20 per cent for sentiment, throwing out the copies of copies. Harmony lies in contrasts as much as in accords. Design is a problem of composition and balance, not of matching or styling.

The charms of the mystic or intricate forms, colors, and patterns of things of other times and cultures stand out in full beauty against the unpretentious simplicity of contemporary design. They are often lost or buried in surroundings which attempt to match or fit through the means of copied and imitated period elements, applied in the desire to create a so-called authentic *milieu*. Art of the Orient, art of the Occident, formal expressions of the past, and formal expressions of the present, will fit together wherever there is a balance of inner or formal values and whenever choice and composition reflect the spirit of sensitive and appreciative minds.

But we should never fall victim to mere decoration. Our keynote must be comfort and efficiency in all parts of our furnishings and household appliances which are primarily utilitarian. Whether in the choice of "objets d'art" for the satisfaction of our sentimental and spiritual needs we tend to an accent on strictly modern, or strictly antique, or a mixture of both, is a matter of personal preference. As long as we avoid turning our homes into museums or curiosity shops there is no reason for following any exclusive rules or patterns.

Let us have elaborate decoration and fancy trimming where they belong, on Christmas trees, on wedding and birthday cakes, in pageantry, in the ballroom; in short, at festive occasions, because this is when and where we should dress up our houses and windows, our horses, our cars, and ourselves. But let us emphasize usefulness and graceful simplicity in everyday life, for there is beauty and charm in simplicity. In the world of fashion, for example, refined simplicity and adequacy is the hall-mark of true elegance. And what else is adequacy but balanced relationship, intelligent adjustment, rational behavior of rational beings whom nature endowed with the faculty of discriminating and reasoning, of learning through experience, of accumulating knowledge, and of organizing living.

## It Is Not the Fault of the Machine

Why is it, many ask, that the machine age has brought forth so many more badly designed and useless objects than any other previous cultural period. After all, man is still the only designer, the only cause of man-made forms and products. Even the most intricate machine is merely a highly developed mechanical tool. It cannot spoil anything.

Literally, it certainly cannot. But its almost infinite mechanical potentialities have confused man's mind. He has lost control over his tool. The simple human relationship: mind-hand-tool-labor-finished product is disrupted. And the intricate system of drafting-board planning, laboratory experimenting, die and pattern-design, die and pattern-making, parts-production, staggered, mechanized assemble, final check and makeup is still far from being the organically integrated process which it has to become before its products can be the perfect and humanized expressions and realizations of thought and form concepts which we appreciate so much in the hand-made products of the past as well as of today.

The machine, in contrast to the sensitive hands and hand-tools of the craftsman, is a mere soulless and unfeeling means for accelerated production. It stamps out with equal concern and efficiency a million poorly designed shapes or a million well-conceived ones. And because mechanized production makes the endless multiplication of a badly conceived form possible on a fantastic scale, an article intended for mass-production should go through a process of testing that would leave no possible objection disregarded. Especially should its human qualities be checked and rechecked: how well it fits and serves and answers human needs and benefits human health and well being; how well it is adapted to the functions of the human body and mind; what sociological implications are involved in it; whether its design is in every regard the best and most timely under given circumstances.

No manufacturer in possession of the means of mass production should be allowed to make his own individual uncontrolled and unchecked decisions as to the design and number of products which he throws on the market. Because of the large-scale and fateful consequences and repercussions of any mistake made in this regard, whether due to ignorance or lack of sense of social responsibility, there will have to be introduced sooner or later, agencies of check and control, committees of public-spirited and social-minded professional experts, including psychologists, physicians, sociologists, engineers, scientists, designers, architects, artists, manufacturers, economists, and above all, plain consumers, who would represent the interests of the public at large.

## CONCLUSION

Even though remedies are already known, evils will keep spreading unless every single human being recognizes that his personal attitude is of paramount importance and decisive influence, that every time he either produces, promotes, buys, or uses the wrong thing, he thereby increases the unhealthy, the ugly, the harmful. For sound and steady progress in any field of human activity, whether in the sciences, in the arts, or in human relations, the interest and support of the masses is a factor of vital importance. Without the active participation and interest of everyone there will be no acceleration of progress in spite of all our wonderful means of building a better and sounder world almost overnight. Every voice added, every intelligent choice made or criticism given in stores and sample fairs where badly or poorly designed things are offered to us, will mean a step forward in the direction of real improvement. Therefore the training of our sense of discrimination and of intelligent appreciation of real qualities is of paramount importance.

It is true that when we examine closely industrial products of our so-called Machine Age, we find only a few which can stand a thoroughly critical examination if we consider the almost unlimited possibilities of perfection which science and technology offer. But the few are promising signs of successful attempts in the right direction and encourage our hopes for the future, particularly when we take into account the still immobilized forces of the beneficial influence which awakened public conscience will some day exert. For the time being there is no ground for over-optimism in this regard, because of the still all-powerful grasp that a too commercially minded advertising system has on the mind of the masses. Exploitation of human weaknesses and ignorance used to be worse, but it is still bad enough.

Science provides us with the means to arrive at clear concepts of the soundest and most efficient methods of satisfying our material and spiritual needs and desires. Technology offers us the tools to make available to every single human being the best, the most fitting and most pleasing means to answer these needs and fulfill these desires. But the majority of men are unaware of these facts, and in spite of a general feeling of dissatisfaction with the misery and ugliness that surround them, they muddle dreamingly along, failing to realize how much their awakening would speed up the process of better and happier adjustment.

We must learn to live with open eyes and open minds. We must first want improvement, and then do our part in bringing it about. And we must realize that nature has endowed us with intelligence not that we may misuse or disuse it, but in order that we may develop it to our highest capacity. Constructive criticism will help to bring about clarification of issues and will check the senseless overproduction of ugliness and misery which lack of foresight and absence of intelligent planning and design have brought about. In this sense the criticism and intelligent appreciation on the part of each one of us of the things which surround us constitute a real creative effort.

# CHAPTER VI

## POETRY

### by

### DAVID DAICHES

The arts differ from each other not only in virtue of the medium each employs (words, musical notes, colour and line, etc.) but also in the way in which the medium is handled. Poetry, like fiction, uses words as its medium, but in poetry words are exploited differently; aspects of language with which the novelist is only slightly concerned are of primary importance to the poet. For the poet employs the intellectual meaning of words, and he also uses their associations and suggestions, their sound and rhythm, and the musical and other patterns they form in combination with each other. Yet obviously this does not sufficiently distinguish poetry from other forms of literature; for a novel, too, will use aspects of language not employed by the writer of purely scientific prose — the sound and rhythm and "colour" of words—only in a less degree than the poet. Is the difference between poetic and prose literature, then, simply one of degree? Is it simply that in poetry the rhythm is more regular and the dependence on the suggestions and associations and the music of words is greater than in prose? And if this is so, where are we going to draw the line between the two kinds of literary expression?

The answer to these questions is suggested as soon as we begin to ask ourselves a further question: What is it in the poet's subject matter or in his way of apprehending his subject matter that makes him use language the way he does? This may sound a somewhat evasive way of posing the problem, for after all we cannot tell much about the poet's way of apprehending his subject except through inquiring into the manner in which he has expressed it. But it is clear that if the expression is discerned by the experienced reader of poetry to be adequate, to be the inevitable expression for that particular subject matter, then there must be something either about the subject matter or about the poet's way of apprehending it that was essentially poetic, that made poetic expression appropriate and inevitable. Again, however, we have the question: What is the subject matter apart from the poem? The history of poetry provides proof enough for the contention that there is no naturally poetic subject, that anything, if apprehended in the proper poetic way, can become the subject of poetry. So we cannot say that the difference between poetry and prose is that poetry, dealing with a poetic content, naturally finds a poetic form, while prose, dealing with a different kind of content, uses only the devices of expression appropriate to that content. There is no such simple mechanical relation between form and content in any art. But we can say that if there is a poetic way of expression there must be a poetic way of apprehension in terms of which that kind of expression is the most complete and the most satisfactory, and that the difference between prose and poetry is not simply a question of the different degree to which certain aspects of language are employed: the difference between the two forms of literary expression lies primarily in the mode of apprehension in terms of which the kind of expression chosen becomes not only the best but the only adequate one.

If this seems to suggest that poetry is a state of mind and not a form of art it is because of the difficulty of discussing the nature of any art except in terms of supposed intentions and presumed effects. When we talk of an artist's intention, or of the way in which he gets his original motive to create, we are not—if we are engaged in an aesthetic discussion—talking in psychological terms at all; we are arguing from the nature of the finished work of art and trying to explain its nature and its value on the assumption that art, representing a *transference* of insight from artist to audience, can be helpfully discussed by considering the work as though in its original form it was a state of mind. That enables us to clarify certain questions relating to the artist's method and procedure, which in turn helps us to see more clearly what the work of art actually is and where its value lies.

The poetic method of expression becomes the necessary and inevitable one in virtue not of the subject matter which the poet is endeavoring to express but of the quality of the insight which he has brought to bear on that subject matter. This is not to say that poetic insight can exist without poetry, for one of the main tests of poetic insight is that it must seek expression in poetry. And we can say that the insight of the poet differs from that of the prose artist just because of the different use of the medium of language to which each is driven. The poet employs all the denotational, connotational and emotional resources of language, but this in itself, as we have seen, would distinguish poetry in degree but not in kind from prose. A more significant differentiating factor in poetry is that the poet uses these aspects of language in such a way as to make some of them *comment on* the meaning and significance indicated by the other resources of words: this comment provides increased specification and particularization (the meaning is restricted to just *this* and not *that*) and at the same time, paradoxically, it provides new enlargement and enrichment—so that the significance of the whole is at the same time specified and universalized. Good poetry is the result of the adequate counterpointing of the different resources of words (meaning, associations, rhythm, music, order, etc.) in establishing a total complex of significant expression. The subject matter capable of such expression is, theoretically, unlimited in scope, yet in fact any subject matter which finally finds itself expressed in a poetic manner is bound to have certain qualities. For in poetry you do not sit down with a subject $x$ and proceed to express it through a medium $a$: you sit down with a potential subject which becomes more specific and more universal (simultaneously) in proportion as it becomes poetic expression, until when the poem is complete it becomes not the subject $x$ with which the poet had started but a complex $xa$, a unique organic product of subject and medium. The form, in fact, is an aspect of the content—a characteristic of any work of art. The subject of poetry must therefore have both a certain specificness and a certain universality; but these are not qualities that exist in the "subject" abstracted from the poem which gives the subject expression; they are, rather, qualities of the poem. For the subject of a poem cannot be expressed except by repeating the poem.

A poem therefore is not distinguished from a work of prose literature by the fact that, in giving expression to its meaning, it uses resources of language that are not employed by the writer of prose: it is distinguished from prose literature in that whereas in prose the aspects of language employed reinforce each other as gestures emphasize speech, in poetry the aspects of language employed, being as a rule more various, are employed in a more complex and paradoxical way—one set of qualities providing instructions for interpreting the meaning that emerges from another set, not simply emphasizing, but modifying, specifying, enriching, reminding, disciplining, liberating, restraining, urging on—doing any or all of these things (even distorting and contradicting) in the service of the final totality of meaning. And the "meaning" is not a pure intellectual meaning: it is a complex welding of emotional and intellectual significance. Poetry moves further away from prose and nearer "pure" poetry according as the different elements of the medium are used in counterpoint rather than in simply repeating the melody simultaneously an octave higher or lower. Thus to describe a dance in tripping words and in a dance rhythm is the simplest kind of poetic effect: in a great poem that effect would be enriched and complicated by all kinds of countersuggestions and expansions deriving from a subtle use of sound, suggestion and association.

Consider, for example, these three stanzas:

> Methinks this world is oddly made,
> And everything's amiss,
> A dull presuming atheist said,
> As stretched, he lay beneath a shade,
> And instanced in this:
>
> Behold, quoth he, that mighty thing,
> A pumpkin, large and round,
> Is held but by a little string,
> Which upward cannot make it spring,
> Or bear it from the ground.
>
> While on this oak a fruit so small,
> So disproportioned, grows,
> That, who with sense surveys this All,
> This universal, casual, ball,
> Its ill contrivance knows.

Here the use of those resources of language other than simple denotation is limited to the reinforcing of the meaning by a simple but monotonous rhythm and a certain contrivance that keeps the sentences of a similar length and pattern and provides a regular alternation of rhyme to mark the end of each phrase. Put beside these three stanzas other three in which the actual "content" is no more profound but where the technique is much more so:

It is an ancient Mariner,
And he stoppeth one of three.
'By thy long beard and glittering eye,
Now wherefore stopp'st thou me?

The bridegroom's doors are opened wide,
And I am next of kin;
The guests are met, the feast is set:
May'st hear the merry din.'

He holds him with his skinny hand,
'There was a ship,' quoth he.
'Hold off! unhand me, gray-beard loon!'
Eftsoons his hand dropt he.

Here we find, in first place, that the rhythm, rhyme-scheme and verse form do not serve simply to give neatness or emphasis to each proposition made: they function in a much subtler manner. The contrast between the wedding guest's mood, expectant of secular celebration, and the new mood that is suddenly thrust on him by the stranger, is deliberately ignored by the placid flow of the simple stanzas, and as a result becomes all the more intense and mysterious, all the more effective as preparation for the strange story that is to follow. The deliberate introduction of the direct speech of each of the speakers without any break in the flow of the rhythm, the simplicity of statement suggesting an uncanny foreboding ('he stoppeth *one of three*'), the casual-seeming juxtaposition of the two worlds—the everyday and the unusual—the use of normal adjectives in a context which gives them an abnormal suggestion ('*skinny* hand'), the quiet dropping of an antique word in the midst of an almost colloquial diction (which nevertheless is not colloquial because of the use of the "thou" forms), the internal rhyme in the third line of the second stanza indicating a certain jollity and confidence that contrasts strangely with the foreboding suggested by images in the previous and succeeding stanzas—these are just some of the devices indicating that in this poem the poet is not using the resources of language in simple cumulation but in counterpoint: Coleridge is not using any more of the resources of language than Lady Winchilsea (the author of the first three stanzas quoted), but he is using them in a more poetic manner. In both poems rhythm and rhyme-scheme are simple—they are actually simpler in the second—but it is the way in which rhythm and rhyme are counterpointed to the meaning put across by the other resources of language employed that distinguishes the poet from the accomplished versifier. Poetry is more than a series of propositions reinforced by regular metre and rhyme. This is why—to take a modern illustration—Edgar Guest writes verse and Elinor Wylie wrote poetry.

Language as an art medium has both a formal and a denotational aspect: like colour and form in painting, it can stand for something in the world of experience but it can also possess a pattern independent of its representational significance. It is possible to figure out the *dialectic* of a poem—to some extent at least—regardless of its *meaning*. Unlike musical sound (which is rarely denotational, and when it is, as in the cuckoo notes in the Pastoral Symphony, it is for a deliberately unusual effect) words represent things and say things at the same time. Thus the appreciation of music is both more difficult and more simple than that of poetry—more difficult in that there is no denotational starting-point or jumping-off place to help the listener get started, as it were, and simpler, in that the composer has not to reckon with the listener's interest in the content rendering him insensitive to form. This latter danger often occurs in painting and poetry. The work of art is *mis-read* through the reader's having an attitude to certain fragments of the meaning that prevents him from reading it as the aesthetic whole that it is. Further, in painting and poetry the denotational aspect has a greater variety of possible degrees of importance, the extremes varying from "purely" abstract to "purely" representational art. Colour and form may or may not have reference to anything that exists in the real world, while language, on the other hand, always has a meaning, a "denotatum," so long as it is language and not mere sound, so that the distinction between abstract and representational art is in poetry a difference in tendency only. The problem as far as poetry is concerned is therefore this: How does the poet establish the "denotational" aspects of his poem, how does he make clear to the reader how much relative credit he is to give to each of the different aspects of language as used in poetry? This problem does not exist in music, and it is less acute in painting, where the abstracting or universalizing of form is immediately visible to the eye. But in poetry it is very real. How is the reader to know whether the line "Childe Rowland to the dark tower came" is the initial event in a series of related events whose aesthetic significance emerges from the nature of the plot pattern or is a purely lyrical statement to be understood as a symbol of romantic action? The answer is just this: The difference must be made clear by the adequate use of aspects of language other than the simple denotational: These aspects must be exploited in such a way as to predispose the experienced and sensitive reader to the proper interpretation. The status of the wedding guest in Coleridge's "Ancient Mariner" is not made clear by the words considered simply in their representational capacity, but by the combined effect of all the aspects of words, poetically used. And if Coleridge had expressed his meaning in words considered simply as denotational or representational symbols and then reinforced that meaning by employing the sound and rhythm of the same words, he would have produced, instead of genuine poetry, that kind of emphatic rhetoric of which Macaulay provides some of the finest examples. This is not to say that Macaulay's verse is bad, but that the standard to be applied to it is not a strictly poetic one.

It is sometimes claimed that the poet, like the painter, can ignore the representational aspects of his medium and produce a purely "abstract" art. But the fact is that words are never entirely divorced from their meanings even when we think we are so divorcing them. When Edith Sitwell writes, in "Ass-face,"

> Ass-face drank
> The asses' milk of the stars . . .
> The milky spirals as they sank
> From heaven's saloons and golden bars,
> Made a gown for Columbine
> Spiriting down
> On sands divine
> By the asses' hide of the sea
> (With each tide braying free),

it may appear to the superficial reader that she is using words in a purely formal and non-representational manner, but the fact is that she is using words in a non-literal and *symbolic*

167

manner, which is quite a different thing, for the symbolic meaning of a word is a product of its denotation and depends on it. Perhaps Gertrude Stein comes nearer than anyone else to using language non-representationally, but even her poetry employs no technical device for blocking the intellectual meaning of words in their poetic context, and it must be judged for what it is rather than for what it might have been intended to be. And language, whether in poetry or in any other context, always has in some degree, however slight, a representational aspect. The poet uses this aspect in conjunction with other aspects, as it were contrapuntally.

Poetry, then, is distinguished from the other arts by the medium which it employs; yet this is not sufficient distinction, for there are other literary arts which employ language, the medium of poetry. It has therefore to be further distinguished by the manner in which it employs its medium, language, and this again is determined by the kind of apprehension which the poet brings to bear upon his subject. It is poetic sensibility that determines whether or not language is to be employed poetically. "Sensibility" is, however, an unfortunate term, for it has been used in a variety of senses, many of them imprecise. But obviously there does exist a quality of imagination, a way of apprehending and patterning experience, that is a necessary condition of adequate poetic expression. We must distinguish here between art and craft. The ability to employ the techniques and tools of poetry with skill merely (such as that possessed by the agile parodist or the competent imitator of complex and difficult verse forms) does not in itself guarantee the production of great poetry, since great poetry demands that such skill should be put at the service of a proper poetic apprehension of experience. But, paradoxically, such a proper poetic apprehension of experience (which results in the ability to illuminate through style, through the way of expressing the content) can never be judged independently of the style, the form, for to the reader it must always appear as though this insight is *created by* style. In other words, though two separate requirements are necessary for the poet—a type of skill and a quality of imagination—in the finished product the latter can only be presented through the former in such a way that it appears to arise and follow inevitably from the former's existence. Thus prose paraphrase is not even a differ-ent expression of what the poet says, for poetic content becomes the specific content that it is in virtue of its form, and what the poet says is expressible in no other way. Great poetry is, therefore, independent of subject matter in the sense that anything can be discussed poetically: any tract of experience can be patterned and balanced and harmonized by style into a unique and illuminating content. What, then, is "sensibility"? Obviously not simply the ability to be "affected" by experience in a sentimental or any other way, for such ability bears no relation to the production of art at all. Nor is it the quality of imagination that determines and controls the insight which is the goal of style, for that quality cannot be diagnosed previous to the production of the specific poem nor does it in any real sense exist independently of the poet's technical skill. Indeed, what is his technical skill but the ability to creat insight out of language, so that in "describing" a sunset or an old man on a country road the poet, by his handling of language, creates a pattern and a significance that, objectively considered, does not depend at all on that sunset or that old man? The point is clearer in the case of music: what is Beethoven's "view of the universe" apart from his music? The paradox about art is that insight is determined by the medium; if this were not so, great poets would necessarily be great philosophers, which they are not. So we begin by distinguishing between art and craft, only to discover that in the great artist the "craft" cannot be separated out—it becomes apparent only in the inferior artist, where, in fact, there is no art but craft only. All we can say of poetic sensibility, therefore, is that it is the *kind* of experience of thought and feeling relevant to the particular insight which the poetic handling of language both produces and is produced by.

If there appears to be some contradiction in this argument—that there both is and is not a type of insight that exists previous to poetry and urges the poet to create his work—this is because the whole relation between form and content in art is basically paradoxical. Form expresses the content, yet the content does not exist independently of the form. This is what distinguishes art from all other kinds of expression.

It is a commonplace that in literary expression the place of any part of the statement in the total pattern of the whole is of more significance than it is in non-literary statement. Poetry is that kind of literary statement which depends to the maximum degree on the order of the individual word, and that is because in employing the resources of language in the manner that has been indicated, the order of words serves an extremely important function. Often the poet arranges the words in such an order that until the total complex of meaning is achieved no premature leakage of meaning can occur, and the poem remains obscure until, on a complete and careful reading, the meaning finally "explodes" (to use Gerard Manley Hopkins' term). This suspension of meaning until the total pattern is complete is only one of many means the poet may employ in order to make sure that the reader reads the poem in the proper way, reads it for what it is and not as a series of propositions simply. Rhyme and metre are, of course, the more obvious ways of safeguarding the poetic qualities of a poem (and they serve other

functions, too) but this should not blind us to the fact that
all kinds of delayed-action devices can be used with tremendous
effect for the same purpose. Indeed, what is, say, the sonnet
form but a device for keeping the reader from premature
interpretation until the poem is complete? All, or nearly all,
poetry is obscure in the sense that the meaning does not
progress in simple distinguishable stages but is kept partly
hidden until the form has been completed. This is particularly
true of poetry which does not use a specifically poetic diction,
for when such a diction is used it is less necessary to safeguard
against misreading, the diction alone being sufficient to warn
the reader against any simple propositional interpretation.
That is why poets whose diction is not specifically poetical—
Donne, Rilke, Eliot—are more careful to guard against the
escape of premature meanings by keeping the whole in suspense
until the form is complete than poets like Pope or Tennyson
who can afford to be more propositional in structure because
both their diction and their strict metre help to serve as
reading instructions. Thus a poem which employs a poetic
diction tends to show less "obscurity" than a poem which
includes in its vocabulary everyday speech: when the poet does
not compensate for this lack of a poetic diction by this kind
of obscurity, then he runs the risk of falling into the trap
into which Wordsworth fell in such a poem as "Simon Lee
the Old Huntsman":

> Few months of life has he in store
> As he to you will tell,
> For still, the more he works, the more
> Do his weak ankles swell.
> My gentle reader, I perceive
> How patiently you've waited,
> And now I fear that you expect
> Some tale will be related.

What is wrong here is not an "unpoetic" diction—for any kind of diction can be properly employed in poetry—but a complete lack of any devices to prevent the statements from becoming merely propositional. At the other end of the scale is a poem like Rimbaud's "Une Saison en Enfer" where the precautions taken against the poem's being read literally as a series of propositions are perhaps excessive and produce more expectations of poetry than actual poetic communication. It might be maintained that in Rimbaud this disparity between expectation and actual quantity of poetic communication is part of the effect intended and is itself an important kind of poetic effect (as in some of the songs in Shakespeare's plays). It is in surrealist rather than in symbolist poetry that we must look for the most extreme antithesis to "Simon Lee the Old Huntsman," for the pure surrealist builds up the poetic preparation all the time and that is all—the final "explosion" of meaning never comes, for the poet never had any in mind.

If poetry at its richest and most mature demands what we have called, by analogy with music, the "contrapuntal" use of the different resources of language, it must nevertheless be admitted that in simpler and less profound kinds of poetry the "melodic line" of the poem often appears to be unenriched by any such complex use of the potentialities of words, sense being moulded simply to the sound and rhythm. Herrick provides many examples of poems of this kind:

> Cherry-ripe, ripe, ripe I cry,
> Full and fair ones; come and buy.
> If so be you ask me where
> They do grow, I answer: There,
> Where my Julia's lips do smile;
> There's the land, or cherry-isle,
> Whose plantations fully show
> All the year where cherries grow.

The poetic interest here appears to arise from the fact that the poet has taken an apt but rather obvious analogy and neatly wrapped it 'round eight lines, metrically equal and rhymed in pairs. We appreciate the deftness with which form and content have been wedded. Yet even here, by such devices as the shifting of the pause within the line so that it occurs in a different place in each line, and the setting of the actual rhythm—which is not strictly regular—against the regular metrical scheme which is nevertheless suggested, the poet has achieved something more than a neat idea neatly expressed. Further, it will be noticed that the content falls into three parts: there is the statement, the anticipated question that arises from the statement, and then the answer. Thus while the verse form is dual (eight lines, in couplets) the idea it expresses is triple. And this gives a new meaning to the whole. The poet arrests attention by a street cry ('Cherry-ripe!") expressed in a line which by itself is not poetic at all:

Cherry-ripe, ripe, ripe, I cry.

In this line the basic metrical scheme is not yet set up, and the repetition of the high-pitched monosyllable "ripe" is compelling, but compelling like a shout rather than like a work of art. In the second line the pace is slowed down, the metre becomes evident, and the dramatic status of the author becomes apparent. When, in the third line, the poet moves into a hypothetical dialogue with a line consisting of equable monosyllables with no pause (or an equal pause) between them, the first line now becomes, in retrospect, poetic. The fourth line, building on this new discovery of the reader's, takes advantage of the suspense in the meaning provided by the ending of the third line in the midst of a dependent clause and prepares for the transition from the market place to the lovers' bower (as it were) with especially effective pause (again, running *against* the metrical scheme and for that reason all the more noticeable and effective; for the pause is on the rhyme word) at the actual moment of transition—the word "There" being the link between the two halves of the "conceit," between the idea of the cherries as fruit and as lips, just as a sustained note on a single instrument can bridge two sections of an orchestral work. The basic meaning of the poem derives from a simple contrast between the two interpretations of "cherry-ripe," yet as a dramatic poem it is triple in form—the author cries his cherries, his audience ask where they are, and he replies. There is thus a constant—and effective—tension between dual and triple form in this poem. There is also a tension—and tension in this sense might be described as an apparent conflict of meanings which results in an enrichment of the total meaning—between the purely descriptive and the purely dramatic aspects of the poem. Slight as it is, the poem is nevertheless a "conceit" expressed partly dramatically and partly descriptively, having for its most obvious function the communication of a compliment and deriving poetic effectiveness largely from the tension between the dual and triple aspects of the poem as finally produced. In fact, even in this "simple" little lyric we have an example of the functioning of those laws of poetic expression described above.

Criticism could probe much further, and examine the exact significance of a word like "plantations" in this context or dwell on the paradox of the poet's offering to sell to all comers cherries which turn out to be his Julia's lips. The lover who offers to sell his mistress's favours to the public is not paying her an unmixed compliment. The critic could inquire whether, in the reversal of the usual situation where the lover is the slave of his mistress without openly rejecting the traditional position, the poet may not have achieved something quite different from a poem of simple compliment—a truly paradoxical poem whose total complex of meaning cannot be expressed in any paraphrase. Yet "Cherry Ripe" is, as poems go, a fairly simple lyric, and the fact that so many of Herrick's poems achieve their greatest effect as songs, set to music and sung, is testimony to their relative simplicity. For only a comparatively simple poem can gain as a poem by being set to music. The richest kinds of poetry—a sonnet of Shakespeare, a lyric of Donne, an ode of Keats—do not leave room for any further expressive device, just as no one would dream of setting words to a late Beethoven quartet. But to a simple dance tune one might well put words, and enhance rather than spoil the effect of the music.

Simplicity in poetry is obviously a relative matter, and the foregoing analysis of Herrick's "Cherry Ripe" will show that an apparent simplicity often conceals a very cunning art. Put a poem by Edgar Guest beside the simplest trifle by Herrick and it will be at once apparent that while both poems will appear equally simple the former is inferior because it does not employ language poetically—it is just a commonplace idea expressed in rhyme and metre. The most commonplace idea—such as the comparison between lips and cherries—if given adequate poetic expression ceases to be commonplace and takes on a new richness of meaning. And adequate poetic expression means a lot more than merely expression in rhymed and metrical lines.

What then, about the ballad and the folk-song? Here again it must be observed that the simplicity of such poems is very different from the simplicity of the commonplace modern versifier. Dr. Johnson's parody—

I put my hat upon my head
And walked into the Strand,
And there I met another man
Whose hat was in his hand—

misses the point because it misses this distinction. For folk poetry at its best is not the trite statement in verse of an obvious or silly situation: it is the endeavor to achieve adequate poetic expression of an emotional situation without the use of any references other than those suggested directly by experience. To limit oneself to such first-hand devices is to make poetic expression more difficult—for no help can be sought from literary allusion or from any other kind of indirect association—but gives it a peculiar effectiveness once it has been achieved:

Foweles in the frith,
The fisses in the flod.
And I mon waxe wod;
Mulch sorwe I walke with
For best of bon and blod.

Here is a poem of despairing love which for sheer intensity of expression is difficult to match in any literature. Conscious or not, the art with which it is constructed is of the highest kind. First there is the reference in clearly articulated and unemotional lines to the contented life of the natural world; then, in one sombre and striking line, the contrast between nature and the speaker; and finally, in the concluding two lines, the reason for this contrast. The variations in metre, counterpointed to the basic metrical scheme, correspond to and intensify the different elements in the content. The isolation of the third line—the pivot, as it were, of the poem—and the slowing down of the rhythm in the fourth line, beginning impressively with two funereal beats, combine with the helpless matter-of-factness of the concluding line to make the poem die away in an echoing plangent note. The poem is over before we realize it: the total meaning has been achieved with complete economy, and it reverberates in the mind. The poem, it will be noted, does not begin with a statement in the first person, but only moves into a personal statement in the third line; and this movement from descriptive to confessional expression provides the element of paradox that enriches the total poetic significance. We have here more than versified propositions, for the propositions are arranged in such an order that the total meaning is different from the mere sum of the separate lines. This is what distinguishes it from Dr. Johnson's mock folk poem. The distinction is even clearer if we put beside Johnson's four lines one of the most famous quatrains in early English poetry:

> Western wind, when will thou blow,
> The small rain down can rain?
> Christ, if my love were in my arms
> And I in my bed again!

It is not true, of course, that all folk poetry is good: much of it is quite poor. But the kind of simplicity that characterizes folk poetry is not necessarily the kind of simplicity that makes for bad poetry, such as we find in "Simon Lee the Old Huntsman" or in the numerous parodies of Wordsworth, such as "The Baby's Debut":

> My brother Jack was nine in May,
> And I was eight on New-year's-day;
> So in Kate Wilson's shop

Papa (he's my papa and Jack's)
Bought me, last week, a doll of wax,
And brother Jack a top . . .

In the latter case we have a trivial subject matter expressed in
a series of versified propositions, with no additional illumination provided by the manner of expression. The typical
folk-poem takes an experience that has continually impressed
its significance on the minds of generations of sensitive people
and gives it poetic expression without going beyond the
limits of that experience in finding devices to enrich the total
meaning. It is this limitation of reference that makes the
folk poem, when it is successful, so impressive: such limitation
constitutes "simplicity" only in a very special sense.

This is also true in some degree of the ballad. Yet in one
sense the ballad is less "simple" than in many kinds of sophisticated poetry, for the very primitive nature of its approach
guarantees that kind of simultaneity in expression which is
a tendency alike of the primitive and of the poetic mind. The
poet is continually seeking for devices that will enable him to
express a complex whole in all its complexity and all its
wholeness—in other words, he is seeking for maximum simultaneity in expression. It is also true—up to a point at least—
that the more primitive man is the less able he is to analyse
into separate parts what he wants to express. Poetry is thus
in one sense itself a primitive mode of expression: it tries,
by using simultaneously and in counterpoint *all* the resources
of language, to express the totality of an experience as immediately as possible: it communicates not through sequential
propositions but through a single ever-expanding whole. The
term "primitive" in this sense has no pejorative implication:
it refers simply to the synthetic rather than the analytic
approach to language. The aim of the poet is to achieve a

178

certain synthesis; his medium, language, is analytic in nature; the achievement of a synthetic effect through an analytic medium represents the poet's greatest triumph. Prose, which is a much more analytic method of expression, does not exhibit the same paradox to the same degree.

Many ballads—perhaps the majority—are, of course, simply versified narratives and as such exhibit few if any of the qualities we have been discussing. But many of the Scottish ballads possess these qualities in high degree, showing a combination of dramatic and descriptive techniques and a skill in exploiting the cumulative effects of language that cannot easily be matched in any literature. The opening of "The Lass of Lochroyan" is a striking example:

> 'O wha will shoe my bonny foot?
> And wha will glove my hand?
> And who will lace my middle jimp
> Wi' a lang, lang linen band?
>
> 'O wha will kame my yellow hair
> With a new-made silver kame?
> And wha will father my young son
> Till Lord Gregory come hame?'
>
> 'Thy father will shoe thy bonny foot,
> Thy mother will glove thy hand,
> Thy sister will lace thy middle jimp,
> Till Lord Gregory come to land.
>
> 'Thy brother will kame thy yellow hair
> With a new-made silver kame,
> And God will be thy bairn's father
> Till Lord Gregory come hame.'

Among other things, it will be noted that the repetition here is not simple repetition, but new meanings attach themselves to a phrase each time it recurs and reflect back, too, on earlier stanzas. And the significance of the whole is kept in suspense until the ballad is completed  The opening of "Clerk Saunders" is a good example of the poetic technique of the ballad at its best:

> Clerk Saunders and may Margaret
> Walked over yon garden green;
> And sad and heavy was the love
> That fell thir twa between.

> 'A bed, a bed,' Clerk Saunders said,
> 'A bed for you and me!'
> 'Fye na, fye na,' said may Margaret,
> 'Till anes we married be.'

The ballad would require quotation in its entirety for any adequate demonstration of its technique. But enough has perhaps been said about the ballads and other kinds of "simple" poetry to indicate the difference between simplicity in poetry and triteness in verse.

The history of poetry provides the most important clue to an understanding of its nature: it is obvious that any definition of poetry which is not to be contradicted by the evidence provided by literary history must be able to embrace the works of such different poets as Donne and Tennyson, Chaucer and Laforgue, Dante and Burns, Pope and Blake. Poetry as a term may refer either to a way of handling language as a literary medium or to individual poems. We have been discussing it so far in the first sense. But though it is possible to define in general terms the qualities which characterize the

180

poetic handling of language it is clearly more difficult to define a *poem* in an equally broad manner: "The Lady of the Lake" and "Le Bateau Ivre" are not easily described, even in the most general terms, in a single definition. The fact is that the poetic use of language permits of tremendous variation and can serve many different purposes. In Scott's narrative poems the poetic use of language figures in a much less organic capacity than it does in a poem of Mallarmé or of Donne: poetic expression in "The Lady of the Lake" or "Marmion" is in a sense decorative in function: the main narrative line is determined by the simple propositional value of the sentences, but at intervals the resources of language are used poetically to amplify and enrich the meaning in a manner comparable to but by no means identical with the way in which incidental lyrics are used in Scott's novels. This is not to say that narrative poetry such as Scott writes consists of versified narrative interspersed with lyrics, but it does mean that the central core of meaning, which is a narrative *continuum,* does not depend on purely poetic techniques for its expression, and poetic techniques function as a sort of commentary on this central core rather than as an organic part of it. This is also true, in some degree, of poetic drama, where poetic expression enriches but does not determine the main line of the action. Yet even this is to make too rigid a distinction, for in the greatest poetic drama the enrichment becomes an organic part of the meaning of the action, particularly when, as in Shakespeare's tragedies, the action is itself largely psychological in nature. Nevertheless even in Shakespeare the poetic effect is limited to the individual speech or passage; it is the poetic expression of a phase of the action, not, as in a Shakespeare sonnet, the total meaning of the whole work. In other words, poetic drama uses the poetic handling of language to express situations within the context of the play rather than to determine the general line of plot development. An adequate criticism of a poetic drama would therefore have to discuss the plot (in terms that would be equally appropriate to prose fiction) as well as the poetic technique employed to specify and enrich the meaning of the action at any given point.

The manner and degree in which the poetic use of language figures in a work of literature will depend on the scope and nature of the work. The lyric, which the nineteenth century critics tended to regard as the highest kind of poetry, differs from the long poem in that in it the pattern and significance of the whole is achieved by the simultaneous (or almost simultaneous) poetic use of all the resources of language, and the degree to which language is thus poetically used remains constant throughout the poem. This hardly warrants the conclusion, however, that the lyric is the topmost in the hierarchy of poetic forms, for the most appropriate employment of poetic expression—that is, its employment in such a way as to provide maximum significance in the parts *and* the whole— in any kind of poetry will make it adequate and impressive as a work of art, and there seems to be no more reason for distinguishing, say, the lyric from the epic on the grounds that the former is "purer" poetry than for considering a short musical composition superior to a symphony. The most effective art is always that in which the resources of the medium are most adequately used with reference to the scope and the scale of the work, and there is as much reason for believing, with the neo-classic critics, that the epic, because of its larger scope, is the highest kind of poetry as for awarding the palm to the lyric for its greater intensity. Differences in poetic texture are bound to exist in poetical works of different lengths. Literature, like music and unlike painting, depends for its expression on the passage of a certain period of time; continuity is indeed part of its medium; it is communication in time, not in space. The longer the time—within limits, of course—required for the expression of a work of art the more opportunity the artist will have for employing all those devices which depend on anticipation and retrospect, on the accumulation of significance through structure. Even the use of "episodic intensification"—to use in a different sense the phrase that Professor Schücking coined with reference to the structure of Shakespeare's plays—which we will find in most epics and other kinds of long poem, will add to the poetic effect of the whole by gathering up and enriching the meaning so far achieved, reflecting back on and giving new significance to what has gone before, and at the same time anticipating and preparing new meanings for what is to come.

In any general discussion of poetry it is important to remember that it is the way and not the degree in which the resources of language are employed that differentiates the poetic handling of language as a literary medium from other kinds of handling. The use of sound effects, for example, to combine with other aspects of language in producing the total significance can vary tremendously from poem to poem. In such a poem as Wordsworth's "Lines written in early Spring" there is no emphasis on the purely musical quality of words at all: sound, as an element in the meaning, is employed only in its rhythmic aspects, in the use of rhyme, and in the effective alternation of one- and two-syllabled words:

> I heard a thousand blended notes
>> While in a grove I sat reclined,
> In that sweet mood when pleasant thoughts
>> Bring sad thoughts to the mind.

To her fair works did nature link
The human soul that through me ran;
And much it grieved my heart to think
What man has made of man.

In the course of the six stanzas of this poem an idea, which is limited and defined through the intellectual meaning of the words used, is enriched and expanded into the expression of a mood in virtue not only of the denotation of the words but of the complex of significance which emerges from effects of metre and rhyme, the selection and organization of images, and similar "poetic" devices. Use of the sheer musical sound of the words—their incantatory value—is hardly found in this poem at all. Put it beside, say, the "Ballat of our Lady" by the "Scottish Chaucerian" poet William Dunbar, and it will be seen how poems can differ in the *degree* to which they employ incantation as a part of the poetic medium:

Hale, sterne superne! Hale, in eterne,
 In God is sicht to schyne!
Lucerne in derne for to discerne
 Be glory and grace devyne;
 Hodiern, modern, sempitern,
 Angelicall regyne!
Our term inferne for to dispern
 Helpe, rialest rosyne.
 *Ave Maria, gracia plena!*
 Haile, fresche floure femynyne!
Yerne us, guberne, virgin matern,
 Of reuth baith rute and ryne.

The solemn chiming that rings through this poem provides a single sustained emotional note against which the groups of

short lines speak their meaning, and the totality of significance
that results is expressible in terms neither of the sound nor
of the sense, but only through both together. An example
from another Scottish poet, Robert Burns, will show a use of
sound midway between that of Wordsworth and Dunbar:

> O, my luve is like a red, red rose,
>   That's newly sprung in June.
> O, my luve is like the melodie
>   That's sweetly play'd in tune.
>
> As fair art thou, my bonie lass,
>   So deep in luve am I,
> And I will luve thee still, my dear,
>   Till a' the seas gang dry.
>
> Till a' the seas gang dry, my dear,
>   And the rocks melt wi' the sun!
> And I will luve thee still, my dear,
>   When the sands o' life shall run.
>
> And fare thee weel, my only luve,
>   And fare thee weel a while!
> And I will come again, my luve,
>   Tho it were ten thousand mile!

In the Wordsworth poem, the reader's first reaction is to
the work in its propositional aspect, and this is modified and
altered as the poem proceeds by the effect of metrical, imagin-
istic and other devices. In Dunbar's hymn the initial reaction
of the reader is simply to the organ effect of the sound, and
then this is both specified and enriched (for the paradox of
poetic expression is that it both delimits and expands the

meaning simultaneously) by the impingement on the musical background of the denotation of the words employed. In the Burns poem, neither the propositional nor the melodic aspect of the expression strikes the reader first; the words are in themselves trivial and the metre is in itself commonplace; but propositions, imagery, analogies, metre, rhyme and pattern together communicate simultaneously to the reader that note of passion with the undertone of melancholy, that mixture of recklessness and sadness, of tenderness and swagger, that distinguishes this, as a love *poem*, from a proposal or a confession. Yet all three poems use language poetically and are distinguished from non-poetical literary expression in the peculiar combination of complexity and directness that marks their use of language rather than in any quantitative superiority in the number of aspects of language employed.

If we distinguish poetry from verse it can only be because verse differs from prose in degree rather than in kind (using rhythm with greater regularity, sound effects in a more symmetrical pattern, etc.) while poetry differs in kind also. Verse can be good or bad on its own standard, without being judged as poetry at all. A verse-writer like W. E. Aytoun produced some first-rate verse but cannot claim consideration as a poet. On the other hand, when Wordsworth fails as a poet he does not automatically become a good verse writer— as Scott often does when his poetic inspiration fails. The more conscious the poet is of the purely poetic aspects of language as a literary medium, the more likely he is to produce either good poetry or else something which is neither good poetry nor good verse: when Hopkins fails he does not fall into competent pedestrian verse, nor does Donne: with such writers it is all or nothing—either the meaning "explodes" poetically, or it never achieves unity of meaning at all. A poet like Keats, when he fails, succeeds in writing indifferent

186

poetry (not, like Scott, good verse, nor, like Hopkins, simply poetry that doesn't come off) because Keats' failures, most of which occur among his earliest writings, derive from an immaturity of taste coexisting with an adequate poetic technique.

Chaucer's "Troilus and Criseyde," Shakespeare's "Since brass, nor stone, nor earth, nor boundless sea," Donne's "Death be not proud," Milton's "Paradise Lost," Dryden's "Absalon and Achitophel," Prior's "Lines written in Mezeray's History of France," Gray's "Elegy," Burn's "Tam o' Shanter," Wordsworth's "Prelude," Keats' "Ode to a Nightingale," Tennyson's "Break, Break, Break," Yeats' "Byzantium"—these are a few examples of great poems in English, and the reader who tries to compare them will be struck more forcibly by the tremendous differences between them than by any similarities. Any work of art impresses us first of all by its uniqueness, its tremendous and splendid isolation: here is a new and original illumination, we feel, the expression of a complex of meaning which has never found expression before or since, here is a new pattern imposed on the human situation. Yet the nature of art can never be made clear by that concentration on individual examples which is so often the critic's duty. Only by a painstaking series of comparisons and inductions can the critic ever hope to come to some conclusions concerning the nature and value of any of the arts. A poem is unique in the sense that it is a unique example of a universal activity, and for its proper understanding that universality as well as that uniqueness must be inquired into.

Art is more than virtuosity in handling a medium. Virtuosity, technique, is the means to an end, and the end is that special kind of illumination which produces in the reader a combination of insight and recognition—a simultaneous (and pleasurable) reaction of "how strange" and "how familiar."

Philosophy communicates insight with recognition, mere journalism will communicate recognition without insight: poetry communicates both at the same time. For, when all is said and done, poetry remains a unique way of communicating a unique kind of knowledge, and therein lies its value. The complex of significance which develops from a poem gives to the experienced and sensitive reader more than the pleasure of recognizing technical skill, more than the insight that derives from a new pattern being imposed on an aspect of experience, more than the recognition of what he has in some sense known but never been able to express or never been able to realize that he knew until the moment of reading. It gives all these things. "I think," wrote Keats to John Taylor at a time when he was struggling profoundly with this whole question of what poetry is and should be, "Poetry should surprise by a fine excess and not by Singularity—it should strike the reader as a wording of his own highest thoughts, and appear almost a Remembrance." *Almost* a remembrance: for poetry reminds us of what we had never known before reading the poem. If this is a paradox, it is because art is a paradox, soothing and exciting simultaneously. It is an over-simplification, but perhaps a suggestive one, to say that the function of art is to provide its audience with an immediate experience of the essential paradox of the human situation.

# CHAPTER VII

# THE DRAMA AND THEATRE

by

## BARRETT H. CLARK

### I

Man—at least man who reflects and is able to coordinate his ideas and occasionally put them into words—seems driven by some force to inquire into and explain what he feels and sees and thinks. Even the man who cannot think in an orderly manner and is less gifted with the power of analysis than the average, even the man who confesses that he doesn't know, is likely to make some mental reservation to himself when he says that he hasn't the answer. It is not always the case that he doesn't actually know, but that he will not try to put his answer into words. Ask anyone what he thinks about an eclipse, or the outcome of a war, what medicine to take for a cold, or the value of radio in education, and generally, no matter who or what he is, he will have some kind of answer for you. It may be stupid, it may be good, but it will probably be based on a distinct assumption, directly or indirectly reached as a result of some process of thought.

Most people, even those we are accustomed to regard as unintelligent, are curious, and even those who are incapable of setting their ideas in order will be found to have some pretty clear notions about life. I believe there are fewer people who really don't know what they think than we commonly suppose. Everyone has been surprised on occasion to hear an uneducated man—a farmer, say, or a taxi driver—explain how he has "figured out" this or that problem. He has reached some conclusion on the destiny of man, perhaps one that may coincide precisely with what Socrates himself "figured out" more than two thousand years ago; and occasionally we will be struck by the "common" man's inherent gift for hitting the nail on the head. He can sometimes sum up in a few words far more effectively some philosophical truth than we are able to find in whole chapters of scientific discussion in the formal treatises.

Not that the conclusions of every layman are always logical, or brilliant, or acceptable, or seem to us to be true. Nevertheless, anyone with half an open mind will perceive about him at all times and in all quarters overwhelming evidence of man's universal curiosity, of his tireless quest for an explanation of everything that is going on in himself and in the world about him. Our current expression about the man who "knows all the answers," is not without significance.

Even during those eras of the world's history when little or nothing was recorded of the thoughts of man, and among the so-called backward races and tribes where no one could reduce his thoughts to writing, a body of religious and semireligious thought had become traditional and just as effective as though it had been recorded on stone or paper.

As we know, religious beliefs are the result, among other things, of man's effort to explain himself, his world, and his future destiny in terms he can understand, terms more or less acceptable to him and his fellowmen.

Laws, customs, tabus, moral codes and constitutions are all in the last analysis the result of man's attempt to establish systems to guide the individual and his group in what is presumably the "right" direction, to protect man from the forces of evil and destruction.

The same universal and inborn instinct that drove man to inquire into the nature of the world, to classify the phenomena that surrounded him and to pass judgment upon them, has led him—particularly after he had tentatively solved the problems of securing food and shelter and physical protection from his enemies—and still continues to lead him, to inquire more particularly into the nature and meaning of phenomena of a less pressing nature. Among the phenomena of this sort that have concerned man for at least twenty-three hundred years, and doubtless for a much longer period, are those that have to do with what we call the fine arts. What is Art? is a question that is today as timely, as interesting, as hotly discussed, as it was in the days of Aristotle who, in the Fourth Century B.C. wrote what is the most exhaustive treatment on one of the arts, drama, that has survived. There is not the slightest evidence to show that the problem of the nature, structure and ultimate purpose of drama has yet been satisfactorily settled. The extent to which writers, to mention only one category of commentators who have studied the problem, have argued the matter since the time of Aristotle's *Poetics,* is almost incalculable.

It might seem that after so much discussion it would be possible for us to accept a brief summary of the best of those writings on the nature of drama and agree that Aristotle and his followers were essentially right and had reached certain conclusions to which the majority of us could subscribe. But this is not the case. There seems to be no disagreement on the specific gravity of gold, or the chemical composition of water, nor on the exact minute and geographical location of the next solar eclipse; but if we ask a hundred critics to tell us whether a certain play, or poem, or novel, just published, is basically good, and demand to know why, we are likely to get almost as many different answers.

It would also seem reasonable, after some three thousand years of playwriting, to suppose that we might find somewhere a relatively satisfactory definition of a play, an answer to the question that might be asked by the hypothetical Martian,

What is a good play? or even, indeed, just What is a play? It is easy to point to several plays which by universal agreement are known to be good plays, like *Hamlet,* or *Agamemnon,* or *The Misanthrope,* and say These are good plays. So far so good, but if the questioner insisted on knowing Why?, and asked for some simple standard of taste and judgment by which he could determine why *Hamlet* is good and why the new play that opened last night is not good, then the trouble would begin.

There can be no doubt that if we set all the drama critics to work on this problem (and directly or indirectly they are always working at it, whether they know it or not), we would get a good many interesting ideas, suggestions, and comments, many notions and hints that would seem sound and true to us; but would we come any closer than we now are to a satisfactory solution of our problem? Probably not. We must remember that a man can say many fine and true things about any subject, and yet fail to utter one word that will explain or define it. Most of us, in the democratic countries, feel very deeply that our form of government is the best yet devised, but when we listen to men of good will speak on the benefits of freedom we are painfully aware that their contribution to democracy is rather in deeds than in words. Fortunately we are already "sold" on the commodities offered by Liberty, and not in the position of "prospects" who have to be persuaded.

In college one of my instructors had an apt phrase which he threw at those of his students who gave him answers which, without being incorrect, shed no light on the matter under discussion: "Mr———, what you say is perfectly true, perfectly general, and perfectly meaningless." Personally, I have always thought that Matthew Arnold's dictum on poetry, that it was "a criticism of life," deserved the same answer.

Several years ago I compiled a large volume, *European*

*Theories of the Drama,* which bore the subtitle "An anthology of dramatic theory and criticism from Aristotle to the present day." This ran to five hundred closely-printed pages in double columns, and included the substance of the theoretical comments of fifty-four writers, many of them famous names in the dramatic literature of the world. A careful study of these texts shows an immense variety of viewpoints. They fail, however, to show very much of the fundamental nature of drama, except that it reflects an infinite number of human reactions to life. The entire collection might conceivably prove useful to a playwright, but only if he could make up his mind which critic or playwright, or which school of critics and playwrights, to follow. If he tried to take the advice of each of the fifty-four writers, he would never write anything at all.

Now it must not be imagined because there is no agreement, or apparent agreement, among playwrights, critics and philosophers as to what a play is or should be, or what makes a good play or a bad one, that therefore they do not know. It is a fact, of course, that a man may live what we call a "good life" and be utterly incapable of telling us either what a good life is or how to live it. It is possible, and this was actually the case with the French classic dramatist Pierre Corneille, that a man may write a beautiful and moving play, and at the same time a good deal of nonsense about how such plays are written. The Abbé d'Aubignac could, and did, write a fairly logical treatise on how to write a good play, and in order to show how good his treatise was, he proceeded to write a perfectly absurd tragedy.

We are all familiar with the man who can do things effectively and yet give us the wrong advice on how to do them. One centenarian tells the reporter that he attributes his longevity to abstinence from alcohol, and the next one tells us that he lived to be a hundred and four on a constant diet of strong liquor.

Now, take the famous line from the Roman poet Horace, that poetry should give both pleasure and profit. To which it is possible to say, Of course. Pleasure, indeed, for if poetry does not arouse pleasure of some sort, it will not be read, and then what becomes of the profit? But what does Horace mean by profit? Most followers of the Roman poet took it to mean moral profit, and proceeded to decorate their verses with what used to be called "noble sentiments." The modern followers of Horace, particularly the writers of "socially significant" literature, claim that profit means simply that which will profit the proletariat, or the state itself.

It may be said, then, that though there is wide disagreement in the written records of the past as to the nature, and still more, as to the purpose of art, the disagreement among commentators need not be assumed to be so great as may at first appear when we study their writings. Words have different meanings in different eras and of course with different writers and readers. Many of the words used in these discussions are so general as to be almost meaningless, unless we inquire closely into the author's own particular definitions. Such words as Imagination, Unity, Feeling, Sentiment, Pleasure, Sublime, Useful, are so trite as to be worthless until they are redefined. I knew an intelligent lawyer once who wrote a book on dramatic technique; he used words like Theme and Crisis, Climax and Development, but he had a private code, known only to himself, which on investigation by outsiders showed that what he called Theme must mean what most others called Characterization. His book was nonsense to most readers, but it was not nonsense to the writer. No layman, reading philosophy for the first time, can have failed to note that many philosophers seem to be writing nonsense.

Even where such disagreement among the theorists of the arts is as great as it seems on the first reading, there is probably less divergence of opinion on the fundamentals among them than there seems to be, even after we understand exactly what we are talking about. It is consoling to reflect that art has a way of getting created, and when created, of making its proper effect, no matter what is said about it.

Narrowing our discussion now to the theatre, and through the theatre to the play, we find the same sort of confusion of standards as I have indicated in the first part of this paper. Man's efforts to explain life, his various methods of reconciling himself with nature and his fellowmen, have been reflected in his art and in his attempts to explain art. The same thing, of course, is particularly true in the art of the drama, which is a sort of synthesis of life, shown by actors playing before their fellowmen. (This is not a attempt at defining drama, only a statement of what seems to be a fact.)

The confusion above referred to, the disagreement on fundamentals and details observed in the other arts and functions of man, runs through all formal discussions of drama. That this should be so is only natural, and I believe it will always be so, because the raw materials of drama are more directly drawn from life than is the case with say music or architecture. Living men and women are the *sine qua non* of drama, and the more directly the playwright comes into contact with life the more deeply is the spectator touched with a sense of the aliveness of the characters; and hence the more difficult it becomes to reach conclusions on drama that are acceptable to the audience, simply because life itself is a matter on which we have not yet made up our minds. It is really impossible to consider a play apart from its characters— or, shall we say, the art of a play apart from its subject matter. I call to mind the old story of the Tired Business Man whose wife dragged him through the art galleries of Europe. He soon wearied of the endless series of Madonnas and the usually inept Christ Child lay figures, and when asked how he enjoyed the great paintings, he said that he didn't—"You see, I don't like children."

If critic and layman alike were always in agreement on the material and treatment of drama, it would mean, since drama is so directly concerned with life, that mankind had reached a very advanced, if not degenerate, stage of development. Thus, so long as life holds for us some slight glimmer of curiosity, offers us problems and gives us any basis for argument, thought, disagreement, so long will drama appeal to us.

Originally the treatises on drama were largely concerned with its form as well as its content. The rules became chains, though every so often a free spirit, like Lope de Vega or Molière, would change the rules or disregard them. Lope, for instance, tells us (1609) that when he got ready to write a play he locked in "the precepts with six keys, I banish Terence and Plautus from my study, that they may not cry out to me . . . and I write in accordance with that art which they devised who aspired to the applause of the crowd." And Molière wrote, "To hear you talk, one would suppose that those rules of art were the greatest mysteries in the world; and yet they are but a few simple observations which good sense has made upon that which may impair the pleasure taken in that kind of poems . . . I should like to know whether the great rule of all rules is not to please, and whether a play which attains this has not followed a good method?" Shakespeare, on the other hand, disregarded the academic rules, but so far as we know, said nothing about the matter.

Out of the great welter of theory and practice, interesting as some of the theory was, and good as some of the practice proved to be, the writers of plays in spite of rules and discussions, managed to go on writing; and few, if any, were very much affected by what was said of the art they practiced. The really great writers gave us of their best, and the others did their part according to their abilities. Each was actuated by a number of motives, and each wrote what was in him, whether he thought that in so doing he was placating the shade of Aristotle, or pleasing the reigning Duke, or helping a housewife escape from her husband, or bringing about the fall of Capitalism, or preparing a place for himself in some theologian's heaven. They were all, knowing it or not, trying to reproduce for their fellowmen something about life which had struck them as worth noting.

In the final analysis it makes little or perhaps no difference what motive or purpose drove any writer to set down his dreams on paper: Scott wrote most of his novels to pay off a debt of honor; Shaw to convert the public to his own brand of Socialism; Ibsen to awaken the public conscience; Euripides to win a cask of wine or a branch of laurel; Bulgakov to show his fellowmen how corrupt the old regime in Russia could be. Such aims were not, naturally, the only motives that governed the shape and content of the work of these men, but each writer looked into himself and contemplated his world in his own peculiar way.

Because the drama has always been a popular art, one that must appeal immediately to large numbers of people; because its subject matter is definitely linked to the doings of men and women; because it rearranges and holds up in relief to man the multifarious doings of man, it has persisted, in one shape or another, from the very beginnings. Despite financial difficulties, despite its occasional eclipse as a paying business or a mere court function, it has always maintained its hold on the public imagination. It has, as we know, been damned as decadent and dying by the critics of every generation, yet it has spread and in spite of censorship and political upheavals, ministered to a world in which the most interesting study was man himself. Our interest in the theatre springs from that fundamental instinct that is in all of us to learn what man is like and to remold the world into shapes that give or seem to give it some meaning. It is one of the many means man has devised for expressing himself to himself, and passing on to others his wonder, doubts, ideas, and convictions.

That drama, even when it appears in its most explicit and articulate forms, even when the dramatist seems to have explained successfully the phenomena he treats, does not settle very much, or even anything at all; that Shakespeare and Sophocles and Ibsen do not enable us at all times, or even at all, to live more useful lives, has nothing to do with the case. Unless we happen to agree with those who demand that all art shall serve some immediate utilitarian end, we are content to have seen reflected in a play some part of human life excitingly and beautifully set forth. To what extent the spectacle of Hamlet striving to solve his problems is actually going to help you and me with our own problems, makes little or no difference. To demand of Shakespeare that he should do more than reshape a part of the world as he saw it is to ask more of the poet than he could give. That he should serve as guide rather than an expositor is to demand what no artist can deliver.

At this point it might be wise to ask just what is the function of art, in order to determine how much we can properly demand of the artist who expresses himself in dramatic form. The most I might do in this place is to try to outline what has been said during the past twenty odd centuries by those considered best qualified to speak, but it is not my purpose to go into the matter to that extent. I think it enough to make it clear that in my opinion—which reflects that of the modern philosopher Benedetto Croce—art is not limited to the recognized masterpieces or their derivatives, but is basically the product of man's attempts to express himself. It is therefore not a thing apart from life, a decoration added to it; it is not a subject for specialists alone. It is by and large the material and visible result of man's eagerness, his inner necessity, to set forth, expose, reflect and more or less to interpret as much as he can of the life of man.

This is not a definition, but a simple statement of belief, and it is applied here specifically to drama.

As I have said, drama is a popular art, and it is therefore no wonder that everyone considers himself qualified to be a critic. In a way this is true, and it should be true. Not that each person thinks himself capable of analyzing purely technical or aesthetic matters, but because the subject matter of drama is life, and anyone may discuss life, and quite properly believe he has every right to do so. The most perfect play ever written, if it is based on a patently untrue premise, will be rejected by the layman, not on technical grounds but on the broader and sounder basis of truth; and the layman will be entirely right. It is hard to imagine any layman who would deny his ability to judge Nora in *A Doll's House,* because this involves judgment not primarily on Henrik Ibsen the craftsman-artist but on a woman in an understandable situation. In a word, Ibsen is really behind the scenes, where he belongs; he has simply thrown before the public a situation and people that are public property. The particular situation he chose, and the exact details with which he set it forth, were as it were distilled from an infinite number of situations and details known not only to this playwright but to the whole world as well. The essential facts in the case we feel to be true; and they are true—truer, in fact, than the real facts of all the cases from which this one was crystallized, because the playwright, being an artist, chose only what would illuminate his characters and throw his situation into high relief. As a result of the artist's process of reshaping a part of the world as he saw and understood it, we get a sort of quintessential stream-lined picture, or reconstruction. So well did Ibsen accomplish his work that the so-called "imaginary" Nora is no longer a fiction at all, but a reality more real than reality itself. That is why we speak of a woman like Ibsen's heroine as a Nora, precisely as we apply the names of other fictional characters to persons known to us in life. Henry, we say, has a Hamlet complex; Louise is a Becky Sharp; and Bill is a Babbitt.

The same passionate curiosity about life that drives the dramatist to make little imaginary stories to be acted out by players on the stage sends all of us to the theater. People have always gone to the theater, and I think they will always go, even when what we know as the theater, or even only part of it, is transferred to celluloid films or sent over the air by electricity, or even when reduced to the medium of black ink on white paper; even, indeed, when the plays are not very exciting, or not brilliant or not too obviously true.

Playgoers demand entertainment. They want to be amused. Of course they do, and they are entirely right. Even the most academic and crabbed critic feels precisely the same way. For obviously no one will go to the theatre unless he is interested, and if he is interested he will go again, even if it costs him money. Entertainment does not of course mean light or super-ficial fare alone, and to my mind it is the proper word to apply to a tragedy of Euripides, to Hamlet, or the divine foolery of the Marx Brothers. *Hamlet* itself, aside from the superb decoration of the poetry, holds us by its humanity, its uni-versality—which is another way of saying that it feeds our instinct by satisfying to some extent our craving for some kind of illumination. It provides for us a partial answer to that eternal query, What is life about anyway?

Shakespeare, however, scarcely provides a complete and satisfying answer, but he does go some way in the right direction, and offers us certain partly acceptable conclusions. The mere spectacle of men and women perplexed by the same problems that perplex us; governed by the same passions, rising to heights of nobility which we can at least conceive if not attain, and sinking to depths which more of us can understand through actual experience—this spectacle, I say, set forth with the glamor of verbal beauty and clarified by the poet's vision, is in itself a sort of consolation to humanity for its inability to live up to its noblest ideals, and at the very worst it does set forth the ideals. If, for example, Shakespeare cannot tell us why man must suffer for his misdeeds, he can and does at least provide us with the spectacle of man suffering with dignity and fortitude.

Or, to reduce still further to simpler terms the argument I have just outlined, the theatre-goer recognizes in drama those persons and situations with which he is more or less familiar as part of his own existence, and in living vicariously the artist's reconstruction of life he achieves what we call pleasure through recognition. That Shakespeare saw and felt what we see and feel proves that we are akin to our fellowmen, that the world of the past is a part of the living present.

A playwright, anyone with enough ingenuity to put a play together and get someone to produce it, can by some strange chemistry we cannot yet analyze, see more than most of us can see, and is able somehow to mould his characters into shapes that even though they are before us for only a very short time we somehow feel are human. This is something of a trick when we remember that in most plays no character is on the stage much longer than an hour. Take the character of

Father in *Life With Father,* and concede that he is on the stage nearly two hours; yet here in essence is all that we need to understand, the essentials of a man whose half century of life had first to be epitomized in three books, and then again reduced to the length of a play that requires little over two hours on the stage. The playwrights who ultimately squeezed into those brief hours in the theatre the characteristics that developed during a lifetime, like all playwrights who know their business, were able to see more of life than most of us can see, and what is more, to express it in terms that make the beholder see a good deal of what they saw.

During the course of a lifetime how many of us have much chance to speculate on man and the world? How many, even if we had the time, would know how to go about it? Most of us are forced to take from others almost all our ideas in predigested form. Our morals, our religion, our philosophy, are all passed on to us by others, and we usually accept them without question.

Because we are most of us so busy merely existing, are so largely the creatures of routine, we are forced to rely on others to tell us about life. Crudely stated, then, we pay our money in the theatre to see what the butcher's son from Stratford has to tell us about the life of man that we have not been able to puzzle out for ourselves; to the ex-drug-clerk from Norway for *his* contribution to the vexed problems treated in *Hedda Gabler* and *Ghosts.* That such plays do not completely satisfy us except by reason of the terms in which they are stated—that it is not a solution but rather a statement—is proved by the pleasure we derive in seeing the same masterpieces time after time. We return again and again to experience all over again the same variations on the same themes, even though the dramatist does not solve a single problem that he treats.

Even when the playwright fails satisfactorily to minister

to the needs of his auditors in all respects (and this must be the case in a still far from perfect world) and provided he gives a certain amount of pleasure; even when in trying to achieve some degree of truth in the presentation of character or idea he fails to do so, or achieves something quite different, we still occasionally find in his work some vitality, some truth, some beauty that outweighs what is imperfect, what is no longer timely or true or moving. If this were not so then we would find almost nothing to interest us in the plays of ancient Greece or the masterpieces of the Elizabethan drama. The religio-ethical problem of Antigone as treated by Sophocles, would appeal to us only as a curious bit of anthropology.

It is true, however, that nearly all the plays in the world that have enjoyed any sort of success are quickly forgotten. They serve their immediate purpose and are superseded by others that in turn serve their purposes, and only one in many thousands survives for a generation. Endlessly the playwright sees with new eyes the human spectacle and strives to reproduce and interpret it in his own way: he looks at his material and out of the excitement born in him he offers his own little explanation as to what it is all about. And every so often the spectacle, and the interpretation, and the tentative explanation, more or less satisfies us—for the time being: it gives us about as much of the eternal answer to the eternal question mark as we are prepared to contemplate. If we could believe literally, all of us, that the chief end of man is to glorify God, or to dominate Nature by science, or to do any one thing that has been conceived by man as the ultimate destiny of the human race, how easy it would be to know precisely what to do in order to reach the goal. But the trouble is we don't know, and slowly and fumblingly we are trying to find out.

It would seem, therefore, that the chief end of man is to

try to learn a great deal more than he now suspects about himself before he can begin to know just what the chief end of man is, and to determine whether the direction he has been going is or is not the right direction. How can what we call progress be progress at all unless we can be sure of what we are progressing toward?

One of the chief ends of drama, then, is to reveal some sort of answer to this question over and above the obscure answer we are able to formulate from our own observation and experience. The capabilities and limitations of humanity are sometimes thrown into striking relief by the playwright, who thus foreshortens the picture and enables us to see it highlighted; for the artist sees more than the layman can see, and he understands better what he sees, even if he has no final answers. The dramatic artist works somewhat more directly with his materials than the painter or architect or composer, and in shuffling the cards—that is, the raw materials of life— he throws into relief the spectacle that too often bewilders us on those occasions when we have time or take the trouble to look about us. We not only lack the time but the vision and understanding. The life that is thrown back at us on the stage sometimes takes on some shadow of meaning, and even when it does not, the spectacle itself is often absorbing. If we ultimately find out (and ultimately I think we will find out everything) that life is in itself without aim or meaning, possibly the man of vision, the artist, may succeed in showing what life may become, and even give it a meaning which it would not otherwise have had, a meaning actually created by man. It seems to me that the dramatic poet at his best has striven to give shape to the world and that his so-called "creations" have at times gone far beyond exposition and interpretation and actually achieved creation in the most literal sense.

# THE DRAMA AND THEATRE

## II

Plays are usually written to be acted out by players on some kind of stage or platform where they can be seen and heard by an audience. The place where these actors are seen and heard is called a theatre. The word theatre comes from the Greek, and it means to see or witness. The theatre is a seeing-place, so far as the audience is concerned, and a showing place from the actors' viewpoint. A theatre can be, and usually is, a structure, temporary or permanent, built exclusively or chiefly for the purpose of play production, with a stage for the actors and an auditorium for the public. Any place where a play is produced publicly may be considered a theatre. Churches and barns, private homes and street corners, ships and military camps, wherever shows are given and an audience is present, are theatres when they are used as such. It is the presence of performers and spectators participating in a common function at the same time that constitutes a theatre.

There are unnumbered books and fugitive essays on the form, function, architecture and art of the theatre—considered as part of or separate from the plays that are intended to be shown—and a large number of students for at least two milleniums have devoted their lives to the subject. The present discussion is in no sense intended even to summarize this immense subject: it is no more than a short exposition of certain viewpoints on one fundamental argument affecting the relationship between the play and the playhouse.

An audience may be anything from one person to a crowd of several thousands: in modern times the average attendance at a theatrical presentation is perhaps about a thousand or somewhat less. An audience, a crowd, a mob, is not just several individuals who have congregated for a common purpose: to some extent the individuals become part of a larger composite entity that generates emotions which are usually, if not invariably, heightened and exaggerated beyond what any one member of it may be capable of. The French psychologist Gustave Le Bon (in his study *La Psychologie des foules*) explains how when a crowd has gathered together to see or do something, its collective self tends to lose the "mental attributes in which men differ from one another," and to assume the "attributes in which they are at one," which he declares are the "innate passions of race." Clayton Hamilton, in his *Theory of the Theatre* (1939 edition), expands this idea by adding that even "the most cultured and intellectual of men, when he forms an atom in a crowd, tends to lose consciousness of his acquired mental qualities and to revert to his primal simplicity and sensitiveness of mind."

The Le Bon theory of mob psychology, during the sixty years since it was first formulated, has been somewhat modified, and some of us are not quite so sure today that the individual auditor in a theatre really does lose his intellectual perceptions or undergoes so complete an emotional change as the psychologist would have us believe; yet there seems to be no question that an audience feels and behaves, as a group, in ways noticeably different from those in which individuals feel and behave.

As I see it, the person who becomes part of an audience or crowd does not actually lose his individuality or wholly "revert to his primal simplicity"; he only becomes himself an actor, a participant in the show wherein the other members of the audience become actors in the presence of the rest of the audience. The not unusual statement "I don't go to the theatre to see the play but to watch the people" illustrates this point. Nevertheless, the spectator in a theatre, no matter how cultured and individualistic he may be, does to some extent merge his individuality into the "collective individuality," but without wholly losing his power of judgment.

# THE DRAMA AND THEATRE

Every one of us adjusts his behavior to the person or persons with whom he associates, and in this way acts various roles at various times. Dr. Einstein, alone in his study working at a problem in physics, is doubtless a quiet and dignified gentleman, but imagine him, for instance, attending a baseball game, and grant that he understands and likes baseball. It is not inconceivable that he might leap from his seat, tear his hair and demand in colloquial American that someone "kill the umpire." Momentarily the great scientist would behave like any office boy or stevedore. Presumably he would not actually want the umpire executed, or possibly he might, on mature reflection, admit that the umpire was right; yet, at the moment, and in the excitement aroused by the umpire's decision, the high priest of Relativity would have reverted, with the crowd, to the status of a Neanderthal Man.

Long before Le Bon, or anyone else, tried to explain the phenomena of what we now call mob psychology, and long before there was a science of psychology, the writer of plays understood that men in groups or crowds were in some respects different from individuals, and when they contrived their little episodes or stories to be acted out in public they must have known that spectators would not long remain in their seats unless they were moved emotionally. The Dialogues of Plato were all very well for single readers seated in their studies or in their gardens under an olive tree. But not for crowds. Crowds would fall asleep (even crowds of "intellectuals") or go home if they were called upon to watch players reciting the long and involved speeches of Socrates or Alcibiades, speeches that arrived nowhere except at some point which appealed to the sense of logic or justice, and could give pleasure only to the contemplative mind properly attuned to receive them. In other words, the substance of the Platonic dialogues is largely devoid of action and emotion. The Greek playwrights

207

knew that audiences would not for long respond to anything except action and emotion. The conception of an ideal state set forth in long speeches could not successfully hold an audience, but the spectacle of Oedipus paying the penalty for the misdeeds of his forbears, staggering on to the stage with blood rushing from his lacerated eye sockets, could and actually did; and so could the tragedy of Medea killing her children. He who wished to know what Thucydides thought of the Peloponnesian War might read the History by himself, but he who would thrill to the triumph of Athenian arms as acted out on a stage by players, went to see Aeschylus' tragedy of *The Persians.* The playwright wrote history, it is true, but he left out what was relatively dull and emphasized and heightened ("dramatized") the rest.

It should be clear that because men react as they do when they come together in groups to witness a play in a theatre, the means of presentation must throw into relief what the author has written, emphasizing the story and the characters which give it shape and meaning and point. It should also be clear that the shape, size and character of the building or other place where it is presented largely determine the shape, size, and character of the play itself. Ideally, of course, the playhouse and the actors should be the servants of the writer, but from time immemorial, and for good practical reasons, the playwright has to a great extent written his plays to fit the place where they are to be acted out and the conditions under which they are to be presented.

The legendary Thespis who, according to Greek tradition, was the inventor of drama, is said to have taken his actors about from place to place, giving performances from the back of his cart. If the tale is true, Thespis must have shaped his plays to fit his cart and actors, and his audience. He obviously could not offer a vast spectacle on a platform which presumably was no more than a small ox-cart, nor could he bring crowds onto his "stage" if he had only three or four players.

During the great classic age in ancient Athens the theatre was a vast outdoor auditorium seating upwards of thirty or forty thousand spectators. Such large audiences could not, naturally, follow complicated plots or listen intelligently to involved dialogue. Later on, and elsewhere, theatres were constructed in roofed buildings, sometimes large and sometimes very small; in made-over tennis courts, in gardens and private rooms—and everywhere the playwright, almost without exception, adapted his writing to the physical conditions of the playhouse for which he wrote.

Brander Matthews formulated what almost amounts to a "law" when he wrote in *A Study of the Drama* that the great plays of the world "are what they are, partly because of the influence of the several actors for which they devised their chief character, partly because the theatre to which they were accustomed was of a certain size and had certain peculiarities of structure, and partly because the spectators they wished to move had certain prejudices and certain preconceptions natural to their race and to their era." The three influences mentioned have been felt by "every dramatic poet, great or small, in every period in the long evolution of the drama."

This sounds reasonable, and in many respects it is reasonable, just as reasonable as to say that an American child born and educated in an American town is influenced by the ideas and prejudices that are shared by the other inhabitants of the same town. But let us be careful to note that Matthews does not here claim that every play ever written or produced *must* conform in every way to the conditions created by the physical playhouse, the actor, and the public. True, he developed his theory into what he himself and others have pretty widely laid down and accepted as a "law," or set of rules. "It has," according to another critic, J. E. Spingarn, "developed into a system, and become a dogma of dramatic critics; it is our contemporary equivalent for the 'rules' of the Seventeenth Century pedantry." Spingarn goes on to enunciate an even more dogmatic opinion when he says that "the dramatic artist is to be judged by no other standard than that applied to any other creative artist: what has he tried to express, and how has he expressed it."

The art of the dramatic poet has no necessary, but only an occasional or accidental, connection with production by actors in a theater before an audience. In expounding his thesis Spingarn quotes from Aristotle's *Poetics* a few passages which show that the Matthews' "law," widely accepted as it is, is not simply a summing up of the observation and experience of playwrights and critics from the beginning of theatrical history. It was, as a matter of fact, first formulated by a scholarly Italian critic of the Sixteenth Century. Here is what Aristotle wrote some eighteen or nineteen hundred years earlier:

"For the power of tragedy, we may be sure, is felt even apart from representation and actors."

And again, "the plot ought to be so constructed that, even without the aid of the eye, he who hears the tale told will thrill with horror and melt with pity at what takes place."

And finally, "tragedy, like epic poetry, produces its true effect even without action; it reveals its power by mere reading."

One more quotation is worth giving, this time from Voltaire, who is writing about one of his own plays, in the Eighteenth Century: "What has the stage decoration to do with the merit of a poem? If the success depends on what strikes the eyes, we might as well have moving pictures!"

Here, then, very briefly indicated, are two points of view

on the function of the theatre in relation to the play, each one apparently logical and just, yet each apparently opposed to the other in every respect. The controversy, you see, is also very old, and like so many others in the realm of art, as in life, it has not been settled. A play is *usually* intended to be acted out on a stage in a theatre before an audience, and this being so, the playwright is almost invariably—whether he knows it or not—influenced by the shape of the theatre, the capacities of his actors, and the ideas, tastes, and prejudices of his audiences. But such considerations, according to Spingarn and those who agree with him, while true in a sense, have little or nothing to do with the fundamental merits of drama as an art, no matter how important they may be in the realm of economics as applied to what is now known as "show business." A play, if it possesses intrinsic beauty, need not be acted at all, though it is admitted that often a play may be rendered more attractive if it is skilfully and understandingly presented, precisely as a person may be more pleasing if he is well dressed than if he is not. But the trappings of theatrical production are at best only of small importance, and so far as the actual merits of the play are concerned, of no importance whatsoever.

I have no intention in this place of arguing the matter in detail, and I believe that the more evidence set forth to establish the claims of either school of thought, the more likely would the layman come to believe each claimant in turn, and possibly end the whole controversy by crying out "a plague on both your houses!" It is certain that the art of the drama has flourished so far largely within the theatre and when acted by players on a stage, but it seems equally clear that if—God forbid!—the theatre, the actor and the audience were at this moment to be entirely abolished there could, and would, remain a drama.

A vast amount of time and paper might have been saved, in this as in many other arguments, if the proponent of each of the opposing views had tried to be a little more explicit in setting forth his views. For example, it is likely that Spingarn would have agreed that most plays were composed primarily for the use of actors in a theatre; that the writer who gave the actor what the latter could not properly interpret, or the audience what it could not understand or easily accept, and the physical stage what could not be effectively shown upon it, would not be likely to succeed as a playwright; on the other hand Matthews would, I believe, have admitted that an original genius could, to some extent, require an actor to do what had previously been considered beyond his powers, an audience to accept what audiences had previously been unable to accept, and to disregard wholly or largely the so-called limitations of the theatre.

We know that the genuinely original artist is always breaking the traditions of his art, and by the virtue that is in him creating something that has hitherto been regarded as difficult, improper, or indeed impossible. Such is growth. The celebrated phrase, "This will never do!", applied to the work of a famous English poet by a hidebound critic, should never be forgotten. It is the creator who makes his own rules.

Without going deeper into an analysis of this controversy, it is worth while to consider the theatre as an art form in itself, apart from the play which it came into being to exploit. The stage, while serving primarily as a physical setting against and by means of which a play is acted out, has often provided pleasure and excitement over and above what the playwright intended when he wrote his plays, and occasionally quite apart from anything that a mere writer, as such, could hope to provide. The theatre frequently offers spectacles in which the playwright has, as it were, made the stage itself the principal actor; in which the playwright becomes actually not a writer of plays but a glorified stage director, and by means of certain arrangements of scenery, pantomime, music and dancing, created an entity in which words (the chief instrument employed by most playwrights) have little or no part at all. There are even cases where the playwright, as we understand the meaning of that word, has no part at all in what goes on in the theatre, and the director takes over. Several of the plays of Molière were enlivened by interpolated ballets having little or no relation to the plays in which they appeared. No reader of Pepys' *Diary* can fail to recall the diarist's delight in such plays as *Macbeth,* not it seems because he was moved by the beauty of Shakespeare's language or dramatic effects but because of the music and dancing.

The arts of ballet and pantomime have survived almost wholly without the help of the dramatic poet, because they depend not on the spoken word nor to any great extent on the story, but on the sensuous appeal of color, and music, and the graceful movements of men and women in striking and beautiful costumes, not to mention stage scenery. The art of the theatre, even without drama, can be an end in itself, just as the art of the drama *can* exist without the help of the theatre.

CHAPTER VIII

ENJOYING THE NOVEL

by

VAN METER AMES

The novel is a device for self-development, and a reader will prefer fiction which helps him go beyond the stage he has reached. As mature selves today are primarily concerned with social questions, even so are the novels they find most interesting. But according to a still current view of art, the novel cannot combine art with serious treatment of the problems that absorb thinking people in time of crisis. The gist of the objection appears to be that the novel may properly deal with things felt to be intensely private and personal, not with things considered public and impersonal. This implies an atomic view of the self as having no vital relation outside a limited scope of intimate contacts. But it is the metamorphosis of a narrow self into one of broad sympathies, largely through the effects of science, that is the theme of advanced novels now; whether stress is on the difficulties in that transition, the fear of leaving the cocoon of the past and coming into the open, or the excitement and promise of the prospect.

The fun of fiction begins with the smile of a child delighted to feel himself in the place of another. Overcoming otherness, essential to becoming a self at all, is evident in playing parent, doctor, truck driver, being a gnome, being a giant, and any animal in the zoo. Make-believe makes the child before it makes the man. "Tell me a story" is the request of the "I" for help in self-development. The "I" tells stories to the "me" when the self does develop, and acts them out. The adolescent, uncomfortably aware of self, inhibited or prohibited from expressing openly all he feels, daydreams what he would like to do and undergo. The movies supply imagery he craves. He is susceptible to many forms of imagination, and the one he singles out is more or less determined by circumstance. But still for literate youth reading is the readiest and most satisfactory resource in crossing the shadow-line to full selfhood, especially since the passion of that passage, the romance and adventure of it, is the conventional content of the novel. As long as the adult is hard-pressed he will recall youth wistfully and like to read about it. But the effort to keep young, aided by science, has enabled many people to grow up enough to enjoy growing older. In later life, as in the beginning, the unfolding of the self through imaginative extension, is the joy of living. Realization of this calls for and is fostered by novels expressing the values of maturity. As these are made accessible to the reader, the young may gain sympathy with age and acquire orientation often lacking when all the world loved a young lover.

As one develops a self and achieves self-realization through intercourse with others, reading which quickly and easily widens acquaintance cannot fail to be valued. That experience gained from a novel is vicarious does not vitiate its importance, for the profit of fiction is imaginative. So is the profit of life. Even the physical organism is unsatisfied with bare existence. The psychical and social self must look before and after, must not only be aware of shifting qualities but fit them into long and short range plans of action, shared with fellows and shaped to patterns of feeling, schemes of thought. Otherwise, to use an older vocablulary, the spirit faints, the soul shrivels up. Man does not live by life alone, but by remembering the best of it, dreaming the promise at work in the worst of it, and identifying himself with what he loves. The self would sink into nonentity if it did not reach out to other selves, rehearse their roles and fuse them with its own initiative, give its own twist to the skein of fate, helping to weave a reality beyond though caught in that of biology and physics.

The first novel that one picks up constitutes the novel until subsequent examples extend the class. Then comparison sets in and taste begins to form. Absorbing as a story may be, the reader cannot help feeling it as better or worse than others he has read, along with making subtler valuations. These will emanate not only from the memory of other pages. Judgment of a novel as of any book must be the upshot of interaction between what is suggested and the whole situation of the self, including its desires and tendencies. Words that open the world where it had been unapproachable and make it familiar, that give the equivalent of much experience at home and abroad in overt endeavor, intimate relations and private musing, add cubits to the stature of the self. A man must choose among many selves the one to carry his name, and this one he can seldom develop as he would, in what is called real life. Holding a novel he can overleap the limitations of his lot, and not only become more fully himself in his own person but assume any identity and taste its fate without being committed to it. The surprising thing is that this is not just pretense but realization. It is a chance to be and not to be, which is the being of mind. The animal is literal except for passing playfulness. He is what he is and not what he might become. Unimaginative man too is cabined by heredity, confined by environment. He is duly and dully himself and little else, for his self is never what it might be. Enlightened government, a social reform, might help him. But a man whose predicament does not preclude reading novels can seize freedom in his hands and vault over walls. He may fall or be thrown back, be deluded and not delivered. Then his freedom is imaginary and not imaginative. But there is a natural tendency toward growth, toward preference for authors who deepen sympathy and widen horizons, though the only "ought" about the novel is that a person ought to read what he enjoys.

To see what that means, one has only to recall the first novels to enthrall one's youth. They were novel. Perhaps they had the excitement of forbidden fruit but they gave sudden knowledge of good and evil, closing the garden of childhood, promoting the self to the world of men and women. To read novels then was to grow up with a rush. To keep reading the same ones might be to stand still or lose ground. But reading is a joy when it breathes new life into the self so that it will break free, not physically perhaps but effectively. It may be said that a youth is growing anyway, with or without novels; that an adult is often stuck no matter what he reads. It will be asserted that only what he does can help him, or what is done for him through collective action—not what he reads, unless he reads for information to help him do something. But a novel-reader is never stuck as long as he reads what stimulates him to reach insights which are consummations of enjoyment in contrast to the coasting of indulgence. The pleasure of reading is likely to liberate by showing possibilities beyond those already caught in the nets of experience; and not just because the nets were faulty, for there is novelty. Things happen, they change, and the novelist may enable people to change them further if he is abreast of the time and a critic of it. Books are not the only events in a reader's biography, but whatever he does and whatever happens to him, if he enjoys novels nothing in his story is unaffected by them. Then the question is how most people can have the opportunity and incentive to read novels; and such a question, in one form or another, is coming more and more to figure in the novel. Not that reading is enough—even the best. But the mark of the best is not the seizure, the being held in a chair, so much as awareness that here is something to be cherished and to have consequences, something to alter conduct and the world.

Society as well as personality is on the way to be reconstructed when new values are honored in the novel. Truth is no stranger to fiction when reality is made over in imagination. The process of renewal, going on in the self and in the organizations of humanity, cuts across any snobbishness of taste. What seems worthless stuff to the highbrow, and what seems out of touch with anything of interest to the average man, will from the sociological point of view be found equally indicative of attitudes and trends. And one who would take a position less impersonal, less non-committal toward values, will find data as much in what the multitude admire as in what the few discriminate. A judge will find things to praise and to condemn, both in fiction that is popular and in that which is not. One who is slow to judge but quick to sympathize will respect any whole-souled enjoyment, feeling what it means to others. Though they may not like authors who are all a man would ask for himself, he could ask no more for any reader than to find writers who speak to him as he is and elicit a response that carries him over the verge of himself as he was. It would be a strange failure of imagination if cultivation of it were to keep people from imagining the value of it in any form.

The essence of the novel is imaginative awareness of worth through words, no matter what the particular subject is. Though earth-bound the content must become concentrated and volatile to rise from the pages of a book, even in the vein of romance and adventure. One who no longer reads Jack London need not deny the vividness which others derive from him, or forget the zest it was to read him once. He may yet make a man, who would not think of leaving home, envy a boy wanting to grow up and go on his own over the ocean, over the snow, to know men and dogs, and a mate. However primitive this may be, it has the vim of the creative advance on any level, of doing things in spite of hardship while feeling them to be worth doing and telling. The musketeers of Dumas have the drive and vivacity that make interesting reading because they make life interesting, so far as found there. In fiction these qualities are enjoyed as symbols of the agility and resource, the daring that would be valuable to a live creature in any environment. The lackeys, the court, the king and the cardinal, the costumes and women, are background for swords and words, for horses and roads, for inns and wines of escape from industrial life, from sickness and worry, from anything holding men from a full career.

The novel provides escape, and could not do so unless enjoyed. But it would not be enjoyed as much as it is if it did no more. And complete escape is more than getting away, since to get clear away is to go somewhere. Escape, to be worth undertaking, must arrive at a destination or a half-way station where life can be carried on more freely and fully than before. The adventures related by Jack London endow a boy with the physique of a man and the opportunity to exercise it, according to the imagination of a boy reaching beyond his place and status, but not too far. The romances of Dumas do likewise for a reader, and more or less regardless of his age and sex. The success of many authors continuing to furnish this kind of thing is evidence of the enjoyment it gives, for with the exception of a few professors who feel obliged to keep track of it there is nothing obligatory about such reading beyond the fact that people are bound to have fun. The fun is spoiled for an earnest person, aside from spells of truancy, when he finds he cannot take it seriously, because it does not get him anywhere.

Such a person may turn to Conrad with gratitude, since

his fiction offers more than romance and adventure and these too. These are there in the shape of ships, in ropes and sails, oily engines and strange shores. One gets away in reading Conrad, but arrives at the sense of men struggling to do their duty in the immensity of nature. Instead of forgetting what has to be done, under the spell of make-believe, the reader of Conrad gains a perspective on human effort, begins to realize the value of striving to do right, whether in the vast inhumanity of the sea or in the shadows of a tropical forest. Here is something one ought to feel, whether it can ever be understood or not, Conrad's admirer is convinced. He has the somber and exciting pleasure of exploring reality, becoming aware of depths and distances that not merely outrun the familiar but surround and overarch it. Here is the disillusionment of science, chilling the schoolboy mind by taking away even far places to play hookey, but challenging the boy who wants to become a man, the man who wants to become able to sail toward death and emptiness for the sake of his fellows.

There were touches of that in Jack London and Dumas, but not with this intensity. The difference can be illustrated by photographs of them beside one of Conrad: an athlete's face, the jowls of an eater and drinker, the grave visage of a dreamer and commander. For the first to be a writer, one can believe that he drove himself as he drove a dog team, making tracks on the snow of paper, 2,000 words a day. The second is said to have lain on the deck of a yacht in the Mediterranean, after feasting, to wait for sleep and a plot that would eventually be filled out on blue paper, with facility and with a factory of writers to help. Composition was not easy for Conrad, nor could he be satisfied with a daily stint. He had to struggle and suffer all the way, because his task was not to trek a certain distance, or to concoct and develop a plot, so much as to surpass himself in the effort to make men pause "with delight and wonder" before "the very truth of their existence." To a maturing person, trying to get his bearings and take the measure of the world, this effort is tremendously stirring, especially when felt to succeed, as it often does in Conrad. He makes one feel the adventure of being alive, having relations with other people, and striving to do right in those relations. The exotic setting, which may attract one to him in the beginning, becomes the stage for human drama. The thing that counts for him is insight into the idea of being a man, as a man should be among men, and this is the pleasure of reading Conrad.

When one tires of him it is because it becomes inadequate, though much, for a man to stick to his post, obey orders, be loyal. If only that were enough! Conrad presented many situations in which it was enough, and was not easy. He used every available refinement, shift and complication of technique, for his presentation. The only story-teller's trick he did not use was that of abandoning story for something else. In general his versatility of method was used to good effect, and may be enjoyed by one who becomes aware of it, as well as the narrative. It is interesting to think of him as a disciple of Henry James, and see delicacies of treatment developed for the psychological subtleties of drawing-room characters being applied to rough sailors of heterogeneous origin. One who enjoys Conrad enough to read much of him is almost certain to become interested in his technique, and it is impossible to care about the technique of the novel without enjoying Henry James. To enjoy him, however, is to become dissatisfied with Conrad.

On the surface the fiction of James is more limited. Usually his characters have no work, no occupation, or are free to get away from it and forget it. Conrad's have definite duties that they shirk in peril of their integrity. James dealt chiefly with

American expatriates at ease in a few European centers, Conrad with workers of the world. But though his men range over the globe, they scarcely know what lies beyond the beaches they visit. Wherever they are they know what they ought to do, to whom they are responsible, and fail in their obligations only through weakness or cowardice. Weather may overwhelm them but cannot keep them from doing their best. The complexities of civilization are hidden. Steamships replace sailing vessels without affecting the fundamental sense of duty to visible masters. That they in turn serve an order which might be questioned is an idea repudiated as unworthy of discussion, born in back-slums, threatening to plunge mankind into darkness and despotism. There is no recognition by Conrad that social-democratic notions are justified by any shift in human affairs brought about by the advance of science in conflict with tradition and institutions. At least there is apparently no recognition of this, unless in the very effort to find the whole of morality in the determination not to flinch, wherever one is placed, and to see the truth of existence in something apart from "the hazardous enterprise of living," in something to make men pause "with delight and wonder." These are noble sentiments and fit the novel as a self-contained art form, derived by Conrad from Henry James and Flaubert. If men must simply keep a stiff upper lip and stick where they are, the highest service of the novel or of any art will be to refresh them intermittently with beauty. Brief and detached, the value of this comfort will be much just because it is removed from the insecurity of everything else, though discovered by an artist amid the vicissitudes of everyday.

Conrad was constant in the faith that each situation is surrounded by wonder as by the sea, and shot through with delight as by a sunburst, for the man who can see it or the one who can appreciate its expression. Men are grateful to Conrad as to any artist who offers consolation. When, however, they become sophisticated socially and politically, and believe their disabilities are not a fate to be accepted stoically but a handicap to be overcome by common action, they lose interest in romance and adventure. They do not crave an art of escape and consoling beauty so much as an art to spread beyond pauses in living, break out of works contemplated apart and merge with endeavor.

In this most important respect Conrad did not live up to his masters, Henry James and Flaubert. Concerned as they were with art for art's sake, with perfection of form, and able to give satisfying pause, they realized that the assumptions of the nineteenth century were undermined by progress in science and social thought calling for fundamental adjustments. Even Jack London, though confused, gathered that it is not enough for men to obey and be loyal when criticism and reconstruction are necessary. And a reader who is aware wants a novelist to realize the crisis of the age. Not that Conrad is altogether out of date. There remain, and will remain, opportunities to do and die without question. Nor will the ineffable quality of immediate experience cease to be a wonder courting expression. But we are involved in what men hope will turn out to be a people's war of liberation, to realize social-democratic ideas. It is warned that winning the war cannot automatically win the peace in the sense of guaranteeing the hopes of humanity. Such a guarantee must depend upon collective thought and effort, beyond willingness to obey and die. What is needed is consciousness, not found in Conrad, that new winds of freedom and oppression are blowing.

Henry James and Flaubert, the technicians of fiction, may yet be more appreciated for their social conscience than for devotion to form, after being nearly eclipsed by form-scorning

Russians who went straight to the need of making the basic goods of life more sharable. Neither the structure of art nor the focus of it upon Conrad's "surrounding vision of form and color" could satisfy Dostoievski and Tolstoi. Dostoievski faced with orthodox Christian faith the inhumanity of man to man. Tolstoi came to feel that the teaching of Jesus called for a reorganization of society to get rid of exploitation. Turgenev, though master of a form too subtle to be called architecture, and magical in evocation of people and places for their own sake, was also concerned with social problems. He rejected Dostoievski's quietism and fear of Western influence and (as Professor Tsanoff has observed) instead of Tolstoi's utopian idea of Christian brotherhood had hope in Western science as the means of improving life in Russia. One might say that in *Fathers and Sons* Turgenev's exhibit of disvalues in change, and of disagreeable traits in revolutionaries, removed from wish-fulfilment the promise of reform to lodge it in the logic of events.

The novel-reader is confronted with a contrast. Conrad and a number of writers, serious and deserving to be taken seriously, have sought to express reality or truth as if it could be caught in a self-enclosing perfection of form, glimpsed in the midst of the life process but not of it. The Russian novelists took that process itself and made their exitement over it, including their pondering what ought to be done about it, the stuff and the form of their art, so far as their art had form. And readers of novels have divided along this cleavage. It is obvious in the case of H. G. Wells diverging from James and Conrad despite their expostulation. What it comes down to is whether social-democratic ideas should be aired in the novel or not. James tried it in *The Bostonians* and *The Princess Casamassima* before giving it up half way through *The Tragic Muse* (as Edmund Wilson has pointed out in *The Triple*

*Thinkers*). But James had enough to keep him busy in the analysis of individual character and the personal relations of a few characters at a time, doing this as patiently as he did, along with meticulous care for texture. His devotees think that enough. Other people prefer Wells because they find him concerned with something bigger and more important. They need not minimize insight into the private and personal aspects of life nor deny that problems occur here, struggles, defeats, victories. The question is whether absorption in this sphere should be allowed to take attention away from social problems. If these are to be dealt with they must be faced, and if they are neglected they may lead to such catastrophe that there will no longer be any personal aspects of life worth notice.

Neither the following of Wells nor that of James has seen how a novel could be made an instrument of social purpose and at the same time a thorough work of art. But there are people who like to read them both and who want a combination of their talents. This wish might have been father to authors who actually have something like the concern of James with form and character analysis, something like the social outlook of Wells. Here is not a hybrid but a type of writer whose wholeness leads him to join what had been separate undertakings. If a man is to be a novelist now it is natural for him to use the craft of fiction as it has been developed, and if he is serious he must broach problems that concern thoughtful people. The novel invites such seriousness because it permits meaning to be explicit and free to range over life. The debate between Wells and James as to whether social-democratic ideas, the meanings fraught with controversy and consequences now, can be given full attention in the novel without disrupting it as an art, is to be settled by seeing what art is. Since art is form which is not only sensuous but symbolical, any ideas that can be symbolized in a form of art may belong to it. Analysis of characters and their relations by James was managed through refinement rather than sacrifice of the novel's form. If he did not continue to approach more comprehensive social problems it was not because the form of the novel could not support him further but because he failed it. And so far as Wells has not spent the time and effort to achieve form in what he wanted to say he also has failed the novel. Here the achievement of André Gide is instructive, for, after viewing the novel as a form to be substituted for life he arrived in writing *The Counterfeiters* at the idea that a pure novel would present the chaotic tensions of life instead of merely abstracting a pattern from them.

The novelist can attain form in life-clinging language because it allows selection and emphasis, grouping and fusing of elements through transition and contrast into an organic whole. Language has texture to be respected like the grain of wood or the consistency of oil; while what can be signified is like light and shadow playing over surface and drawn into design. As chiaroscuro comes into the composition of painting, as highlights become accents in sculpture, as sunlight strikes openings in architecture, so the flash and nuance of meaning brighten and shadow a structure of words. Yet meaning is not merely added to a neutral stuff and framework, because what is there for sense is not more structural than what is there for a self. The trick is to internalize designation within a rhythm of thought and feeling, so that the furthest sweep of discourse does not go out of bounds of art. This is possible so far as the life-reference of language is amenable to arrangement. Words and phrases can echo others within the limits of a piece, as epithets of Homer or Thomas Mann call back and forth; as the speeches of a person fasten together; as characters make groups and counter-groups which could not be what they are in isolation or outside fiction. The chief unifying as well as enlivening factor is the author's style, his way of seeing and putting things. The style gives the reader a sense of being escorted by a constant guide, speaking in the same voice throughout, though with modulations that keep attention alert if justified by what is said.

The novel is a form of life-and-language in which words are rarely chiseled or tooled as they are by Joyce but chosen, with an ear less for sound than for sense; the sense they have and that which they may be urged to reveal. If the sound (and look) of words were all that fiction had to stand on, it would be top-heavy with meaning. Actually the foundation of the novel is substantial, because its language forms a secondary suggested medium of any strength, according to what is needed. A person with a book in hand may be transported to the ocean, to the forest, to the body and self of another man or woman—where an author wills—and seem to experience appropriate feelings and attitudes as well as sights and sounds which are the more common stuff of art. The novelist can lay a sensuous base adequate for a superstructure of psychological interpretation and social implication. What is said coalesces with a complex effect caught in a pattern transcended by its reference. There is no contradiction, since language requires words to be patterned, and so much of man's life is lingual that to talk or write is not to press existence into alien terms but to let it speak with its own tongue. Life is wrapped in language and men breathe idiom, yet what is understood in a novel must be imagined, being held within the range of attention while kept for the moment out of reach of a practical response. The novelist evokes sense qualities, emotion, action, characters and situations, felt to be no further than the page, while the fact that only words are there keeps the experience at arm's length, keeps it in the key of contemplation, incipient and ideal. Short of dropping the book the reader must follow implications imaginatively. And when he has finished a novel the consequences in conduct are significant in proportion as he was enabled to have an inner vision of them while meaning, induced by symbols, spread from and returned to form.

Since meaning in the art of the novel centers on self-development, and the most developed selves today are concerned with the relation of science to social welfare, with the right of all selves to realize a full life if science can provide the conditions, the novel must find the symbols for this concern or be disappointing. The novel must come to express the vital issues of the time or sink to entertainment that men cannot fully enjoy at their best. They do not want, because they cannot want, mere romance and adventure, character studies, or mystical glimpses of an unchanging background. They want to know what the novelist can tell them about the breakdown of the social order, the necessity of reconstruction, the hope and threat of science, according as it is used to free men or to oppress them.

To seize life in its depth and sweep, its impasse and gathering pressure, men need imagination, and they find it most adequate in fiction. Poetry is a rival, but if good too hard for most people to read, being condensed and elliptical. Short stories are too short unless charged with poetry. Though science can solve many problems, it constitutes the main one now, and for comprehensive grasp, as found in fiction, scientific writing is divided into too many fields. Philosophy surveys them too abstractly. Serious magazines are largely given to journalism, to articles composed of facts and conjectures that stick closely to facts and dates. So-called "must" books have the same tendency. They tell what to think, or even what to do and how, but within this or that situation, usually ignoring the need of perspective on life as a whole. Interpretations of science, philosophy and religion, help men to get their bearings in the universal and accelerating shift of values, but fall short of fiction in failing to fuse the larger issues with personal insights in a vivid perceptual form. Needing a vision of their world, and prevision of their part in it, men want a larger view than actual contacts offer, a more intimate and dramatic portrayal than informative articles and essays can give. Only in the novel can this moment of history be appreciated with some completeness, with a sense of the human beings involved, their anxious isolation, their growing effort to unite in organizing scattered living into meaningful life.

The gist of the serious novel now is this. Traditional culture and institutions on the one hand are in conflict with science and social-democratic thought on the other, and there is no easy solution. Science and ideas of democracy cannot be scrapped by men who realize their importance. Neither can tradition and its institutions be abandoned lightly. What is called for is a re-thinking of both sides of the opposition, to accommodate them to each other. This is going on all through society, and is not so much being thought as felt and imagined. Men need cues, dramatic rehearsals, illustrations and test cases, such as the novel presents. Here a combination of the talents of Wells and James is invaluable. The power to construct a formal pattern of rich perceptual texture enables the mind to imagine more fully what is offered than if it were merely written in logical fashion. Since ideas are not primarily logical but arise from hopes and fears, the most effective expression of ideas comes in the shape of human beings with whom the reader can sympathize as they mull over and act out his problems for him.

Theodore Dreiser, Ernest Hemingway, James Joyce, Thomas Mann, Marcel Proust, Georges Bernanos, André Malraux, Ignazio Silone, André Gide: these are some of the novelists

enabling us to see the reality of our time. We may enjoy them
not so much because we delight in what they show us as because
they warn us of our predicament. Enjoyment of them is a
serious matter. They are prophets. They see the iniquities
of the old order bringing ruin to persons and nations. They
are also wistful about time-honored values and eager to see
them re-instated, but know this requires renewing them and
working them into the fabric of actual conditions. Some
are more discouraged than others, more attached to what is
doomed, more appalled by the spread of destruction. Malraux,
Silone and Gide, who have most hope, see it in the form of
collective action, but fear the abuse of this may cancel its
gains. They are especially concerned with the problem of
socializing the self without forfeiting its personality, and Gide
is fond of saying in scriptural fashion that only by losing what
has been the self can the living self be saved.

Perhaps just because science more than anything else has
brought about contemporary problems and programs, novelists
have a strikingly divided mind about it. Wells remains con-
spicuous as the only one wholly espousing science. It cannot
be said that he alone in the craft of fiction appreciates the
affinity between science and social progress, but possibly his
eagerness to speed reform, destroying his patience for analysis
of character and perception of the human scene, has blinded
him to the disadvantages of science. Literary men in general
have a profound distaste for scientific procedures and results,
along with acknowledgement of their influence. Often failing
to see or to appreciate the qualities of imagination at work
in custom-refuting hypotheses, men of letters have tended to
note the dullness of little minds which memorize laws and
operations and learn to use them mechanically, as if there were
no hacks in literature. No man of imagination has ever
thought the discoveries of science could take the place of

fiction. But as if writers feared this they have attacked the prestige of the new learning in the pretensions of its hench- men—an easier mark than the modesty of its great names. Yet serious fiction need not be without humor, nor does it fail to take science seriously.

Medicine is often chosen to represent science, as the branch of it most widely appreciable in service and disservice. Tur- genev, seeing the kinship between scientist and revolutionist, portrayed in the medical student Bazároff the crudity that may go with defiance of tradition, yet made him a character whom the reader cannot help admiring even when he thinks the author did not. Flaubert could not have intended to hold against science the incompetence of Charles Bovary as a doctor, and did not make a fool of the pharmacist Homais without making plain that his science was specious. The master of form, at the climax of *Madame Bovary,* stopped the death scene to pay a tribute to a great doctor brought in only to receive it. Proust maliciously enjoyed letting Dr. Cottard be a bore at length, yet the notable thing about him was that his stupidity in company went with a specialized ability of high social value. If the narrator (and author) of *Remem- brance of Things Past* prided himself on not letting science help him, his recurring preoccupation with it, his use of it for metaphor, his hatred of it for changing the world, testify to his respect. Joyce showed annoyance with the medical student Buck Mulligan, but not without humor; and Bloom, the main character in *Ulysses,* speculates much about science; while its disturbing effect upon Stephen in *A Portrait of the Artist as a Young Man* need not be forgotten. Doctors de- scribed by Thomas Mann in *The Magic Mountain* are inhuman enough to make one dread getting sick in mind or body. Yet the whole book hinges on the opposition between unreason and reason, and though the position of science is equivocal it is central. Aldous Huxley in *Brave New World* travestied the triumph of science as the doctoring of people into robots, just fairly enough to suggest in spite of himself the power of science for good as well as evil. Sinclair Lewis in *Arrowsmith* showed that the trouble with medicine is not in scientific method, which he admired profoundly, but in the tendency of a promising method to be commercialized.

The novelist, whatever his feeling about science, is becoming aware that he cannot give a full expression of human life today without recognizing the multiple effect of science upon it, from political to imponderable factors. Seeing the impossibility of turning the clock back he peers ahead and weighs the prospect. The reader, eager to see what the novelist makes out, is intrigued by his oscillation with regard to science. It seems that an adequate modern attitude must keep abreast of it yet be emancipated as far as possible from its limitations, though realizing that these are not fairly represented by the travesties of them often found in novels. The most imposing fiction is a combination of art expressing and science explaining what life is like—the life that science abstracts from and must come back to if it is to be of any use or importance. But life as the prime source and last criterion of science is altered by science, and the effort to seize the quality of this alteration distinguishes fiction now. It enables the reader, pausing for contemplation of values and disvalues, to draw back from actuality and approach more imaginatively.

The ambivalence of the novelist toward science is equaled by his balance toward social action. To write effectively of men he must have sympathy with them and he may love them enough to feel that nothing is better than effort in behalf of common humanity. But a writer combining the detachment of the artist with the impartiality of the scientist will not be a propagandist. Not through indifference but through affection he will refuse to put his eggs in one basket. Sensitive to the complexity of values, to the difficulty of favoring some without sacrificing others, the novelist is cautious about committing himself to specific programs. He may as a man be carried away by a fight, and write a novel in the heat of it, as Malraux wrote *Man's Hope* fresh from helping the Spanish Loyalists. The book is moving, yet inferior as a novel to *Man's Fate* written some years after the Shanghai rebellion of 1927, when events could be worked over in perspective. And even *Man's Hope* admits misgivings about the idea of identifying human good with the success of a party. Hemingway, after vigorous espousal of the Loyalist cause, was accused of being a traitor to it when he wrote *For Whom the Bell Tolls,* because there he was too absorbed in human beings to care very much which side they were on. It is well argued that this novel would have been more significant if it had not "turned off the thinking" about world-dividing issues in the narrative. Perhaps because he was unable to handle them with art he chose the easier course of making them properties for a Hollywood love story in which his old technique was adequate. At any rate, the way this novel was attacked, and the way criticism was split by praise and blame for *Man's Hope,* indicates that the closer a novel comes to taking sides in a controversy the more it tends to forfeit the objectivity of art and of science.

It is true that stainless devotion to art or science will not save a man from being lined up involuntarily when no one is allowed to be an innocent bystander. Nor should an artist or scientist be sorry to have his work help a cause he believes in, hinder one he abhors. There is no reason why a novelist should be deprived of convictions and loyalties or have no part in the struggle for a good life. But he cannot write to the order of a party or afford to be insensitive to nuances qualifying a dogmatic stand. His loyalty is to man, and neither his integrity as an artist nor his fellowship with the scientist will permit a good novelist to risk misleading people by writing anything he does not feel. If his feelings conflict he must confess instead of hiding it. He need not be like a man of action, unshakable in decision. The acts and choices of other men will be wiser if among the books they read are some not committed to a specific program but to revealing the values and disvalues of life in their overlapping complexity.

It was complications that made life human in the first place and they keep it interesting. If a novelist could iron them out of his vision he would lose the stuff of story. So he is not simply lacking in character whenever he fails to present a solid front facing one way or the other. He is a novelist at all by virtue of sympathizing with so many kinds of people at once that he cannot be satisfied to write monographs or monologues but must write dialogues. Knowing that people cannot do themselves justice in speech he must add action and interaction, and penetrate to the drama of feelings and ideas which neither become articulate in words nor obvious in deeds. By fitting everything together that he can sense and express, with all the resources of imagination and technique, he approximates the density and zest of life as it settles down to values, to goods and bads, which despite variety and contradiction have a certain steadiness and stamina in war and peace. Thus Silone appears at times almost to be writing novels of manners, because he cannot resist recording as vividly as possible just what people are like, regardless of his zeal for anti-fascism.

So the greatness of Tolstoi's masterpiece is that it deals with a series of earth-shaking events without losing touch with the intimate business of being men and women, old and young and children, with their roofs over them or off, their land around them or far away, with their things, their purposes, their idiosyncrasies and secrets. If now many readers have gone back to *War and Peace*, it is probably on account of the parallel with recent happenings, and discontent with matter printed the day and week after: lacking the truth of fiction written long before and after such events, with imagination to cross the lines, to make historical figures dramatis personae, to see big and little men as men. Knowing that the truth about a stretch of peace or war cannot be shown until the lapse of participation has voided the recovered facts of their lost significance, people are glad to read about Tolstoi's Peter and his friends. Amid the tumult and the visiting, the love-making and heart-breaking, Peter comes through, thinking. He thinks about good and evil, and what could be done to help his fellow men. He wonders about progress but is discouraged by the difficulties in the way of engineering it. So he tries to find the good at hand, under foot, wherever men are free to exercise their capacities and affections simply and naturally. Though intrigued by theories Peter is inclined to reject them except as they can be interpreted as plans for recovering time-honored values of wholesome living, essentially the same for peasants and nobles. Tolstoi was convinced that so far as there was a difference it would be better for nobles to emulate the life of peasants than the other way round; but did not see how brotherhood could be implemented by enabling all men alike to enjoy the advantages of scientific progress. Hatred of inequalities in the established order made him yearn to change it. Yet he questioned the innovating power of science, while drawn by it, because he loved to celebrate values already achieved.

The art-science tension in the novel is revealed as a past-future tension, suspending the reader so that he must survey the new in the light of the old. The distinction of the novel is not that it can urge this program or that hypothesis, but that it helps men to reconstruct their situation with awareness both of what has been won and what is in the offing, so that neither will be neglected. Reactionaries will object to the suggestion of change; radicals will denounce the implication that change may be unfortunate. But novel-readers, in a position to weigh conditions and consequences imaginatively, will see need for social progress, and will in the long run work more effectively for a better world because they are not committed to the narrowness of parties or the vanity of panaceas.

To read Dreiser, for instance, is to feel that traditional forms of living have been warped, that something must be done if decency and dignity are to survive, though it is a moot question whether a novel of his is strictly an indictment against anyone or anything in particular. Such writing does make one more aware of qualities of life, wistful about what is missing, and disillusioned about an easy reform, yet alert for a chance to do something. Or does it? Does the tone of mechanism mean abandonment of hope, or is it a way of warning men against the loss in accepting a mechanistic view of science? The difficulty of paraphrasing a work of fiction into a message is a large part of the novel's fascination. Not that a novel must be vague and evasive. The point is that the more sensitively it expresses attitudes toward life, the more qualified and oracular it is. A writer's words in a work of art become unusually symbolical, as there appears much more than clearness in their use. They may clarify what is vague but they take what is clear and fill it with suggestion when fiction approaches the complex indeterminateness of the world. Imagination and humor are evoked in the reader until he realizes the inaptness of any rough and ready pigeonholing of a novelist. The reader is moved not so much to match his wits with him as to discriminate the scale of his values, the angle of his assumptions and the drift of his insights. One may be reversed in first judgments by learning what other readers discover in a novel and how they interpret it. Thus one becomes more perceptive, more critical, more able to enjoy the subtlety beneath a surface which does not satisfy when found to be all.

There is danger of obscurantism in this. On the other hand, when men are overwhelmed by appeals for action, not to mention orders and commands, it is salutary for them to call their souls their own and have a chance to get oriented in reading authors who respect their intelligence and imagination, who leave the issue open and the initiative free. A great novelist can be read on several levels. Proust may be understood as a pathetic or sinister example of decadence and snobbery in a rotting civilization, or may be interpreted as denouncing it with wrath. Joyce has been enjoyed as a wordman amusing himself with language, as an aesthete withdrawing from reality into art for art's sake; he has been branded as a hater of culture, smasher of values; and he has been hailed as a champion of humanity against social injustice, voicing a warning to wake the Finnegans. Thomas Mann has developed a grand dialectic between nature and spirit, art and science, past and future. One never knows which side is coming up in his work, or how soon it will slip into the other. And when he speaks or writes in his own person, holding one thesis, his limitation seems incommensurate with his power as a novelist to project the life of a family, a continent, the race.

Private turning points and social goals coincide as the novel reveals the impact of science upon patterns of thought and action, shows the human situation taut between the unpicture must be very careful of the ideas which it advances, familiar past of culture gathering inertia in institutions and former works of art. This is the challenge, the adventure beyond adventure, to be enjoyed in the novel now. It is not a pastime confined to hours of reading but an inspiration that must carry over into what Conrad called the "hazardous enterprise of living."

CHAPTER IX

## THE MOVIES

by

MILTON S. FOX

A great and new art-form has been taking its rise in our time. But we, who have created it, and are its contemporaries, give to it only a limited value. We treat it as hardly more than an extravagant toy. To most of us the movies have come to mean entertainment or diversion (in a very restricted sense), or snippets of "information" about the wide world. Through them we may "kill time," make money, influence public opinion, teach, find distraction or vicarious satisfactions and adventures. We ignore the deep potentialities of the movies. We ignore that we have developed one of the greatest mediums for artistic expression ever devised by man.

The origins of the new art-form are mongrel enough, compounded as it is of scientific technology and the traditional arts. It is without lineage or antecedents of its own kind in cultural history. Erratically, even hysterically, it has made its way from its beginnings in such things as Fred Ott's sneeze, for it had no traditions upon which to draw. There have been, of course, predecessors of a sort. For centuries artists, visionaries, and tinkerers have dreamed of an art in which carefully controlled images could be caused to move, scenes to change, and events to run predetermined courses through the medium of time. But however memorable these predecessors are in their manifold ways—oriental scroll paintings, continuous narrative frescoes and bas-reliefs, shadow plays, colored shadow puppets of Java and China, and novelties such as moving murals, and mobiles—as visual arts-in-time they are hardly to be compared with the movies. The eighteenth and nine-teenth centuries produced many devices, strange, and sometimes pathetically childish; they bore fearsome names—the Eidophusikon, the Phenakistoscope, the Praxinoscope, the Phasmatrope, the Zoetrope, the Kinematoscope.

Evidently it was fast becoming a "cultural imperative" that there be some sort of cinematic medium, a medium in which classical time, place, or bulk would become simply momentary manifestations of a condition of flux. In many ways it seems as though the evolution of the visual arts (and the literary, for that matter) of the West has portended the inevitable appearance of a medium such as we now have in the movies. From the early Renaissance on, painters have sought—have behaved as though impelled—to break down the natural barriers of their art; they have extended the scope of that art, and the range of its effects, through veritable miracles of technical virtuosity in forcing recalcitrant materials to yield.

If we may for the moment consider all the visual arts as related, by virtue of their common and basic condition—visible imagery—we will see how many lines of pictorial development lead us straight to the art of the movies. From the early Renaissance, through the Dutch, progressively through the Impressionists, painting has sought greater spaciousness and a more pervasive feeling of atmosphere. From Baroque and Rococo, through Impressionism, light itself, luminosity, has been increasingly the subject of painting. ("The chief person in a picture is the light," said Manet.) Movement engrossed the later Renaissance, was rhapsodized by the Baroque, became a fetish with the Futurists. Consider time—for even though a painting or sculpture is obviously static, there are many indications of time-state. Giotto seems time-less; Poussin presents an eternal, or absolute, time: the seventeenth-century Dutch present today, or now; the Impressionists, this moment, and some of the crowd, this instant; the Futurists, a relative time-condition. Increasingly, as we approach the twentieth century, sensation, emotion and association predominate; painting becomes sensory and psychological, and the solid world is dematerialized. The artist became many things, but not a mere

(*Courtesy The Museum of Modern Art Film Library*)

**Fig. 53**

Legendry, in the expressionist vein. Big close-up of Paul Wegener, the director, in the title role, The Golem. (German, 1920. Photo. Karl Freund.)

recorder. He moved around, into, and through things. He painted people coming into, and going out of, his pictures. He painted fragments, mere flashes of things. Subject-matter—image material—was dug up in the highways and the byways. Scant indications of real things were buried in associations, and pictures began to whisper allusively to the deep recesses of the mind. The artist worked for "dynamism," and soon gave the horse twenty legs, and not four. Manifestoes appeared, art movements rushed each other along in a succession of "isms"; and as this beating against the gates reached a climactic fury, the movies appeared on the scene. Perhaps this was the answer to a Muse's prayer.

The history of the movies, as we know them, is short; 1895 is the date of what is said to be the first public showing. Less than fifty years have passed, and in that time the movies have developed in a really phenomenal way. On the mechanical side, the inventive genius has been the equal of almost anything which this century has produced; refinements in cameras, films, projection, and gadgets deserve the word wonderful. As a method of narration of stories, or the presentation of facts, it has developed many effective techniques, and some which are sheer genius; and these have made the movies an endless source of delight and diversion for millions. It has been overwhelmingly a popular art, catering to, and expressing, the values of the masses. This very fact, however, while it has given the movies a robustness and directness which are among its chief present distinctions, has also diverted us from its artistic potentialities. Since mass approval and sharp trading practices have at all times determined the growth of the movies, this, one of the most flexible and limitless of all artistic mediums, constantly tends towards standardization and easy repetitiousness.

We must begin to recognize what a great medium for artistic expression we have at hand. We must study its language, its techniques; we must learn what we can do with it; and we must learn how to look at it and how to enjoy it. Obviously it is not suggested that its function should forthwith cease to be entertainment as at present; that we should smother it beneath a pile of doctors' theses, take it away from "the people." It should by all means be predominantly a popular art, not a recondite one. But instead of endlessly trivial scripts, absurd screen life, spurious emotional situations, smart-alec sophistication, fashion-show mannikins, presented in filmically moribund ways, let it deal more often with richly human and meaningful subject-matter and with

**Fig. 54**

The fantastic and magical. An early trick-work film by George Melies, Les Quatres Cent Coups Du Diable (The Merry Frolics of Satan. French 1906).

whole human beings, making full use of film prose and poetry. No medium of artistic expression should be held permanently at so low a level that only in rare moments does it reach above the artistic and intellectual level of, say, Saturday Evening Post literature. What is wanted is a greater variety in the entertainment, a great development of the enormous possibilities latent—even obvious—in the medium; not entertainment only, and predominantly, at a low level. But this is only a small part of the story. How much, how very much, more than entertainment we may create through this medium!

It is important that we come to appreciate the movies as an artistic medium, to love it as a craft, for qualities found in it alone; and to become conscious of style, the marks of personal craftsmanship and artistic imagination on the part of the creative motion picture artist. As a matter of fact, this has already happened to a certain extent, for the most universally popular movies of today are precisely those which most consistently use many of the unique characteristics of movie technique, namely, Walt Disney's animated work. Let us not be deluded by the high degree of mechanization in the craft, or the communality of the final work, the combined efforts of innumerable hands; despite these, the motion picture is a medium which can be extremely sensitive to the promptings of creative imagination. Indeed, we have already seen, in the work of certain directors, something of the large promise which the medium holds.

Now, before we go on to an examination of the movies as an art-form, it is necessary to pause for a moment over certain surrounding features. For we will gain perspective in so doing. Any form of expression, and particularly one so public as the movies, is largely conditioned by its social context. We had better look briefly at some aspects of this context.

"Like the farms of the nation, its [the motion picture industry's] product is a daily necessity," said Will H. Hays, spokesman for the industry, in his most recent report. It is quite true that in this country the movies are so closely tied up with the requirements of daily life that it would almost be easier to speak of them in terms of vital, everyday services. These services provide us with water, power, news, food, and so on; the movies are counted on to supply the nation with "glamor," "allure," adventure, success, faith and hope, information (of a kind), and again "glamor" and "allure." There are other things: through the popular film millions have heard an adequate Shakespeare for the first time, and the measured dignity of eighteenth-century language; they have poked around in the alley-ways of ancient towns, have seen

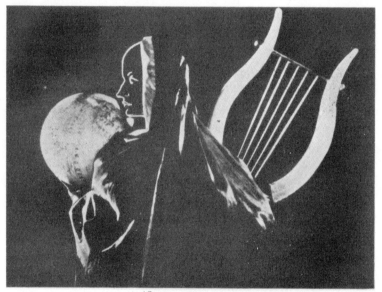

*(Courtesy The Museum of Modern Art Film Library)*

**Fig. 55**

Jean Cocteau's film Le Sang D'Un Poète, in the surrealist manner. With music by Georges Auric. (French, 1932.)

the delicate minuet, and also the inside of a submarine; they have seen how a lady's hand was kissed, how and when to use the second spoon to the right; and surely lovers were never before so thoroughly coached in the proper and most fruitful methods of approach. But primarily the movies provide vicarious satisfaction in fame, fortune, and love. And who is to say that this function is of no importance in twentieth-century living, commercialized and industrialized, tough and self-seeking as it is, skeptical, mercenary, willy-nilly impelled by something called "Progress"?

The movies are regarded as "art"—if only potentially— by an earnest professorial few, who usually don't like readily available examples. But to millions, white, black, yellow, red, in every corner of the earth, apparently, and at different levels of civilization, the movies have long since become a thing so natural, so immediate, so taken-for-granted in the ordinary routine of living (like painting and sculpture in the Middle Ages or the early Renaissance), that any attempt to make them something aloof or special (like painting or sculpture today) seems silly on the face of it. Every few days new movies appear, they are good or "lousy," and that is the end of the matter.

Where movies are considered among the necessities of life, it ordinarily makes little difference who creates them, and fans every now and then erupt in indignation over time and footage wasted for credits. This is understandable: one does not quibble about credits in the other necessities. If one is hungry, one doesn't ask who raises food, and who prepares it; one goes to a place where food may be had—within certain limits, almost any place—and then one eats. Thus millions and millions of people vis-a-vis the movies. Off they go, once, twice, or oftener, every week, to see love, and heroism, and virtue rewarded, and the triumph of integrity, and fun and fantasy, blood, gore, and sodden truth. These people, who don't know what art is, and don't care, like the movies.

For those blissfully unaware of aesthetic matters of any but the most rudimentary sort, it makes little difference whether the form and manner of a film are this or that, so long as the developments are unambiguous and easy to follow, so long as any slight strain upon intellection is soon compensated for by some incident of "comic relief" or "human interest," and so long as all comes out reasonably well in the end: the boy gets the girl and therefore slums are cleared, Louisiana is purchased; or, nobly, he keeps himself from getting her and therefore becomes a great surgeon.

(*Courtesy RKO Pictures, Inc.*)

**Fig. 56**
Abstraction, expressionism, and the fantastic popularized in the interpretation of musical materpieces. (From Walt Disney's Fantasia, 1940.)

To most fans, the movies mean first and last—stars. In common talk, in advertisements, in reviewers' columns, we say, "In this picture Robert Taylor loves Lana Turner," or "See how Cary Grant tames his wandering wife, Rita Hayworth." The fans want to see, in public, what the actor does, or would do, under a variety of circumstances, and the film must not get in the way of the doing. A newspaper review, selected at random, illustrates many of these assertions; writing of "Crash Dive": "It's corny, but good in its way. When our hero, Tyrone Power, a handsome young naval lieutenant, isn't blasting the daylights out of Nazi subs, he's working up to a clinch with the beautiful Anne Baxter. Anne has another boy friend, Dana Andrews, who happens to be Power's superior officer on the submarine. It's hackneyed, to be sure, and so is the action . . . All that remains after the big smash is to know which boy gets girl. The suspense then is not so terrific." Special groups are sometimes irked by this "glamorizing" of the person of the star, as may be gathered from this quotation from a service paper at Fort Belvoir: "There must be a better way of winning the war than letting five or six men do it every time. What about using the Army once in a while?" This runs against the current; pictures may be *plays,* but they are primarily brave, two-fisted men, beautiful and perhaps even obtainable women, or potential lovers. The part-name does not hide the fact that the American movie usually wants to show us how Gable—as Gable—kisses, how Gable smirks when in Amor's clutches, how Gable looks in Civil War clothes, in armor, on horse, afoot, and without an undershirt. The movies are thus an instrumentality through which the actor is generally asked, not to create character and to lose himself in that character, but exactly the opposite, to maintain his off-screen identity. Following this line, the pictures periodically strive to see how close they can come to the old-fashioned peep-show of the penny arcade.

The patron's identification of self and persons on the screen has often been commented upon. No one who heard it will forget the shudder of nervous delight and anticipation which ran through an audience, preponderantly feminine, when Mr. Gable, with excessively (but still characteristically) masculine intentions, pounced upon Vivien Leigh (Scarlet O'Hara), and bore her aloft to his couch, in "Gone With the Wind." In the dark of movie halls, dreams come true. And the movie industry, through a formidable machinery of advertising, and through the pictures themselves, manages to

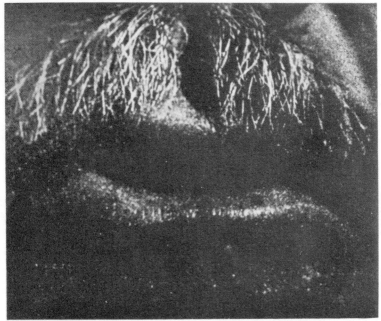

*(Courtesy RKO Radio Pictures, Inc.)*

**Fig. 57**

Very big close-up, inducing an effort on the part of the spectator to catch a dying man's whisper. (From Orson Wells' Citizen Kane, 1941.)

induce and maintain an almost compulsive type of passion for the persons of the screen actors.

It is editorially lazy to make generalizations in the name of "the people"; yet one has but to consult fan magazines, fan letters and queries, the newspaper reviewers, the revolting drivel purveyed by radio and newspaper gossipers, and, of course, the movies themselves, to know what is expected of the movies. Actors, yes. Plot and story, yes. Gowns and costumes, yes, again. But what of scenario, direction, cutting, lighting, photography, sound? One does not expect a popular audience to be overly concerned with such matters—to say nothing of more theoretical matters—unless they are strikingly below the level of slick adequacy which they have attained. But it is in these very matters that the greatness and distinction of the medium primarily lie; and surely the human race is not so rich in expressive vehicles that we can be indifferent to one of the greatest—and our own.

It must never be forgotten, in any discussion of the movies in this country, that movies are "big business"; in the days before Pearl Harbor one of the biggest of industries. The one simple and inexorable fact about business is that one is not in it for fun. It must "pay off." Thus the movies, like any other commodity, must be in consonance with the demands of the market; there is no other alternative. Parenthetically, it may be stated that this is the main reason why it is simple-minded to belabor Hollywood and the picture-makers for everything one may deplore in the movies. It was inevitable, in the social and economic pattern of the twentieth century, that this new medium of expression should become big business, and ultimately be taken over by great financial interests.

Even so, the movie industry has always been ahead of the patron; if it lags behind, the patron hurts the industry in its most sensitive spot, the box-office. Other arts, it is said by the detractors of the movies, have had to conform to the requirements of patronage, and have been great withal. But there has never been an art-form which required so great an outlay of money on plant, equipment, and staff, as Hollywood does today, merely to keep going; and with so many people getting a fat "cut," a chain-belt system for the production of "art" is inevitable, as is also an elaborate system of distribution throughout the world. The heavy investments in developing and popularizing stars, for example, assure that these valuable pieces of property will be used again and again in proven ways, without much variation, until returns are no longer satisfactory. The same is true of types of story, or any other aspect of the movies which happens to "catch on." An old story will serve

*(Courtesy Twentieth Century Fox Film Corp.)*

**Fig. 58**

b. Nature and history in tune with love. (From The Farmer Takes A Wife. 1935.)

to illustrate these points: A director wanted to throw about his actor at a certain moment the aura of mystery, suspense. He called for lighting which covered a large portion of the face with shadow, breaking up the familiar contours, altering the clear shapes. When the producer saw this Rembrandtesque bit on the screen, he moaned. "Look," he said, "I'm paying $5,000 a week for that face, and he goes and hides half of it."

The story may be apocryphal; but back in 1921 the master, D. W. Griffith, recalled, "When I first photographed players at close range, my management and patrons decried a method that showed only the face of the story characters."

The consequences which flow from such influences of property on "art" are matched only by the fact that the movies are a popular—or better, a mass—art. They must have something for everybody who can scrape up the price of admission; they must never, or never for more than an instant, reach so rarefied an atmosphere that the mass-customer will be frustrated (unless the producer is bent upon financial hari-kari). Said Alfred Hitchcock, ". . . the films suffer from their own power of appealing to millions. They could often be subtler than they are, but their own popularity won't let them . . . I have become more commercially-minded; afraid that anything at all subtle may be missed." It is for this reason that the appeals, devices, and modes of address of the popular movies so closely approximate those of contemporary advertising in almost every respect. Both of them, addressing themselves to a mass-audience, must be ingratiating through use of easily assimilated, sure-fire, attractions. Thus the saccharine beauty, the elaborate, stylish chic and polish, the store-bought ease and urbanity, the cheap exaltations, the same half-truths, sentimentalities and puerilities. American business has learned the effective appeals to the mass-mind, and in suitable terms, hammers away at the national mind until the people have all but forgotten that there are other values.

But because the movies reach so great and miscellaneous an audience, further strictures are perforce imposed upon them. The influence of the screen on the formation of attitudes and beliefs has been demonstrated time and again; the educational value of the screen is tremendous. For this reason the motion picture must be very careful of the ideas which it advances, and constantly the makers find themselves in hot water with groups of all sorts: the wets, the drys, the whites, the blacks, the Jews, the Catholics, the lawyers and the doctors, the Argen-

*(Courtesy The Museum of Modern Art Film Library)*

**Fig. 59**

Brutal Realism: one of the screen's most forceful images. (From the epic Potemkin, directed by S. M. Eisenstein, photography by Edward Tisse. Russian, 1925.)

tines, Italians, Egyptians, and the Boy Scouts. It is pulled and tugged this way and that, by the State Department, the woolen industries, the motormen's unions. It is really almost a miracle that, hedged about with such menacing pressure groups, the movies can ever express anything more than valentine sentiments.

Yet the valentine sentiments are wanted; they are the staples, the perennially rewarding items. And so the American movie has always striven primarily to provide recreation and entertainment, "to make dreams." "There are men and women of every race and of every tongue," said Will Hays in 1929, defining the industry's position, "moving slowly forward, seeking something, seeking, searching, yearning—asking for a place to dream . . . And over and above them, and in front of them, attracting them on, offering that which they desire, are billions of flickering shadows—the motion picture." There are some unalterable requirements laid upon the typical Hollywood film, and they are as definitely formulated as they are for, say, pictures on the covers of popular magazines. It becomes almost impossible realistically to discuss the run of current movies, at any time, in any terms save those suited to pulp literature. Yet, let it be emphasized here that there have been many exceptions, some of them of so high an artistic order as to challenge the highest achievements of our time in the older arts.

All of this, given sketchily, and in part only (there are many if's, and's, and but's) results in certain peculiarities in the form of the movie art *as we commonly know it.* It has been necessary at least to mention these matters, for, it seems to me, the form of an art is inextricably linked with its content: what that art wishes to convey, or to evoke, or express, or make manifest—what its intention is, in short. An enforced distinction between form and content seems arbitrary, and unless this distinction is announced as provisional, in order to facilitate discussion, the distinction is false and misleading. There can be no content without some sort of form to make it manifest. In the mind of the creator, that form was evidently the only way in which he could make that particular content manifest. And if, in order to demonstrate the separability of form and content, it is asserted that content may change with time, as when we ignore or do not know some of the symbolism

*(Courtesy The Museum of Modern Art Film Library)*

Fig. 60

Slice-of-life naturalism in the twenties. (Emil Jannings in The Last Laugh, directed by F. W. Murneau. German, 1924.)

or allusions of historic or exotic art, it still remains that, whatever the content may be for us, it is as embodied in that particular form, and would be different in another form.

The forms and techniques of the American movies are in perfect accord with their content and intentions. By and large, they can tell a story suavely and fluently, sometimes beguiling us for hours. Yet it is more common than not that this is accomplished by means other than those uniquely and element-ally of this medium. Methods are taken from the stage, from vaudeville, from verbal story-telling, and developed in a straight narrative manner. The peculiar and crystallizing vividness of pictorial imagery is sacrificed; pictures are used as mere illustrations to the talk. Except for certain fragments, a majority of our pictures could be observed and heard almost as well off the screen as on it. One has the feeling that camera and microphone have been used merely as record-ing agencies, fidgeting about from one position to another only to keep the pictures from becoming monotonous (and to give us a better look at the faces which launch towering box-office returns at topless prices).

What, then, is this medium capable of? If it is not neces-sarily only what the popular commercial film makes of it, what else can it be? What are some of the differentia—the unique charcteristics—of the movies?

Perhaps the most extraordinary facts about this medium are its tremendous range of visual images, whether photographic, drawn, or other visual material, and the utter freedom and flexibility with which it may handle these images as stimula-tions to the mind. A similar freedom obtains with regard to auditory effects of every kind. Surely, in these respects it has no peer in the other arts; none so closely approximates the fluidity, the ebbing and flowing, of our psychological processes.

Literature is tied to the word, and the word is a symbol. Its images, suggested by memory and association, may be intense; but in the nature of things they cannot be so direct or forceful as the perceived visual objects, for these are not only there, tangible to the visual sense, but they too may gain an added intensity from evoked associations. In any case, the

THE MOVIES

movie attacks *directly through two senses,* the visual and the auditory, whereas literature prompts *recall* of their use.

The stage is tied to physical presences; and flexibility of action, place, and to some extent, plot, is necessarily limited. Particularly is the relationship of spectator to presentation

*Courtesy Frontier Films)*

Fig. 61

The documentary film. Dramatization of problems and aspects of daily life. Magnificent shot of terrorized share-cropper, from Na!ive Land, 1939. (Photo. Paul Strand.)

fixed, and this relationship, as spectator-screen relationship (to be discussed more fully later) is one of the most remarkable of the many remarkable things about the movies. In the Preface to *The Dynasts,* Hardy comments on some of the restraints imposed on the drama; he conceived of this work as a drama not to be staged: ". . . no attempt has been made to create that completely organic structure of action, and close-webbed development of character and motive, which are demanded in a drama strictly self-contained." *The Dynasts* requires ". . . a completion of the action by those to whom the drama is addressed . . . Readers will readily discern, too, that *The Dynasts* is intended simply for mental performance, and not for the stage . . . by dispensing with the theatre altogether, a freedom of treatment was obtainable in this form that was denied where the material possibilities of stagery had to be rigorously remembered."

The stage has tried in numerous ways to capture its ancient immediacy with regard to the spectator, and to break the rigid separation of the two sides of the proscenium. In effect, the stage is a box, and one wall is removed in order that we may look in. Since ordinarily we ourselves cannot move around in it, or see it from other sides, the action and composition of the presentation are necessarily determined by what may be effectively seen from in front. Action which includes the body of the theatre, and the soliloquy and the interior monolgue, are among the devices which are intended to get the audience inside the action, and even, so to speak, inside the actor. But inevitably, the mere presence of actual bulk and space enforce a physical separation, establishing scale and position in space. An object which distends a small visual angle and creates a tiny image on the retina must be small or distant, and however we try to identify ourselves with the thing "out there," the awareness of separation must persist. The thing-out-there is necessarily tied to the sound it makes; and any activity (walking across the stage, delivering a blow) must run its full course, visibly, on the stage, taking the same amount of time as it would on the street. Sometimes the consequences of these hard facts are comic: one recalls a corpulent, aging Tristan waddling around the stage, singing his youthful passion.

The movies, on the other hand, are almost overwhelming in their ubiquity. Consider what they may show us. They are shot everywhere; they show us everything—or pretty close to it; and they take us along with them. This is probably as

Fig. 62
George Pal. Puppetoon

close to omniscience and omnipresence as most of us will ever come. There seems to be hardly an event of any importance (or lack of importance), on any value scale, but that is shot by some prescient cameraman. If some new refinement in triviality is invented, some new revelation of the utter banality of which the human mind is capable when it really tries, it will presently be flung upon the screens of the nation. But so will many other things—perhaps even the documentation of some glorious and noble act. Volcanoes erupt, and mines explode, and rats run mazes, and Kaltenborn makes everything clear, and girls wear bathing suits, and men are shot through the head by distant snipers. The whole universe of natural shapes, animate and inanimate, great or small, elemental or tentative, is subject to the artistic intuitions of the movie artist. He can cause the microscopic momentarily to fill the whole of the conscious mind, to become the sole existing reality. Or suddenly, he may present infinite vistas, great magnitudes, or vast armies. The catastrophies of nature can be documented. We can "sit in" on the marvels of life in impossibly small entities.

Never before has so wide a range of image-material been available to the creative mind; yet this is only a part of the resources with which the movie artist may work. Any artist working with visual material must transform appearances somehow, or utilize them in ways which will effect a transformation for some end which he has in mind. "To show something as everyone sees it is to have accomplished *nothing*," says the great Russian director, Pudovkin. And Ruskin, "These ideas and pleasures [of imitation] are the most contemptible which can be received from art." To help him impose his creative will on the raw material of visual imagery the movie artist has at his command a multitude of camera effects, effects of lighting, processing, and trick-work—mechanical and optical resources which may be used to transform, or qualify, the character of any object or appearance. For example, there are various types of lenses, filters, and other devices which effect the light passing through the aperture: screens of gauze or burlap, prisms, smoke, petroleum jelly, water, mirrors. These may lead to all sorts of qualifications of image: soft-focus effects, where everything is misty and blurred (widely used at one time for "tear-jerking" and "romantic" effects, or to suggest a moment of exquisite tenderness, and now, regrettably, regarded as old-fashioned and used only on occasion, as when a director wishes to show the

*(Courtesy The Museum of Modern Art Film Library)*

**Fig. 63**
Charlie Chaplin in The Gold Rush. 1925.

vision of one whose eyesight is failing); or a universally sharp focus (as in "Citizen Kane"); or distortions of shape, to suggest the vision of one demented (as in "Cabinet of Dr. Caligari"), or drunk (as in "Last Laugh"), or a moment of violent emotional shock (as in "Marie Chapdelaine"); and there are many other usages, such as one recently seen in "In Which We Serve"—the watery-wavering transition shots leading from the men on the raft to some associated subject.

Light, of course, is in truth both vehicle and subject of motion picture photography, for it is the light which falls upon objects, is shaped by them, and is reflected back to the raw film through the lens, and there leaves its "message." The lens knows only of degree and disposition of light. But we know how the direction of the light, its mere relative position as a source, will affect the appearance of an object. Shrewd moviemen like John Ford, James Wong Howe, Hitchcock, Lee Garmes, Eisenstein, and others rely heavily on the alchemy of light which transforms filmically nondescript material into powerful stimuli to mind. In this they fall in with a great line of artists for whom, in their own ways, light spells magic; amongst them may be mentioned Tintoretto, El Greco, Rembrandt, Vermeer, Chardin, Guardi, Degas, Manet, Dali. It is almost impossible to judge exactly what contributes most importantly to greatness in art; but surely one of the greatest pleasures to be derived from their work arises from the sensuous play of light, and the counter-play of shadow.

We may pause in this recounting of the resources of movie art to emphasize this all-important factor of light. As we know it on the commercial screen—with some exceptions, naturally—it is artistically valueless. It serves only a revelatory function, so that nothing is unduly obscured. It is completely barren of emotional or expressive values. Again we are reminded of advertising techniques, for this slick, silvery, crisp lighting — over-lighting, if you will — these metallic gleams on the dark side of things, are all precisely the lighting used to set off the latest pattern in silverware, another brand of scotch, or a new hair preparation. From this point of view, it would be possible to cut sections of trashy comedies into many a pictured tragedy, and, if we were to judge by picture quality alone, few would notice any difference. Nothing can justify artistic pretensions which so completely ignore basic sensuous components.

But to return: Objects are transformed, qualified, by different intensities of light, different qualities, different conditions of brightness-contrast. Light may be polarized, or colored; it may be steady or intermittent or moving; it may be a bath rivalling the sun, or a tiny spot; it may involve infra-red or ultra-violet radiation and fluorescence. And the type of film stock, upon which the light exerts its influence and "causes" an image, considered together with the developing and processing, again may effect image-quality. There may be effects of quality due to under- and over-exposure and development, graininess, speed, and color sensitivity; and to the manipulation of exposures and printing, leading to double- and multiple-exposures and trick-work of all kinds. If now we add the further consequences resulting from movement of the camera, we have a really formidable range of image-material upon which to draw. The scope of moving picture imagery has never before been available to artistic expression.

But if the range of image-material is impressive, consider the freedom and flexibility with which the movies characteristically may handle such images——in the camera, in printing, in cutting, and in projecting. The medium is completely free from the ordinary restraints and exigencies of material existence. Objects and events may be associated, not because they are physically, temporally, or causally related, but only because they are psychologically, or narrationally, or rhythmically effective in some particular context—or for the sheer pleasure in the synchronization of sound and image (as in the ever-delightful "A Nous La Liberté"). This, and this alone needs determine what is shown upon the screen.

There are no limits save those of human imagination and the perceptual apparatus: it is no exaggeration to say that the movies can give presentment to anything which can be seen or heard or imagined. Heard melodies may be sweet, but if, as the poet tells us, unheard are sweeter, we may confidently expect to hear them through this medium one day. If the movies too often limit themselves to following action prosaically, merely recording (even though with some taste) the beginning, middle, and end of an event or action, it is also possible for them to parallel mental activities, whatever the state of consciousness or sentiency—whether characteristic of waking hours, or of sleeping, or of the in-between states of reverie or undisciplined association, or in the realm of dream, fantasy, or hallucination.

There is no event too heroic or too massive, no action too commonplace, no shading of thought of mood too slight, but that it may find presentment in this medium. Fairy tale and myth, which almost since the beginning have entranced man, have gained a new credibility from the camera and the sound track: flowers may sing and dance before our very eyes, change to lovely princesses, and back again to flowers; we can be in more than one place at one time; we can have eyes that see evil thoughts inside the mind of the miscreant; inanimate things are revealed as sentient; we hear the voices of the dead. In short, there is absolutely no limitation to the movies' treatment of what we might call "the logic of everyday reality."

The movie artist can disdain gravity, bulk, opacity, distance, scale, condition, distinctions between real and imagined things, between hard fact and fantasy, between physical objects and mental events, between subjectivity and objectivity. He can show us a scene in complete objectivity, or he can editorialize on it through arrangement, context, and lighting emphasis.

He can show us now one detail now another, and they may be separated by hundreds of miles, or hundreds of years. We may look on the world, seeing it as though we had a thousand eyes. We may see the characters from the outside, as onlookers; then through their eyes look at other characters. We can see what the trapped animal sees, what a person sees as he dies. We may move around in the scene, viewing from above and below, from near to and from afar, we may see things move and pass us, then miraculously find ourselves travelling alongside.

In the movies time is ambient, fluid, not a line going straight from yesterday to tomorrow; the movie artist can speed it up, or slow it down. The duration of a gesture, an event, an epoch, is entirely subject to his needs. Through the flashback, the movie maker may reverse time; he may develop two events, an earlier and later, simultaneously; through double exposure and trick-work we may see, at the same instant, a variety of events unfolding coextensively even though they are announced as preceding and following. Sacha Guitry, in such pictures as "The Story of a Cheat," and "Pearls of the Crown," has played some very delightful tricks with time. One must always remember that the treatment of time—in parallel, in counterpoint, or even a timeless fixity, a continuous present—may arise through the oppositions or parallelisms of sound and image, for on occasion we will have a pictorially contemporary image with a voice of a much earlier period, or vice-versa—as when a mother looks on her dead soldier son, and hears an infant's lisping voice. Even this extraordinary range of time-treatment by no means exhausts the possibilities; for through the slow-motion picture movement may be dissected, so to speak; and through lapsed-time photography long-term processes are compressed by a smooth ellipsis and made visible to senses not equipped to perceive growth and evolution directly.

Indeed, this is a most unique characteristic of the movies—their ability to wander, the state of mental flux in which, when at their best, they really have their being. The movies closely resemble the dream, as has on occasion been pointed out. Images surge and flow, tumbling forth one upon another, advancing and receding, or gradually and almost imperceptibly blending and changing from picture to picture, mixing "real" components in "unreal" arrangements with "unreal" components in "real" situations. Color and sound materialize with, or independent of, their original vehicles. The mind is carried along on a stream of fluid images. The illusion is helped, of course, by some of the physical conditions and circumstances of seeing a picture: the usually comfortable seats, the bright, single-purposed focus of attention, the eyes held to the image in the grip of a powerful phototropism, the shutting out of the harsh sounds and sights of routine existence, and the dark vaulted hollow in which we almost seem to float. The enormous popularity of the movies, their persuasiveness, their psychological *reality* ("the camera never lies"), is unquestionably due in large part to this resemblance to dream, in process, and to some extent, in circumstance.

It is now necessary to dwell on certain implications of the foregoing. We have described in a very general way something of the great range of visual imagery available to the movie artist, and something of the freedom of handling of those images as stimulations to the mind. Naturally, mere range of imagery, mere ability "to give presentment to anything which can be heard, seen, or imagined" does not automatically confer greatness of expression—as thousands of movies will attest. What is indicated is the nature of the raw material of the art, with which we have to work, and this invites speculation on how to use it. We are in a better position to appreciate the movie way of telling a story.

At this point the actor comes into view. There is controversy over the place of the actor in the movies; but realistically speaking, any such controversy is quite academic, since the popular movies present us with a *fait accompli* in the shape of hundreds of miles of film per year in which the actor and the person of the star are the be-all and end-all of the filmic universe. A cynical aesthetician once wrote that he could empty any art museum by staging a fire outside; and probably Betty Grable's legs or Dorothy Lamour's "oomph" (and those of their successors) will always seem a more urgent attraction than refinements of film style. Since anything but popular movies exists only precariously or in theory (saving, of course, educational, instructional, advertising, and such-like films), it is almost quixotic to talk of any other type of film style. The coming of television, and movies for television, will probably widen still more the distance between popular movies and movies which are predominantly cinematic in method.

Speaking broadly, in current practice the actors play, the cameras grind. The movie is a record of the actors' performances, and through their actions and talk the story is told. There is a certain amount of cutting from this viewpoint to that, and the inevitable succession of long-shot, medium-shot, close-up; there is some scrambling up and down stairs with the camera in hot pursuit, and an occasional quick melange of images called "montage," or "special effects." The film which results is hardly a form possessing values which arise from the working of the medium itself. It is in reality a photographed series of little tableaux vivants, animated and talking.

Contrasted with this usage is an old tradition—old in relation to movie history. The poet, Vachel Lindsay, one of the early and one of the most perspicuous critics ever to write on the film, said, in *The Art of the Moving Picture,* written in 1915, "The performers and the dumb objects are on equal terms and in his [the director's] paint buckets . . . While the leading actor is entitled to his glory, as are all the actors, their mannerisms should not overshadow the latest inspirations of the creator of the films." In the late twenties, Pudovkin ("Mother," "End of St. Petersburg," "Storm over Asia"), was saying, ". . . that editing is the creative force of filmic reality, and that nature provides only the raw material with which it works . . ." These observations apply also in detail to the *actors.* The man photographed is only raw material for the future composition of his image in the film, arranged in editing . . . "one cannot 'play a part' on the film . . ." Alfred Hitchcock ("Thirty-nine Steps," "Foreign Correspondent," "Rebecca," "Shadow of a Doubt"), wrote, in 1937, ". . . film work hasn't much need for the virtuoso actor who gets his effects and climaxes himself, who plays directly on to the audience with the force of his talent and personality. The screen actor has got to be much more plastic; he has to submit himself to be used by the director and the camera . . . leaving the camera to add most of the accents and emphases. I would almost say that the best screen actor is the man who can do nothing extremely well . . . The picture is the thing."

Now, none of these people object to actors, we may be sure; they are undoubtedly expressing the director's point of view. They feel that images tell, or should tell, movie stories, and that the movie actor provides only one kind of movie image. Indeed, there was a time when some of the great Russian directors declared that they preferred not to use professional actors; yet this is not to say that they would not use human figures (or professional actors, for that matter, in the main parts), but merely that acting, in terms of stage techniques, was not well adapted to the screen. René Clair ("Italian

Straw Hat," "A Nous La Liberté," "The Ghost Goes West"),
explains, "The movie actor has only a few minutes in which
to shape and definitely crystallize a certain emotion . . .
Besides, he is seldom ever given the opportunity of enacting
one whole scene in its entirety; he acts it out in snatches which
will eventually be put together, and will then form a continuity,
*the nature of which cannot be gauged until the film has been
actually assembled.* [My italics.] It is obvious, therefore, that
although the stage actor's talents may serve him well when he
steps before the camera, his stage technique can only be a
hindrance. The congenital incompatibility existent between
these two phases of the same artistic source can never be
bridged."

Acting—even good acting—can more or less adequately
unfold the involvements of a story on the screen, in the same
sense that we tell children a story; first this happens, then
this, then so-and-so didn't like it and did this. This is the
predominant mode of the popular film. Presently the thing
becomes stuffy and eye-wearying, and the film then goes into
shipwrecks, fist-fights, dog-fights, and gun battles, ivory, apes,
and peacocks. When it is necessary to present emotional or
dramatic situations, a person skilled in acting will probably
be better than one with no such experience; but to say that
a picture is well acted is not yet to say that it is a good
picture.

Protracted sieges of acting, or business invented merely to
provide time for the delivery of lines (as at the end of
"Pygmalion," when Leslie Howard walked back and forth toss-
ing an apple into the air) are antithetical to film style, for the
camera then becomes merely a recording instrument, and all
the resources of the film are ignored. There is not shown
"unquestionable evidence of a sincere concern for the manner
of expression," which Dr. Schoen, in his essay earlier in this

book calls, "the one condition for artistic expression." In "The Little Foxes" an attempt was made to neutralize the fixity required for long speeches by showing the characters in conversation, now from this angle, and now from that. An absolute low in cinematic usage results when stage plays, no matter how good, are photographed as they are produced on the stage, the camera stationed in the center aisle half-way back. We then completely ignore our medium.

For consider: there is not only the ability to carry through, or play, a bit of action, but more important, the decision of precisely what shape that action must take in order to be effective before the camera, how much of the persons or scene is to be included, from what distance and what relative position and angle to be shot, how to be lighted, what shall be the movement pattern (in the sense of dance or ballet), how long the piece is to run on the screen, what comes before and what after, through what transition method the piece is to be brought in and out (cut, wipe, dissolve, etc.), what the sound shall be, and how related to picture.

The plain fact is that the movie way—or to use more formidable language, the cinematic mode of presentation—is a form of telling through pictures and visual images. If, in a series of images a bit of business acted out by human performers is most effective, that unquestionably should be used. But more often than not, if an action is given exactly as it would appear to a fixed observer in real life, or even stylized to the degree that all good acting must be, a mere straightforward photographic reproduction of the action turns out to be very dull and ineffective. This would be like the still-life painter whose meager supply of creativeness is spent in arranging his apples and paper-covered French novel, and whose actual painting is the mere subsequent recording of what is before him.

Suppose, to use a very simple example, we want to show a man leaving a room. He is distraught. Will a single shot from a fixed point of view do it? Or a pan shot, the camera rooted as before, but turning slowly to follow him out of the room? Or a shot showing him rising, one showing part of his body as it comes into the frame (picture), the hand grasping the knob, opening the door, and then one of him on the other side of the door? Or perhaps a series of shots; the man getting up, taken from one position; from behind, the completion of the action and the beginning of the journey to the door; perhaps a close-up of feet, perhaps one of worried eyes; perhaps a shot of the thing which troubles him; he hears (and we do) once again the message which has so affected him; perhaps a shot flashing back to an earlier period happily devoid of such problems, voices of many years ago, perhaps in another language; then maybe a travelling shot, the camera, representing his vision, blankly taking in everything before him, things moving by as he advances; or perhaps the camera view distorting or mixing up the appearance of the room, as his agitated mind might; or some sort of prism- or multiple-shot of various images all jumbled together, the person being seen wandering expressionistically in the midst of them. This is pretty elaborate; yet it should serve to make it clear that the mere picture of a man walking out of a room may not be enough.

In all but the first two treatments several things are at once apparent: the story, or point, is advanced by a series of discontinuous pictorial fragments; sound and image need not parallel each other; we have changed our viewpoint and position relative to the person several times, have moved independently of his movement; we have freely varied the relative sizes of things; we have assumed different relationships with the screen, first observing the person from the outside, then

271

seeing what he sees, then seeing, so to speak, how he feels. We have introduced a manipulation of time, for we have heard a message spoken a short while before, and seen a situation of many years earlier. Details may be given great importance— a close-up of a cigarette left to burn, or a crumpled bit of paper on the floor, a swinging pendulum, or the sound of a pounding heart.

It is left to the spectator to grasp the relationships between these visual and auditory images. This is a "language" which must be learned; there are "easy" usages, and there are "difficult." A child taken to the theatre for the first few times finds it very disconcerting to try to follow the short-clipped jumpy bits of pictures, even of the "easy" variety of the popular film. Similarly, audiences often find it difficult to grasp the significance of images-in-a-series when the sequence is of an unfamiliar pattern, as in the case of many a European picture. Let us take an image-series which is not difficult: (1) a view down a lovely, sun-dappled, country road, (2) the roar of a plane, (3) some people running helter-skelter across a field, (4) a close-up of a rattling machine gun, (5) dead bodies sprawled in the sunny grass, (6) the face of a bawling child. In this case the relationship between the separate shots is entirely inferred by the spectator, for nothing was given which inevitably relates one image to the next; the roar of the plane is not explained as spacially or temporally related to that particular road, nor the road to the field, nor the machine gun to the people lying dead, nor all of this to the crying child. Note that one unit in this series was given through sound alone. By means of the selection of highly significant—even crucial—images, our store of associations and memories has been tapped, and the force of the presentation lies in large part in the fact that the mind of the spectator, receiving certain elliptical indications, fuses them, and itself creates the final whole. In this fact lie the great potentialities of the medium.

When, however, the various images are not easy to grasp as physically or temporally related in some way, the real trouble starts. The difficulty of fusing the images increases in proportion as we leave a straightforward presentation of matter, action, and time, and approach idea and association. But in this direction are greatness and poetry. Pudovkin gives an example: "The son sits in prison. Suddenly, passed in to him surreptitiously, he receives a note that next day he is to be set free. The problem was the expression, filmically, of his joy. The photographing of a face lighting up with joy would have been flat and void of effect. I show, therefore, the nervous play of his hands and a big close-up of the lower half of his face, the corners of the smile. These shots I cut in with other and varied material—shots of a brook, swollen with the rapid flow of spring, of the play of sunlight broken on the water, birds splashing in the village pond, and finally a laughing child. By the junction of these components our expression of 'prisoner's joy' takes shape."

This introduces us to *montage*. (The word was used earlier, as "montage," which is Hollywood's way of referring to a quick succession or melange of shots, for example, the scenes of Washington, D. C., in "Mr. Smith Goes to Washington," or a tremendously effective usage in "Cavalcade"— explosions, men marching, falling, girls singing, all becoming more and more grim and hysterical. Usually it is quite hackneyed—pages floating from a calendar, newspaper headlines crowding one another.) There are varieties of montage, as there are varieties of statement or presentation in other mediums. But the common element to the varieties of montage lies in this, that the pictures address us evocatively and relationally, not through straight, objective narration and demonstration. The story is told, or the point made, not through bald prosaic statement or simple enactment; but precisely through the implications of the pictures as they are fused in the mind of the spectator, through the psychological value of *the intrinsic qualities of the pictures as newly created entities.* Desired effects arise through the juxtaposition of images, and the play between image and sound. The images themselves are not mere representations or depictions, but are creations, in that, through the use of filmic techniques, they qualify or transform the originals for some expressive end.

Each picture, in this conception, is but a word, or at most a phrase, and its cinematic value lies not so much in its own qualities and "message," as it does in the aggregate effect of a whole sequence of images, in much the same way that words "make sense"—and even poetry—when the proper words follow each other in a suitable and effective order. In routine prose, the words follow each other methodically, laboriously, without charm; they have been divested of most of their intrinsic value, and become only vehicles for the conveyance of thought. In poetry—or in good prose and good prose is poetic—words fly. "Give Coleridge one vivid word from an old narrative; let him mix it with two in his thought; and then (translating terms of music into terms of words) 'out of three sounds he (will) frame not a fourth sound, but a star . . .'" The passage is quoted by Eisenstein in his book, *"The Film Sense,"* which should be read by all serious students of the movies.

Montage is the poetry of movie expression. It speaks through metaphor, simile, figure of speech. Exactly the right image must be found, and it must have exactly the right duration in relation to the other images. They condition and act upon one another, making an image-series; and these image-series again are conditioned by the adjacent image-series; and through these pictorial symbols and allusions, the common-place and the familiar are endowed with greatness and power and surprise.

We had begun to forget, in an increasingly word-conscious, scientific civilization, how eloquent the pictorial image could be, how loaded with meaning and symbolic values were the simple animate and inanimate objects around us—the grasses, water dripping from icicles, the tensing of a muscle, a child laughing, animals, flowers, the sea. Vachel Lindsay years ago insisted that some of the most effective and dramatic imagery of the screen should derive from such materials. Said he, "Why not . . . make the non-human object hero indeed? . . . The non-human thing is a personality . . . Let buildings emanate conscious life." Lindsay was perhaps the first to formulate clearly the essentially pictographic and ideographic nature of the new movie art; and his plea for the non-human object as hero has been met by beautiful films in which tractors and battleships were heroes, in which rivers and rain and buildings become eloquent, in which an abstract idea like justice, or freedom, is the central "character." The Russians, notably, have made films in which the hero is something other than an individual; and documentary and instructional films have provided us with some of the most poetic realizations yet put on film. Lt. Col. Frank Capra, the Hollywood director, has recently produced "Prelude to War," a sometimes extraordinary piece of picture-telling, again without recourse to exposition through stars or situations.

Picture-telling, through pictographic and ideographic images, is a return; for this is one of the oldest, and still one of the basic, modes of human expression and communication. The movies, the youngest of the arts, are thus in a sense another of the returns to, or rediscoveries of, the primitive, which is so characteristic a feature of twentieth-century culture. As we know, behind all human expression there lies the significant gesture or act, or the warranty of some sort of meaningful objects, and combinations of these. In very rudimentary and primitive forms, the expression partakes merely of the display or the handling of the original material, as in early pictographic writing, which consists mainly of simple pictures of the objects or events having to do directly with the account. Presently, however, it was found that qualities carried over, and that certain images or acts could stand for a variety of things; it was found that objects, gestures, and images took on meanings which were not directly perceptible in them; that images and objects as well, have, so to speak, spheres of influence, and that their significance is altered when these spheres collide; and finally, that through suitable juxtapositions of pictures or objects, by a kind of metaphorical process, new concepts were created which were not contained in the original ingredients. Thus the whole universe became endowed with meaning, eloquence, poetry, magic, and more than a little mystery.

This, of course, is the montage method. But now, in this period of reaction in the arts, it is the fashion to look down upon the *avant garde* movements of the recent past, in much the same way as a boy, putting on his first long trousers, suddenly becomes contemptuous of the furniture of his immediate past. At the risk of being considered slightly old-fashioned, it is here maintained that the purest form of movie expression is to be found in the conception of montage; it is the mode which offers hope for the development of a great movie art. Even today the popular film owes much of its greatest effectiveness to usages derived from montage principles. But this does not say, most emphatically does not say, that all moving pictures should be developed through montage principles. The more prosaic form of the average popular film is exactly suited to its intentions and requirements. Yet all movies should be primarily visual, or, at the very least, a balance between visual and auditory stimuli. Alfred Hitchcock has said, "There is not enough visualizing in studios. There is a growing habit of reading film script by dialogue alone. I deplore this lazy neglect of action, or if you like, this inability to visualize . . . I try to tell my story so much in pictures that if the sound apparatus broke down, the audience would not get restless, because the pictorial action would still hold them."

And what of sound? I do not wish to undervalue its importance. If the visual scope of the film is unprecedented, so is the auditory. Sound should weave in and out of the fabric of visual images, enriching, enforcing, making a whole which is of great complexity. At its finest, sound, too, will be developed according to montage. But talk must not be forced to carry the burden of meaning, making the pictures mere illustrations of the talk. An old comedy of Larry Semon's innocently burlesqued the too frequent tendency of picture-makers to fall back on verbal explanation when they do not know what to do with the pictures. Near the end of this silly film appeared the subtitle, "Now is the time for all good captions to come to the aid of the climax." Hollywood itself has recognized the abuse of sound, and in some recent pictures the increased use of silence is notable; "background" music is slowly giving way to carefully worked out supporting sound and musical scores, which may be used as aural parallelism, or counterpoint, or as aural commentary (as in the case of a grave bit of music with the picture of a fool).

Let is not be supposed that we have touched on all the resources of film art; for even a matter so taken-for-granted as the transition from one image to another may be of considerable artistic consequence. Cut, dissolve, fade-in and fade-out, focus and de-focus, all may be said to have psychological analogues. It should not be a matter of indifference how and

277

in what connection they are used; they are not, in best usage, equivalent, and in themselves have evocative and rhythmical possibilities. Movement—ancient and perennial delight in the movies—makes many an otherwise dull film dance. There is, as movement, action in the photographed objects—horses running, men fighting; movement in the camera (and therefore movement relative to the scene), as it approaches, turns from side to side, swoops, falters—or dances, as in the beautiful "Carnet de Bal"; finally there is the sense of movement which comes from the cutting—the phrasing: a staccato succession of short shots, or alternations of short and long, or a continued flow of the same sort of material. In this sense the movement becomes largely psychological—the feeling of fixity, slow change, or rush. The film may have a variety of tempos, creating a pattern in this respect. We are yet the primitives of this movie art. But one day great masters will use its vast artistic resources, akin in various ways to the ballet, to poetry, to the stage, to music, and to painting—and yet so distinctly its own.

Chapter X

MUSIC

by

Glen Haydon

Of all the arts, music is in many respects the most intangible, the most elusive and hence perhaps the most difficult to treat linguistically. Except for abstract art, painting is ordinarily a representative art; the artist has a subject, a landscape, a person, or a scene, which he is somehow representing in his picture. But music is not in this sense a representative art; it is not attempting to portray anything that exists independently of its specific expression in the particular musical composition. Nevertheless, properly viewed, what at first may seem to be a disadvantage in this respect, may prove to be one of the very great assets of music for purposes of discursive treatment. We constantly hear artists bemoan the fact that people do not see the artistic values in a painting because they get misled and befuddled by the subject of the painting, improperly taking what the painting is a painting of as the matter of prime importance in the work of art.

In music, most certainly in absolute music, this problem does not arise, at least not in the same way. Pure music is not a representation of anything; it does not attempt to represent a person, place or thing. It represents only the specific, concrete, particular values it embodies by virtue of its unique nature. The individual's enjoyment of music, therefore, depends upon his capacity to respond adequately to the specifically musical values embodied in the particular musical composition. It depends upon a sensitivity to sound, and especially to sound presented in a tonal rhythmic pattern.

The sense of hearing is one of the most basic of all the sense modalities. Biologically, man has been largely dependent upon a keen sense of hearing for survival. This keenness is not merely in the capacity to hear sounds, but also in the ability to discriminate among sounds, to interpret their meaning in relation to his well-being. The failure to detect the impending danger indicated by a warning sound, might have meant death.

In the processes of individual, social, and cultural evolution, the sense of hearing has come to provide a channel for a unique type of enjoyment—the enjoyment of music. The physical laws governing the vibratory motions of pulsating bodies resulting in sounds and the physio-psychological laws governing the response of the organism to these physical "disturbances in the air" known as sounds, have given rise to a remarkable and unique form of art—the art of music.

But the enjoyment of music involves more than merely auditory sensation; it involves tactile, kinaesthetic, and somatic responses that reach throughout the whole organism, manifested in glandular changes, bodily movements and attendant emotional reactions. Because music sounds the way moods or emotions feel, because auditory patterns of sound get translated into patterns of feeling, music becomes a deeply moving art.

## MATERIALS

If we regard material as the stuff out of which the artist fashions the work of art, then just as the sculptor uses stone as his material, so the musician uses physical sound. But the composer's work is probably more nearly analogous to that of the architect who makes a blueprint of the edifice to be constructed out of building materials. The composer writes a score which is a "blueprint" for the guidance of the performer, and, as the architect considers how the materials used will look in the completed edifice, so the composer has in mind how the tones of his score will sound in performance. This seems so obvious that it scarcely deserves mention, but, in view of the common confusion on the subject, it seems necessary to emphasize the fact that the raw material of music is physical in character, that it is the physical vibratory motion or pulsation of the air or of the transmitting medium. Of course, it may be argued that the material of music is the vibratory motion as heard; and there is no objection to this view so long as a similar view is maintained with respect to the other arts, namely, that the material of sculpture, for example, is the stone as seen, or that the material or architecture is the brick, stone, or what not, as seen.

The material of music, then, is essentially sounds, which we may further distinguish as tones, vocables, and noises, with all their qualitative richness. If we analyze this qualitative richness, we discover four basic elements, intrinsic orders, or dimensions. These fundamentally characteristic dimensions or intrinsic orders of musical materials may be distinguished in terms that represent approximate physical and psychological correlates, namely, frequency-pitch, intensity-loudness, overtone structure-quality, and duration-time, or perhaps, sense of time (we apparently have no unequivocal psychological term for this last dimension). Although these dimensional elements of musical materials can scarcely conceivably occur in isolation, for they represent aspects of an indivisible whole, nevertheless they afford valuable and significant means of analyzing the materials of music for purposes of learning and understanding. (For further details the reader must be referred to the technical literature on the subject.)

These several dimensions afford the basic means of bring-ing order into the total chaotic mass of sound materials. In terms of frequency-pitch relations, tones are organized into scales. Intensity-loudness provides the basis for the patterns of dynamics found in musical compositions. Overtone structure or quality provides the foundation for the tonal distinctions represented in the main by the characteristic sounds of different instruments and by the conventional qualitative differences of the individual instruments. Duration or temporal factors underlie the various metrical or rhythmical schemes manifest in music. On progressively higher levels of organization and abstraction we arrive, in terms of these intrinsic orders, at our familiar concepts of melody, harmony, counterpoint, orchestration, and structural rhythm. At this point it should be observed that just as in psychology sensation tends to merge imperceptibly into perception, so our discussion of materials has brought us well into considerations of matters of form.

## FORM

Form may be thought of as (a) the means by which the materials of music may be organized for the expression of meaning or content, that is, as the intermediary between material and content; (b) the organization of materials *per se,* that is, the area in which the aesthetic principles of design are evolved; or (c) the certain explicit type of organization, or patterns, common to a number of different works of art; for example, the particular forms of music such as sonata form, fugue, minuet, rondo, and the like. Passing over form in the first sense, let us consider how the principles of design, basic to form in the second sense, are evolved. In general, the principles of musical design, however they may be expressed in detail, depend upon physical factors inherent in the nature of the physical materials of music and upon physiopsychological factors characteristic of the organism which responds to the physical stimulus of music. In other words, they grow out of the intrinsic nature of the materials and out of the nature of the organism as it reacts to the stimulus.

The physical factors are expressed in terms of the intrinsic orders of sound: frequency, intensity, overtone structure, and duration. The more rudimentary physiopsychological factors are stated in terms of the more or less closely corresponding dimensions of pitch, loudness, quality and sense of time. For details concerning the various factors the reader must be referred to the standard literature on acoustics and psychology. For present purposes, a few general remarks will suffice. First, the powers of pitch discrimination determine in part the limits of interval size that may be effectively used in musical scales. Secondly, the limits of loudness discrimination lay the foundation for the dynamic patterns used in music. Thirdly, the powers of quality discrimination underlie the differentiations expressed in orchestration. Fourthly, the discriminative capacities in the realm of time are determinative of the rhythmical structure of music. Other psychological factors that are important for the principles of design in music are memory, span of attention, span of comprehension, habituation or the long-time development of taste, emphatic response, and the so-called laws of association which are basic especially to the formation of the concept of types. Here again the details must be left to technical works while we pass on to a discussion of some of the resultant principles of design.

## The Principles of Design

The principles of formal design may be most generally stated in terms of unity in variety. Simply expressed, a work of art must have unity, for lack of unity leads to chaos; it must have variety, for the lack of variety leads to monotony. The crux of the creative problem, in this respect, is to discover ways and means of obtaining a satisfactory balance between the two extremes. In music, unity is obtained by such devices as the use of a predominant tonality or key; by the repetition of a given motive or melody; by the exploitation of consistent harmonic or contrapuntal procedures; and in many other similar ways. Variety is obtained by the introduction of contrasting melodies, harmonies, rhythms, tonal qualities, dynamic levels, and the like; by the juxtaposition of varying tonal centers through the use of the devices of modulation; by the use of variation in a musical-technical sense; and by numerous other methods.

In general, the principles of design, however they may be stated in detail, operate most significantly in a given work of art through the perception of relations obtaining between corresponding elements in the several dimensions of tonal materials and among co-ordinate features in the tonal-rhythmic structure. Thus, in the dimension of pitch, melodic contours in an antecedent phrase are related to corresponding contours in its consequent phrase. Similarly, dynamic contours are exploited in relation to co-ordinate dynamic contours; quality contours in relation to quality contours; and agogic nuances in relation to agogic nuances. The point may be illustrated by means of the following simple example.

The melodic contour (b) of the consequent phrase takes its formal significance largely through its relation to the melodic contour (a) of the antecedent phrase; for example, the fourth eighth note in (b) is felt as a change in contour in relation to the fourth eighth in (a), and the second measure of (b) is felt in relation to the second measure of (a) as a shift to a lower pitch. With respect to dynamic contour, whatever pattern is used in (a) would probably be approximately repeated in (b) since the change in the pitch contour would probably give sufficient variety in such a simple melody. If, however, the melody should be repeated, variety might be obtained by performing it forte the first time and piano the second, or vice versa. The same observation holds, with necessary changes, with respect to the dimension of quality; here the contrast might be obtained in the repetition by a change in instrumentation. Likewise in agogic matters, an almost imperceptible lengthening of the cadence notes in the first phrase would probably entail a corresponding effect in the second phrase. In short, in the several dimensions, and in various complexes involving combinational elements of each, corresponding elements may be exploited for purposes of unity and contrast.

## EXPRESSION

Expression in music means essentially the communication of musical ideas from the composer to the listener. These ideas are intrinsically musical ideas having no existence apart from their particular musical expression in a given work of art. The notion that music is essentially the expression of anything existing independently of the specifically musical idea can only be labelled as a misunderstanding of the essential nature of music. If emotions as independently existing find expression in music, this expression is always a secondary matter so far as absolute music is concerned. Music that is made subservient to a literary text, program music, and functional music of all types—such as religious music, film music, or patriotic music—emphasizes what is intrinsically a secondary aspect of expression in music. Pure music expresses primarily the specific beauty it manifests in its tonal rhythmic structure. Even the "expression of eternal truth," if this is thought of as something existing independently and in the abstract, is beside the point so far as musical expression is concerned.

The felt qualities of music, constituting its essential expressive content, attain their powerful effects through the translation of the tonal-rhythmic patterns of music from the auditory sense modality into tactual, somatic sensations which underlie man's feeling, affective, or emotional nature. But this essentially sensuous nature of the musical experience which constitutes its foundatioin, is profoundly affected by intellectual considerations. It is in this relation that learning through the ordinary analytic and synthetic processes plays its important role.

Music is a language with its own characteristic phonology, accidence, and syntax. The study of music theory is the study of these things and is the only road to musical literacy. Just as illiterate people understand and enjoy much of spoken language, so musically illiterate people enjoy music.

### The Aesthetic Object

If two people, one of whom is aesthetically sensitive, trained and experienced in music and the other not, attend a symphony concert, we may assume that the one will hear and appreciate the works of art presented on the program, whereas the other will hear only a relatively unintelligible conglomeration of sounds. The aesthetic object, the source of genuine musical enjoyment, is more nearly the tonal-rhythmic pattern of sound as perceived by the experienced musical listener rather than that perceived by the second listener. If the second individual finds something to enjoy in the experience we may be sure that the musical masterpiece performed is only partially grasped; that the aesthetic object is of the same type, but much thinner in aesthetic richness; and that the enjoyment is of a lower order of aesthetic excellence. Of course, the pattern of sound pulsations transmitted through the air constitute the physical work of art, but unless the listener "understands" music he will not actually hear it.

# MUSIC

## The Aesthetic Experience

The aesthetic experience in both cases is the reaction of the individual to the same objective stimulus but the experience is richer in the first instance than it is in the second. The problem of the enjoyment of music, in these terms, is that of enriching the aesthetic experience. The road to the enjoyment of music is most surely traveled through the study of the language of music. We cannot maintain that the goal is attained by the study of musical syntax only, but we can insist that it is the only way to musical literacy and that it will greatly aid in the enjoyment of music.

## The Language of Music

Music speaks to man a varied and, in a way, mysterious language. If we attempt to analyze the nature of this language we discover many difficulties because of this complexity. The following is an attempt to think through some of the fundamental characteristics of music as it acts upon man's nature as a language. In looking for the basis for the enjoyment of music, we shall have occasion to examine the nature of the materials of music which afford the fundamental means which music has of affecting man's nature. Then we shall look into the organization of these materials in temporal patterns that operate in the presentation of sounds for more extended and enduring enjoyment. Finally, we shall try to point out something of how the materials and forms of music in their affective character result in aesthetically expressive meanings of transcendent beauty.

It seems that man naturally enjoys sounds. The child loves to shake his rattle, to beat on anything that will make a noise; and primitive man seemed to take great delight in pounding on drums, in making gourds rattle, and in finding different ways of making sounds. Furthermore, it is interesting to notice in passing, that many if not all of these sounds are emotionally expressive; that the lalling of a child expresses his contentment and that his crying expresses his discontent or discomfiture.

Even at this very elementary level we may see the nature of music in embryo. If we follow the development of music in the growth and maturation of the child or in the history of civilization we find a gradual process of refinement in the discrimination of the several dimensions of sounds; in pitch, the distinctions between low and high tones that result eventually in the concept of scales; in dynamics, the several gradations running from soft to loud; in quality, the innumerable differences represented by the great variety of musical instruments and by the subtleties of tonal nuance possible to each; and in duration, in the differentiations of short and long that crystallized in the stylized concepts of musical meter and rhythm.

The enjoyment of sound as sound is primarily a sensuous enjoyment, and this remains a fundamental factor in all musical enjoyment. But as sounds, the raw materials of music, are exploited in musical compositions, there emerge new values in the tonal-rhythmic patterns as factors in the musical experience that depend not merely on the senses but also upon the perceptual intuition of the relations involved. It is in this area that music as a language becomes articulate. Music, to be enjoyed at this level, must be within the range of our comprehension; we have to "understand" it. Music that is so complex in its structure that it is beyond our powers of comprehension so that we cannot perceive at least a modicum of its structural pattern is likely to be uninteresting to us. We get lost in the tonal rhythmic intricacies and have to fall back on the enjoyment of the cruder, more obvious, aspects of the composition such as the basic rhythm, or perhaps snatches of melody or harmony. Let us turn now to a consideration of some of the principles of design the mastery of which, in actual experience, enables us to extend the scope of our musical comprehension and enjoyment.

First let us examine some of the elements of the rhythmical nature of the music. A person could possibly be practically tone deaf, that is, he might not be able to perceive differences in pitch at all well, and yet he might respond quite readily to the rhythmic patterns of music. Who does not respond to the thrilling rhythms of a swinging march or waltz or other dance music? It seems to be inherent in our nature that we should tend to perceive the temporally successive pulses of music in patterned groups of twos or of threes or multiples thereof. Hence the preponderance of binary and ternary metrical schemes. One of the simplest of these corresponds to the trochaic tetrameter of literary prosody, which may be musically represented as follows:

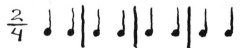

We may describe this pattern as a musical rhythmic phrase consisting of eight beats divided into four sub-groups of two units each. In such a plan we have the nucleus of a scheme that admits of an almost endless amount of exploitation and expansion.

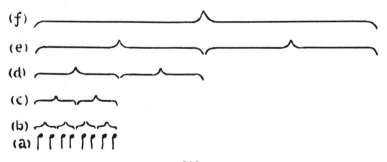

Starting with a single pulse or time value as our unit of measure, represented by the first quarter note (a), we may add a second unit similar to the first in length and combining with it to make the larger unit of the "measure" which consists of a strong followed by a weak beat (b). We may call this larger unit a motive and extend it by adding another similar motive to form a larger unit which we may call a "sub-phrase" (c). To this sub-phrase we may add another of similar dimensions and get a phrase as the next unit in our expanding system (d). If we take this phrase as an "antecedent" phrase and add a "consequent" phrase of similar structure, we get a simple "period" (e). Similarly, the period may be expanded into a "double period" (f); the double period to a "section," the section to a "movement"; and so on. In this process of accretion we are expanding the form and adding innumerable and varied details; but we do not exceed the limits of comprehension, provided we understand and perceive what is going on, because at each stage in the process, at each level of abstraction, we have essentially not more than two corresponding factors to relate to each other. There are numerous technical ways of varying the procedure while still observing the basic principle; that is, our units are either binary or ternary or some combination thereof.

If we superimpose upon this metrical-rhythmical foundation a series of tones employing different pitches, we may arrive at the more specifically musical feature known as melody.

This melody consists of two phrases, the first of which we call the antecedent phrase and the second, the consequent. The antecedent phrase begins, psychologically, at a point of rest, the tonic, and moves to a point of tension, or suspense, the dominant or fifth degree of the scale and the consequent phrase moves back to the tonic. Notice how, even in this very simple melody, the idea of motion is omnipresent. We "move" from note to note; or the melody "moves" from one degree of the scale to another. Further, we may feel many differences in the several kinds of motion involved. The repetition of a tone is perceived as a kind of hopping up and down in the same place; the progression from one scale degree to the next is called "conjunct" motion; that from one scale degree to another that is two or more degrees removed from the first tone is called "disjunct" motion. Conjunct motion is movement by step; disjunct motion is motion by skip. Thus a melody is a kind of patterned motion; and we can scarcely tell whether the use of the terms implying motion is literal or figurative.

It is interesting to notice, too, how the idea of tension comes into the analysis of melody. The word tension refers to a quality that comes to be felt in a tone by reason primarily of its relation to the tonal-rhythmic pattern, or more precisely, because of its relation to the tonality and to the rhythmic pattern. This feeling quality is probably most obvious in tones giving rise to the feeling of a need for resolution. For example, if we play an ascending or descending scale and stop one degree short of the octave there arises a strong feeling of incompleteness, a feeling that can be satisfied by the adding of the final note of the scale. Each degree of the scale has its own peculiar feeling quality, a fact that can be easily demonstrated by playing the same note in two different scales; for example, play the C scale descending and stop on the note D, then play the B♭ scale descending and stop on the same note. In the first instance the D has a feeling quality of "twoness" in the scale which is the unique characteristic of the second degree of the scale. In the second instance, the feeling quality of the D changes from "twoness" to "threeness"—to a feeling characteristic of the third degree of the scale and not of another degree. Further, it should be noted that the feeling quality of a tone may be modified by changing its relation to the rhythmical or metrical phrase; for example, a D coming as the last note of an antecedent phrase has a very different, though not entirely different, feeling quality from a D occurring as the penultimate note of a closing phrase.

Thus, of the various musical-technical means of bringing order to the chaos of possible sounds for the purpose of musical enjoyment, melody is one of the most important. As we examine the order peculiarly characteristic to melody, we find it in each characteristic dimension of tone: in the pitch dimension, the organization of tones, in terms of underlying scalic schemes, into pattern which we may call pitch contours; in the loudness dimension, into dynamic patterns that are more vague for want of well-defined units for comparison, but none the less important; in the quality dimension, first of all, in terms of the medium of performance, and secondly, in terms of textures obtained through the simultaneous combinations of tones which we usually regard as one aspect of harmony; and in the duration dimension, in the rhythmic patterns evolved on the background of a basic pulse, which result, in combination with the other patterns or contours of the several dimensions, in the over-all forms of music. With extensive possibilities of variation in each dimension, what inexhaustible resources are afforded in a system of relations combining the variables of four dimensions! In the light of comparatively limited extent of the psychological span of attention and comprehension, it is not surprising that the most common contour-patterns employed in each dimension are remarkably simple.

In the simple melody previously discussed, a half dozen

pitches of the diatonic scale provide the materials for the pitch contour characterized by a rising movement to the fifth which continues upward to the sixth of the scale before coming to a momentary rest on the fifth at the end of the first phrase; and by a descending stepwise movement to the tonic in the second phrase. The total contour, consisting of a rising movement followed by a descending movement which is nicely broken by the cadence, may be graphically indicated as follows:

The loudness contour, equally simple, might be graphically represented by some equally simple line. The quality contour, with respect to medium, would be practically constant. If sung by a solo voice, for example, there might be slight changes in quality brought about by an almost imperceptible vibrato at the half note of the cadence; or by the changes in quality due to the different vowels in the text. If the melody were harmonized, a definite quality contour would result from the shifting of the harmonies. The rhythmic contour, brought about by the comparison of comparable elements in the rhythmic design, is likewise of the simplest type, which we may describe as a swing from one element to the corresponding one on each level of organization in a binary type of expanding pattern, ranging from the progression of note to note to that of phrase to phrase. In melody we find one of the chief sources of musical enjoyment. Those untrained and inexperienced in music will doubtless get the greatest enjoyment from listening to comparatively simple melodies; with more experience, especially if accompanied by training, one comes to "understand" and enjoy more complex melodies without necessarily having one's enjoyment of simpler melodies lessened.

Next to melody, harmony is probably the most important

means of bringing order into the chaos of possible sounds for the purpose of musical enjoyment. Whereas melody deals with tones in succession, with tonal "lines," as it were, harmony deals with the ordered relations of simultaneously sounding tones. These "ordered relations" are of two essentially different types: one has to do with the character of the simultaneous combinations of tones called chords, and the other has to do with the "progression" of these chords one to another, which may be called the function of chords. Just as the feeling quality of each tone in a melody is conditioned by the tones that precede and follow it, so the feeling quality of each tone in a chord is affected by the other tones of the chord. Thus, the way a given note in a melody "feels" is determined both by its relation to the other notes in the melody and by its relation to the chord that accompanies it. Further, the feeling quality of a chord is modified by the chords that precede and follow it and by its relation to the chordal structure.

The ordinary chords of conventional harmony are classified according to the number of notes present or implied in the structure, according to the principle of superimposed thirds, or in terms of certain other principles familiar to students of harmony. Thus the common chord, or triad, consists of three notes called the root, third, and fifth:

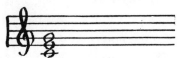

Chords of the seventh are created by adding another third to the triad making four note chords with the seventh between the top and bottom notes, the most characteristic interval in the chord, whence the name:

For further details concerning the classification of chords, the reader must refer to technical books on harmony. So far as the enjoyment of music is concerned, we need only point out that the proper supplementation of the melody with a chordal accompaniment greatly enriches the sonorities of the tonal complex presented to the ear.

Even more important than this elementary classification of chords is the subject of chordal *function,* for it is in this region that some of the subtlest and most exquisite musical effects are obtained. We have already spoken of the felt quality of chords; this quality in chords is most clearly established by means of cadences. These qualities are so numerous that music theory makes little or no attempt to give suggestive names to them but prefers the neutral terms of tonic, dominant, subdominant, and the like. We cannot go too much into details, but we do want to illustrate the fundamentally important point of the feeling quality of chords. Let us therefore consider only the three so-called primary chords: tonic, subdominant and dominant—the triads on the first, fourth and fifth degrees of the scale.

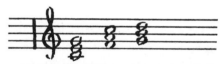

We strongly establish the tonic character of the C major chord by placing it after the subdominant and dominant chords as in the so-called perfect cadence:

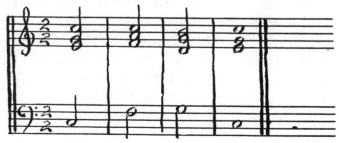

This tonic quality is characterized by a feeling of rest, stability, or finality. We may change the feeling quality of the C major chord from tonic to dominant by relating it to a cadential pattern that establishes the new feeling quality, in other words, by introducing the C chord in the key or tonality of F major, the key in which C is the dominant:

The C major chord now has a certain quality of suspense, of incompleteness, or lack of finality; in fact, the technical name of a cadence ending on a dominant chord is *imperfect* or *half* cadence. The process of changing the significance of chords, when it occurs in the course of a particular composition is called modulation, and with countless ways of effecting modulations into the various keys, the composer has at his disposal an almost limitless range of expressive possibilities.

Another important means of enriching the tonal-rhythmic structure of music for musical enjoyment comes under the heading of *counterpoint.* By counterpoint we mean, in the simplest terms, the simultaneous or overlapping presentation of two or more different melodic lines, or the presentation of the same melody in several voices with a larger or smaller time interval between the entrances of the different parts. We may get an idea of what is meant by the first procedure by assuming that a pianist sits down at the piano and plays "Yankee Doodle" with the left hand and at the same time plays "Dixie" with the right. From this somewhat crude, but none the less effective, example we can readily see how it is that we can recognize the two tunes presented simultaneously and how the total musical effect might be enhanced by such a procedure. The second procedure may be illustrated by a familiar round, such as "Three Blind Mice," in which the same melody is sung successively by different voices while the other voices continue to sing through the melody.

Actually, of course, harmony and counterpoint are overlapping concepts, for most, if not all, contrapuntal compositions have their harmonic aspects and vice-versa. We ordinarily simply classify a given composition according to which feature predominates. Because of psychological limits of our span of attention or comprehension, that is, because of our incapacity to attend to or comprehend more than a certain limited number of simultaneously presented lines of organizational complexity, we find that most compositions tend to exploit predominantly one manner of treatment at a time. Thus, as the contrapuntal treatment gets more complex, the harmonic treatment is likely to remain relatively simple; or as the harmonic texture and treatment grows in prominence the contrapuntal aspect of the music tends to remain within reasonable limits of complexity. If the level of complexity increases in both directions, the result is likely to be an instance of what Bosanquet calls "difficult beauty"—a composition that only the trained and experienced musician could hope to understand and enjoy fully.

Dependent upon and in many ways growing out of the melodic, harmonic, and contrapuntal principles of tonal organization which we may subsume under the heading of manners of treatment, there is another important means of bringing order into the realm of tone, namely, compositional pattern or formal design. If we take a motive consisting of a few notes or chords as our compositional unit, and expand it by the musical-technical devices of repetition and development, we may expand it into a larger musical idea or *theme*. On the basis of this theme we may construct by application of the several manners of treatment characteristic conventional forms such as the binary and ternary song-forms, rondo, sonata, fugue, and the like. These typical musical forms are the primary solutions of the problems of aesthetic design that composers through the ages have gradually achieved. We cannot go into details but must be content simply to observe that these forms, each in its own characteristic way, provide the means of reducing the multiplicity of details in a more extended tonal rhythmic structure to a certain over-all simplicity of structure, so that in the end there emerges a pattern that is within the limits of human comprehension. In the sonata form the whole divides into three main sections, called exposition, development, and recapitulation, which provide basic units for purposes of comparison and contrast.

Unless the listener is equipped by natural aesthetic sensitivity, experience, and training to perceptually intuit a large measure of the relations implicit in a given musical composition at the several levels of integration already suggested, his enjoyment of music is going to be slight in relation to what it might be if he were better equipped in all these respects. In other words, the failure to perceive the larger implications of the formal structure forces the listener to revert to a level of enjoyment corresponding to his powers of integration, a level that in extreme cases might be reduced to the simple enjoyment of the beauty of material, or of snatches of melody here and there, or of sections of harmony from time to time. It is at this high level of integration that the materials and forms of music in their affective character result in aesthetically expressive meanings of transcendent beauty.

# MUSIC

## Functional Music

In program music, dance music, and other types of music where music looks outside its own intrinsic means for assistance in conveying its message, or where it is subservient to other ends than its own, the enjoyment of music is modified by extraneous considerations. In program music, for example, the individual's enjoyment is modified by the fact that his attention is diverted to some extent from the music itself to the program, and to a consideration of the relation of the music to the programmatic ideas it is striving to express. In dance music, one's enjoyment is conditioned by questions of functional appropriateness; and so, likewise, in religious music, patriotic music, and all types of music with text, extra-musical factors condition the response of the individual.

In view of the great variety of individual differences among people, it is not at all surprising that a person should enjoy some type of functional music more than so-called absolute music; or that he might prefer music for the dance to religious music; or that he might be more responsive to the art song than to opera. Since the quality of one's enjoyment of music depends upon natural endowment, training, and experience, the highway to an enriched musical experience seems obvious. Repeated and continuous listening to good music undoubtedly lays the foundation for a fuller enjoyment of music; but the full richness and refinement of musical enjoyment can only come as one's understanding of music is improved through study and training.

# Chapter XI

# THE PROBLEM OF CRITICISM

by

George Boas

I

When critics write essays on works of art, they will be found upon examination to be saying a complex of two elements: (1) that they either like or dislike the work of art which they are criticizing; (2) that they approve or disapprove of it. The former is an expression of those reactions of pleasure and displeasure which certain experiences seem to have, even when they do not center upon works of art. Thus the color of a flower, the taste of a new dish, the sound of a bird, and so on, may without any reflection at all appear obviously pleasant or disagreeable, and no "principles of criticism" are needed to tell one that they are pleasant or the opposite. A child knows whether he likes certain foods or not; his liking has nothing to do, as far as he knows, with any question of their dietetic value, of their wholesomeness, of the high regard which doctors and other experts have of them, of the traditional consumption of them in all western European homes since the Flood. He just likes them or dislikes them.

It is of course possible that by dint of argument a parent may persuade a child to eat a food which he dislikes or to refrain from eating foods which he likes. These arguments may take the form of dietetic evidence or simply the form of rewards and punishments. But the fact that a child is brought to the point of changing his food-preferences does not imply that the foods in question have become either pleasant to his taste or unpleasant as the case may be.

## THE PROBLEM OF CRITICISM

An analogous situation obtains as regards works of art. If you like to listen to Lizst, argument from musical experts may induce you not to listen to him, but it cannot change the pleasantness of the sounds which his works produce in your ears into unpleasantness. If you dislike listening to him, knowledge of the fact that he was the inventor of the tone-poem, a great admirer of Wagner, a friend of all struggling musicians, a great piano virtuoso, a perfect example of nineteenth century baroque music, the creator of more difficult cadenzas than any other composer, will not make you turn from disliking the sound of his music to liking it, even though it may persuade you to be more tolerant of his music when played. You still like or dislike him regardless of what you yourself may say when in the presence of critics.

Approbation and disapprobation are quite different. They are always expressed in the form of certain principles or rules or standards. Thus a critic may disapprove of a play because it lacks unity, of a novel because vice triumphs in it instead of virtue, or of a picture because its subject-matter is sordid, or of a musical composition because it contains consecutive fifths, or of a piece of sculpture because it is not "true" to its material. He may approve of a play because it holds one's interest to the very end, of a novel because of its acute psychological analysis, of a picture because of its vigorous painting, of a musical composition because it is restful, of a piece of sculpture because it symbolizes the spirit of America. It is of no importance at this moment whether these principles are valid or even whether they make any sense. They are forms of argument which are used—and every one of them has been taken from a real essay in criticism—to justify or condemn certain aesthetic practices.

We have been made familiar with the possible—though not inevitable—conflict between liking and approbation in morals. It is an old story that one may see the better and pursue the worse. One likes to gossip but believes it to be wicked; one enjoys gambling, but thinks it anti-social; one is selfish, but believes in altruism; one dislikes one's wife, but believes marriage vows to be binding. In fact, most moral problems consist in harmonizing our likes and our principles of approbation; most moral casuistry consists in finding the reasons, as we put it, for doing certain things which we do not feel enthusiastic about doing. We find ourselves disapproving of what we like, approving of what we dislike; we hope to reach the point of approving and disapproving of what we like and dislike respectively.

In matters of art we go to a course in English literature and find that the poems which we have always enjoyed are considered by our teacher to be very poor poems. Being at bottom fairly docile, we try to like the poems which the teacher tells us are great, and our effort consists, let us assume, first in refraining from saying that we like those of which he disapproves, next in refraining from reading them, next in reading attentively those of which he approves, and it may very well be that before the end of the course we actually find ourselves having "outgrown" the poems which we used to admire. Exactly what psychological processes are involved in this change we do not know; all we can say is that our taste has changed; since we have taken on the taste of someone older than we and presumably more expert—or at any rate the taste which he has expressed *ex cathedra*—we say that our taste has not merely changed, but has improved.

Now if we call what we like our *taste,* since the word might seem to indicate a spontaneous untaught reaction to certain experiences, then we can truly say that there is no arguing about taste. You either like a thing or you don't. Nor can most of us give the reason why we like it. If we are reflective, we may generalize on our tastes and say that we like serene and calm music, like Bach's *Come, Sweet Death*— when transcribed for orchestra by Stokowski—or clear prose, like that of Voltaire, or spicy odors like that of geraniums. The question of whether such taste is *good taste* could never arise until someone questioned it, and no one would question his own taste until he had discovered that it was not universal. An American might not see anything peculiar in eating bacon and eggs for breakfast; a Frenchman might think it anything from comic to gulttonish—everyone knows, he might say, that the proper breakfast for a human being is coffee and rolls. In so far as a man's taste is that of the entire species, it might be fitting to say that it is normal, and if there is any reason to believe that it is better to enjoy whatever everyone else enjoys, then one might maintain that such taste was better than that which is peculiar and individual.

How taste in this very simple sense arises can be studied only by a psychologist. There is no more reason to believe that it contains any mysteries than there is to maintain that good eysight and good hearing are mysterious. A person who never heard of optics could still have normal or supernormal eyesight; a person who knows nothing of acoustics can hear as well as any psychologist. If you were to ask such a person why he saw so acutely, he would be at a loss to tell you. His ignorance of ophthalmology and the psychology of vision does not prevent him from telling what he sees and only a slight acquaintance with his fellow-men suffices for him to know whether his eyesight is better or worse than theirs. Similarly if he finds certain experiences agreeable or disagreeable, he has no need to know why, where "why" means the psychological causes of his pleasure and displeasure. In fact, there is reason to believe that if his pleasure and displeasure were explained to him causally, they would become just a shade less pleasant and unpleasant. But that is irrelevant to the issue here being discussed.

Again, if someone says to a man who enjoys the taste of alcohol, that he should not enjoy it since alcohol is a dangerous drug, leading to the formation of anti-social habits, causing men to waste nutritious grains in its manufacture, eating out the lining of the stomach, producing locomotor ataxia, prejudicing the welfare of the future generations, the drinker may discover that he has tastes which are bad morally and socially, but he can never be convinced on such grounds that he does not like alcohol. He may, as we have suggested above, be induced to give up drinking, but that is not giving up his taste. He has simply yielded to argument which is directed towards the reform of his behavior, not to the elimination of his likes and dislikes. The argument has not been either about the existence of his taste, or about its harmony with that of other people; it has been merely about its supposed evil effects. He has been given reasons for disapproving of drinking; he has not been given the causes of anyone's liking or disliking the taste of alcoholic liquors. We are thus differentiating between "causes" and "reasons"; the former being usually—though not necessarily—unconscious and determinative of likes and dislikes, the latter conscious and implicative of approbation and disapprobation.

At this point we must indulge in a bit of psychological speculation which can be judged only by its reasonableness. It seems probable that human beings are so constituted that they tend to find reasons for their likes and dislikes and tend to like the things of which they approve and dislike the things of which they disapprove. In other words, the ethical problem of harmonizing our beliefs and our actions has a strict aesthetic parallel. Psychoanalysts have maintained for years that most of our beliefs are "rationalizations" of our desires; a notion which occurs at least as early as Schopenhauer with his doctrine that the reason is created by the will for its own aims. Nor is it very far removed from the Marxian belief that "ideologies" are determined by our economic interests. Regardless of these special theories, it is a matter of common observation that when a principle of aesthetics is pronounced before us, in our reading or in lectures or conversation, which agrees with our taste, we tend to adopt it with much less reluctance than that with which we would adopt a principle which ran contrary to our taste. Similarly, if we have been convinced either by the logic of persuasion or that of conviction of the truth of certain aesthetic principles, we find ourselves beginning to like works of art which agree with the principles in question and to dislike those which disagree with them. The matter is not quite so simple as stated here, for there is some reason to believe that (1) no one would ever accept a principle which ran counter to his taste without a greater impulsion than the forces of logic and (2) there are some people so constructed that they are more uncertain of their taste than we appear to have indicated.

## II

The remarks of critics, we have said, are indicative both of what they like and that of which they approve. It can easily be seen that unless all men like the same things and approve of the same things, criticism will inevitably be various.

To begin with there are a great many writers who maintain that regardless of what a critic may say, he will always be confined to an expression of what we have called his "taste." They will maintain either for psychoanalytic or other reasons that principles of approbation are never more than rationalizations of taste and that therefore they are worthless. One need not believe in this theory to understand it, and we are more interested in understanding it than in arguing either pro or con. Assuming then that a critic will confine himself to an expression of his taste, what will be the nature of his criticism?

First and foremost, one must conclude that it can never transcend that which is immediately given in perception. It must be something which can be seen or heard or smelled or tasted. It must be sounds, colors, shapes, odors, and the like. If such a person talks about "form," it must be perceptual form, shape, pattern, structure, as these things—as this thing—appear before our eyes and ears. It is only in a metaphorical sense that one can "see" an allegory, an illustration, or any other element inherent in a work of art which might be said to require interpretation. Any two human beings see the same pattern when they look at a Chinese character; but one interprets the character as meaning a man or a house or a cosmic principle or human immortality, or what you will. Such a person knows that what he sees is not merely a visual pattern, but also a visual symbol. The other person, ignorant of Chinese, sees something which has no meaning beyond itself; he may nevertheless like or dislike what he sees and he may be able, if gifted verbally, to tell other people about what he likes. But however gifted he may be, he will be forced to confine his remarks to the vigor of the brush strokes, the balance of the whole character, its simplicity or complexity, or whatever other traits may be taken in by the eye. Such remarks are not necessarily otiose. It is a commonplace that one can see something which is pleasing without being aware of its details. People frequently grow rapturous over flowers without being able to describe them accurately. They have a general impression of agreeable color and form and odor and texture, and no specific impression of any details.

Such a critic, therefore, even if he confines himself to the expression of his taste, in our narrow meaning of this term, is performing a useful service. It is true that his remarks will not seem very persuasive to people who do not share his taste, but at the same time they may induce someone to look at the object of his remarks more closely. He does not explain why a flower with such characteristics is more pleasing than one with other characteristics, nor does he imply that Nature would have done better to stick to this flower-pattern and reject others. He states simply that he finds his flower pleasing and informs anyone willing to read him about what the flower is like. There is certainly nothing legislative in his comments nor is there any appraisal. He is strictly descriptive.

There probably has never been a purely descriptive critic, for even when we consider the work of such a writer as Anatole France in *La Vie Littéraire,* a writer whose conscious program was the pronouncement of his taste and nothing more, one sees that he always goes beyond description to approbation. He establishes his taste as a norm and seems to be telling his readers not only what he likes but also what they should like, whether they actually do or not. He thus sets himself up as a standard, for he ridicules books which he does not find to his liking and thus tries to induce his readers to see them as ridiculous. This is probably inevitable, however confused the logic of the position may be. Were one to explicate the dialectic, however, the first principle of such a type of criticism would be, *Those works of art are great which the critic likes.* One has then only to discover the general characters of such works of art, and one has a set of traits which will distinguish great art from small art. Insofar as the taste of the critic is characteristic of the taste of men in general, one might conclude that an artist who knew these rules would be sure of producing works of art which would please everybody—the word "everybody" being interpreted liberally.

The matter, however, is not quite so simple as it sounds. For only few readers approach a book without knowing what critics have said of it. They know that it has been praised by John Doe and condemned by Richard Doe. They know, moreover, something about the author, at least what other books he has written when he has written other books. They have read advertisements or reviews of the book. They have been introduced to it by friends who have praised or condemned it. They consequently never approach the book with a neutral mind. Nor should they be expected to. Readers cannot be asked to dehumanize themselves, to become "objective," to forget everything they ever learned, their whole past experience, to wipe off their minds all traces of their education. And consequently so trivial a factor as boredom may enter to upset the calculations of the critic—or those prophets of public taste known as merchandisers. People simply grow tired of certain types of art and their aesthetic fatigue may account for much of the change that the history of art shows.

Among the factors which influences a person's approach to a work of art are such things as one's knowledge of who likes it. One's awareness that the artist who made it belongs to a certain movement or artistic school, or was in a certain state of mind when he made it, are not without influence on our attitude. This has been clearly brought out in Richards' *Practical Criticism,* where even a poem of Ella Wheeler Wilcox was highly esteemed so long as the estimators were given no clue to the author's identity. One may say that such matters are childish and beneath serious consideration. But again, they are matters which are inevitably known to the reader— or spectator—and are read into the work of art whether they should be or not. A sketch by Delacroix may have no interest whatsoever until it is known to be by Delacroix. Then it fits into a larger context, as, for instance, the beginning of one of

his paintings. Is there any reason to ask one to forget that
it is the beginning of the painting in question and to estimate
it out of its context? Only if one arbitrarily decides that drawings should be seen as meaningless lines. But no one ever
saw anything a complete detachment. Any set of scrawls
is going to suggest something to an eye; that something need
not be illustrative or allegorical or even relevant to human
psychology. But except for the very rudimentary colors and
shapes whose agreeableness and disagreeableness depend on
childhood experiences so far buried in the mind as to be to
all intents and purposes forgotten, one's pleasure or displeasure
will be determined by suggestions and associations which are
bound to go beyond the object before one's eyes.

It is not difficult to imagine what some of these associations
may be. Any product of human creation is created by a definite
human being living at a definite time in a definite place.
Most of us have this information before we approach the work
of art in question. We read this knowledge into the work of
art or, if you prefer, we see the work of art with this knowledge
in our eyes. The three bits of information may, and usually
do, have differing degrees of clearness. We may be more
aware of the artist's biography than we are of his milieu,
his school, his time. Or we may know more of the tradition
into which he fits—as for instance in the case of certain
Italian primitives—than we do of his biography. But we
certainly must know that no artist ever floated like a cork on
the stream of history, barely getting wet. Even when he tries
to revive an artistic style of an earlier period, he cannot avoid
coloring his revivals with the tinge of his own time. The
archaistic Roman statues are seldom mistaken for really archaic
statutes by archaeologists; the neo-classicism of the early nineteenth century—the poems of Delille, the drawings of Flaxman
and the statues of Canova—would never be confused with

309

their ancient analogues. If one knows this, one cannot avoid seeing it. What would be gained from pretending not to see it?

Now when one is aware that a certain statue, let us say, is an early nineteenth century imitation of a Roman statue, one's liking or disliking that statue is going to be colored by that information. Similarly if one knows that a given book was written by a child of thirteen rather than by a man of thirty, that knowledge is going to color one's taste. If one thought that *The Young Visiters* had been written by Barrie rather than by Daisy Ashford, one would have read it as a literary fake and disliked it. Finally if one dislikes a certain style or school or period for religious or political or other reasons, as for instance the so-called Jesuit style of architecture, one is going to dislike churches built in that style. The writer of this essay when young discovered from reading the *Stones of Venice* that the dome of Santa Maria della Salute was made of wood and not of stone so that when he first saw the dome, he saw it as Ruskin wanted him to see it, with all the moral prejudices that that great aesthetic moralist was able to stir up. It was only later—much later—that he was able to ask, "Well, what of it?"

Critics are frequently engaged in the process of substituting the personalities of artists, their periods, schools, national traditions, and the like, for the works of art conditioned by them. By writing a biographical essay on Michelangelo, they induce their readers to see the sculptor's personality in his art and hence, if they do not like his personality, they will induce their readers not to like his sculpture and painting. Or they will see the Baroque as one of the effects of the Counter-Reformation and since, let us say, they admire the Counter-Reformation as a process of self-purification within the Church, they will read this process into the paintings and sculptures and architecture of the Baroque. As a result they will expect their readers not merely to admire the Counter-Reformation, but also to enjoy the works of art which it theoretically created. Or they will hate the Germans and they will point out why they hate them in an article denouncing a national tradition which has undoubtedly been the curse of Western Europe for about one hundred and fifty years. They will see in German music all the *furor teutonicus* of Goering, with the result that their readers when they hear Brahms will hear the voice of the Nazis.

Logically there is no connection between these things. It does not follow that because a German is cruel and blood-thirsty and unscrupulous and megalomaniacal, that the music which he writes will have the same traits or, what is more important, will create them in people who listen to it. But on the other hand, no one ever listened to music with an absolutely vacant mind. Nor can he be expected to. If listening to *The Ring* awakes images of Hitler, that fact is a fact and cannot be denied. I choose *The Ring* deliberately because its composer had a definite social purpose in mind—as comes out in his prose writings—and the question which is bound to arise in such cases is which context is the music to be heard in: in the context which the composer intended or in one deliberately worked up by the listener?

## III

So far we have been dealing with expressions of critic's likes and dislikes, with his taste. We now turn to his principles of approbation and disapprobation.

In the last analysis the logical basis of principles of evalua-tion is bound to be a fiat, a declaration of faith that certain things are good and others bad, a postulate or definition. For from the statement, *This is,* we cannot deduce the statement,

*This ought to be,* unless we also assume—and it will always be an assumption—*Whatever is, is right.* If we argue, *That which all people consider good, is good,* we are still basing our reasoning upon an assumption of value, an assumption of the uniformity of human nature, an assumption of the indifference of historical events to evaluations. All formal reasoning rests ultimately on unproved premises and there is no cause to think that reasoning about values differs in any respect from reasoning about other matters in this particular.

We are not, fortunately, obliged to justify any special postulates of value in this brief essay. But we are interested in pointing out in what region of discourse they lie. Thus certain critics will use value-theories which differ profoundly from those of other critics; some, for instance, basing their criticism upon what they believe to be certain eternal values, others admitting a frankly relativistic position, in which the system of relations includes geographical, temporal, sociological, and almost every other conceivable human interest. Let us for the sake of simplicity and regardless of common usage, call whatever positive value a critic finds in a work of art "beauty." We shall then find, as has been pointed out elsewhere,[1] that the sentence, *This is beautiful,* in actual practice means any one or combination of the following eight expressions.

1. That the artist thought he had succeeded in creating the work of art as he had planned it.

2. That the artist succeeded in creating the work of art which the critic believed him to have planned.

3. That the artist found his work of art useful—in any one of the many ways in which works of art can be useful.

4. That the critic has found the work of art useful.

[1] See the writer's *Primer for Critics,* ch. 1.

312

5. That the artist found great value in creating the work of art.

6. That the critic found great value in watching—or imagining—the artist's creating of the work of art.

7. That the artist enjoyed observing—or listening to or reading, etc.—his work of art after it was created.

8. That the critic enjoyed observing—and so on—the artist's work of art.

Usually these sentences are not expressed in so pedantic a manner. If they were, there is no doubt that they would never be confused with each other. The ambiguities appear only after some analysis of what critics actually say.

Thus to begin with, critics seldom make a sharp distinction between the two kinds of value which are supposed—and rightly—to inhere in any work of art. The former is what may be called its terminal value, the latter its instrumental. Terminal value is believed to be good-in-itself, something which does not necessarily have utility, but is self-justified. It appears in such expressions as *Virtue is its own reward, Beauty is its own excuse for being.* Readers who have a little knowledge of the history of philosophy know that Aristotle maintained that happiness had such value; it was the justification of all human striving, all human action; it was that for which other things existed and which did not exist for anything else. It has frequently been maintained that aesthetic value is precisely of this type. The most usual expression of this idea in modern times is that which runs through the "art for art's sake" movement; it appears in Oscar Wilde's famous epigram, *All art is utterly useless.* When philosphers of art point out that we are not supposed to take a "practical" attitude towards works of art, they are maintaining something which is probably close to this point of view.

On the other hand, some critics have been equally forceful in insisting that art which does not serve some useful function has no excuse for being. It is sometimes difficult to tell whether they are maintaining that such works of art are ugly or whether they may be beautiful and yet should be eliminated. In Tolstoi's case it is fairly clear that he so disapproved of works of art which did not meet his ethical demands, that he disliked them intensely and saw them as ugly. His attitude, and we may assume that of all people he at least was sincere, developed to the point where he disliked that of which he disapproved and could see no beauty in moral evil. Plato's case is somewhat different; his disapprobation of the poets who teach harmful lessons is based entirely on moral grounds, but he never tells us exactly what he means by "beauty" and his treatment of it in the *Symposium* is such that we suspect he saw no difference between what might be called beauty and what might be called goodness. That is, he would probably have been willing to make such a distinction for purposes of discussion but would deny that the two things could be separated in fact. An act which was morally wrong might be aesthetically right for purposes of conversation, but in actuality one could not devote himself to the aesthetic aspects of the act and thus annul its moral aspects. And since ethics is the evaluation of all acts, whether those of artists or of anyone else, the ethical judgment had primacy over all others. Human acts are individually complete wholes and must be judged in their entirety, he might have reasoned, had the question arisen.

When one judges anything by its effect upon conduct, one is fastening one's attention upon its instrumental value rather than upon its terminal value. It is thought of as an instrument for the attainment of goodness or evil, not as something good or evil in itself. That works of art can have some effect upon morals may not be obvious, but neither is the denial of the assertion.  For generations people have believed rightly or wrongly that looking at pictures might stimulate good or evil thought which would lead to good or evil acts, that reading books might influence one's conduct; Aristotle and Plato believed that even listening to music would change one's behavior. It would indeed seem strange that so large a part of our life should be utterly without effective influence upon our action. This influence may not be exactly what might be anticipated: reading moral tales like those of Maria Edgeworth may not make a boy more moral; it may make him simply a hypocrite. But if reading does not have some effect which will eventually result in changed behavior, then it might reasonably be concluded that education in the sense of "book-learning" is little more than pleasure and pain.  We are not here interested in debating this issue, but the question must be raised because of its reasonableness.  It is furthermore at the heart of a whole school of criticism which as a matter of fact was the dominant school up to about a hundred years ago.

Our first ambiguity thus resides in the doubt whether the value-terms in critical statements mean terminal or instrumental value.  We have indicated merely one kind of instrumental value—the moral.  There are of course others: the economic, for instance, whose influence upon the history of art is usually obscured but is nevertheless much stronger than critics have been willing to believe, the religious, the psychotherapeutic, the patriotic, and so on.  The consideration of art as an instrument for the attainment of all of these values has determined both the form and the content of works of art; they have been cherished and despised in all of these contexts, and it would be the height of obscurantism to eliminate them from any study of criticism.

The second ambiguity occurs in the very meaning of the word "art."  At times this word means the finished product, what is usually called the "work of art;" at times it will be found to mean the process which terminates in a work of art, or what has been called "artistry." There is at least a logical possibility that the value of one is irrelevant to the value of the other. We know, for instance, that in mathematics we can arrive at the right answer in what is called an inelegant manner. A proof of a theorem which is called inelegant is not given a bad name because it reached the wrong conclusion, but because it is in itself clumsy, roundabout, based on too many assumptions, and the like, considerations which are purely technical. In the field of ethics we speak of good deeds badly performed, such as tactless charity. Similarly in the field of aesthetics, one can think of good plots badly told or a good pictorial composition badly painted, and so on. The distinction is of course artificial, for there is no act aside from its perform-ance, and there is no picture really aside from the technique which eventuated in it. Furthermore a work of art is in some sense a whole which cannot be analyzed into form and content except for purposes of conversation. Yet in conversation it is possible to emphasize what might be called the technique of a work of art, to think of that technique while it was alive and in process, to see how a man reached a certain end without thinking of the end which he has rescued. Whether one should do this or not does not concern us; the fact is that many critics have maintained that problems of technique, of artistry, alone should concern the critic. He should interest himself not in whether the work of art is in itself worth while or not; he should interest himself solely in how it was produced.

A third ambiguity lies in the point of view of the critic. Every work of art can be thought of from either the point of view of the spectator, the reader, the audience, or from the point of view of the artist who made it. There can be no denying that what Beethoven, for instance, heard in one of his string quartettes is something more or less different from what his contemporaries—to say nothing of us—heard in it. An artist is presumably expressing what he knows intimately; he is trying to communicate something to us who depend precisely on what means of communication he may use to discover his meaning. All of us have had the experience of not making our meaning clear even when we are using a language with which we have been familiar from childhood. The difficulty may reside in the inadequacy of our language, which may be simply our limited vocabulary, the obscurity of our ideas, or the nature of what we are trying to communicate. How much the more difficult is the situation in which the subject-matter does not lend itself to linquistic expression, when it is not what is commonly called an idea, but is, for instance, an emotional state, the nature of which is hidden from the artist himself. In such a case the artist is bound to find a value— or its absence—in his works of art as well as in his artistry which need not be the same as that found by a critic. Critics like to flatter themselves that they understand an artist's purposes and motives; their technique usually consists in attributing to the artist the emotions which his work of art has stimulated in them. That is about as sound as arguing that when a child angers his father, the child is expressing his own anger.

During the romantic period it was common to maintain that the real value of art lay in artistry from the artist's point of view. The work of art might be destroyed as soon as created, the value for the artist lay in the process of creating it, not in contemplating it once created. This notion, which is similar to that expressed by Novalis in the parable of the Blue Flower which may always be sought and never found, is probably sound psychology. At any rate there is some reason to believe that many artists write for the pleasure of writing and not for the pleasure of reading their books once they are written; that many painters paint pictures not to look at them afterwards, but for what is sickishly called "the joy of creating." No one, to be sure, ever had one isolated motive for doing anything, but the sacrifices which many artists have made to paint or write or carve in their own fashion, regardless of public opinion, fame, starvation, poverty, and the other rewards of virtue, are evidence enough that if there is no value to an artist in artistry, whatever the end-term may be, there is no explaining why many artists continue their work. But when one argues from this to the conclusion that spectators should identify themselves with the artist, should try to recapture the value which the artist found in making his work of art, one is guilty among other things of advocating an impossible program. Critics need not try to identify themselves with artists for the simple reason that they are not artists. They may be artists as far as the art of criticism is concerned, but when they are criticizing a painting, they do not and cannot become painters, to say nothing of becoming the painter who painted the picture they are criticizing. Critics are spectators, listeners, readers, and one of their tasks it to point out what value the work of art or the artistry has from the point of view of the spectator. That value need not be the value which the artist found in his work of art. If it should be, well and good; that is a happy accident. It is interesting to know every-thing that can be known of course. But it is more interesting to know those things which are true or plausible and relevant to general experience, when the person communicating them thinks that he is saying something true. If a critic is willing to say that his criticism is entirely speculative, no one can object to his indulging himself in such sport. But let him suffer no illusions about the precise import of what he has to say.

It would be desirable if critics would make certain verbal

distinctions when they are in a field of probable ambiguity. If they are talking about the work of art, they would be charitable to say so; if they are talking about the artistry, that could be easily told. They could distinguish between the two kinds of value—the distinction after all is a commonplace in philosophy and easily grasped. They could also avoid confusing the point of view of the spectator with that of the artist.

## IV

When one has made certain distinctions, it is inevitable that misunderstandings arise. We shall devote this section of our essay to anticipating some misunderstandings.

In the first place, the fact that one distinguishes between instrumental value and terminal value does not mean that if something is useful it cannot also be beautiful. Any instrument or tool may be said to have been devised as a means toward a certain end, but that does not imply that it cannot be valued as an end in itself. In fact, there is reason to believe that many of our *objets d'art* are obsolete—or obsolescent—tools. One thinks of an open fire on a hearth as essentially an instrument for warming a room; but in a modern house it is utilized not for warmth but for looks. Our lives are filled with objects and activities which are valued both for their utility and for their beauty. Speech, for instance, may be thought of in terms of its clarity, its adequacy to what it is trying to express; or it may be thought of in terms of style, beauty of phrase, rhythm, and the like, none of which need be relevant to its more utilitarian ends.[2] Or one may have something which is usually thought of as primarily an *objet d'art* and yet find it in actuality valued as an instrument: pictures in the hands of a picture-dealer may be valued by him

[2] This does not mean that the writer of this essay admires decorative prose; he dislikes it intensely.

above all for what they will bring in the market.

Values are determined by evaluation and the only way which we have at our disposal—whatever may be the way of the angels—for knowing what value anything has is to see how it is valued. There may exist some people who have an intuition into the values which things have, a direct communication with supernatural powers which reveals to them secrets which the rest of humanity does not share. But if we are in the realm of discussion, such mysteries may be set aside as not suitable. It should never be forgotten that the correct answer to all problems in natural science is, *This happens because God so wills.* And yet such an answer throws no light on anything. So in our field, it would be senseless to deny the existence of intuited and eternal values, senseless because by their very nature they are discovered by a process which eludes all investigation. But the people who believe in them must also grant that if they exist, they form no part of what might be charitably called science. Hence if we find a thing or a process which actually is valued both for its utility and its beauty, then we have to conclude that it has both instrumental and terminal value.

In the second place, there is no contradiction in maintaining that a work of art has positive value from the spectator's point of view and negative from the artist's—or of course the reverse. In more concrete terms, there is no reason why a reader should find a poem ugly which its author found ugly, or that a poet should find a poem beautiful which a reader has found beautiful. An artist might be expected to demand certain things from his works of art which the public does not demand. It would be folly to deny the desire of all people to have others agree with them. We might expect a unanimity not only of ideas but also of emotions. All knowledge rests upon the universal meaning of words, all truth is supposed to be un-

touched by the accidents of time and space and human preferences, and similarly all human beings are supposed to react in
about the same way to the same stimuli. The fact that the
same stimuli are never found in two sets of experience except
under laboratory conditions ought to convince people that there
will be a large gap between the findings of laboratory psychology and living experience. No one would deny that if one
could take two human beings whose psychological makeup was
exactly alike and submit them to exactly the same stimuli,
they would react in exactly the same fashion, whether the
stimulus was an electric shock or a painting by Piero della
Francesca. But no one ought to deny that no human beings
have the same psychological makeup and that they do not look
at Piero in the same way with the same resulting judgments.

What you see in a work of art depends to some extent upon
what you are looking for.[3] There have been people—and
periods—when one looked above all for subject-matter in a
painting. It was taken for granted that all paintings were
illustrative, even anecdotal, and the value of the picture de-
pended on the value of "what it had to say." To confront
such people with paintings by Braque would leave them either
puzzled or disgusted. We have shown elsewhere that even
when a given work of art is highly esteemed over a period
of years, it is not always valued for the same reasons and
may indeed be highly valued for opposing, if not contradictory,
reasons. Proudhon and Zola both admired Courbet's paintings,
but their principles of approbation were close to being contradictory. The Mona Lisa has up to very recent times been
universally admired, but the critics of the sixteenth century
admired it for its fidelity to "nature," those of the nineteenth
century—following Gautier and Pater—saw it as a symbol

[3] This is beautifully demonstrated in a paper by Meyer Howard
Abrams; "Unconscious Expectations in the Reading of Poetry," ELH,
Vol. 9, No. 4, Dec. 1942, pp. 235 ff.

of "enigmatic womanhood." If you ask which was right, you are asking a foolish question. For no one in the sixteenth century could have seen it as a symbol of enigmatic womanhood for the simple reason that women did not become enigmatic until a certain form of romanticism had become popular. A glance at *Bartlett's Quotations,* that repository of platitudes, will convince one that before Goethe women were only too well understood. Men may not have admired them; they certainly said harsh things about them; but they thought they understood them only too well. The history of ideas shows among other things that there are fashions in ideas and ways of thinking as in clothes, and that a problem, for instance, does not always disappear because it has been solved; it sometimes disappears because people are tired of it. The element of intellectual boredom as a cause of historical change may not seem very profound; it will indeed seem revoltingly superficial to a large proportion of the few people who will read these lines. But that is attributable to the shortness of the public memory.

If this is so, then it is inevitable that different people will approve of works of art and artistry for a variety of reasons. The question now arises which of these reasons are legitimate and which are not.

Leaving aside the matter of intuition and revelation, is there anything in the nature of art which makes one kind of appreciation more relevant than another? To argue this matter thoroughly would require several volumes and certainly more information than the writer of this essay possesses. It may be asserted with some confidence, however, that the clash in opinion arises over the epistemological question: Is there such a thing as immediate knowledge? By "immediate" I mean—in this context—a supposed assertion which will spontaneously arise when a human being is confronted by an experience. It is sometimes said that when a human being with normal eyesight is confronted with a patch of, let us say, redness, he will without any reflection—meditation—say, "This is red." He is not inferring anything; he is simply observing. Such knowledge is held to be indubitable; it is the basis of all other knowledge; it is the proper thing to say on such an occasion, the assertion which will unavoidably be made; it is embedded, so to speak, in the experience of redness.

Let us say dogmatically—for we cannot do more here—that such a point of view seems highly questionable. It is true that if one asks for the logical evidence for most assertions, one will be given after lengthy analysis a list of assertions which are based upon sensory perception. No one would deny that the best proof of the color of something is observation. But it must also be noted that when confronted with a patch of redness, one says, *This is red,* only if one is asking oneself—or has been asked by someone else—*What is this color?* It is not true that all knowledge consists in answers to questions of identification. We also have questions of causality, of practicality (what shall I do?), of purpose, and so on. The desire to identify what is before one is only one of the many equally legitimate impulses to knowledge which may arise. And what is more, when one is asked to identify something, one has to have in mind some scheme of classification which may simply be taken for granted. It is no more essential or fundamental or natural or primitive that the question, *What is that?* be answered by giving the color or some other sensory content, than by giving one of a dozen other possible identifications. Thus the red patch may be a piece of cotton or wool, a flower, a flash of light, a signal, a symbol, and there is no saying in advance which context provides the "right" answer, unless the context is also given in advance. If a given experience really exists in a variety of contexts, then a variety of identifications is right. If red is the color of a strontium flame and the question arises in an elementary course in chemistry, it is just as correct to say, *That is strontium,* as to say, *That is red,* and a great deal more intelligent.

We are maintaining that the context appropriate to judgments is not given in the content of an experience, but is assumed before the experience is had. When we are walking in the country and someone says, pointing to a flower, *what is that?* we know beforehand that he wants the name, popular or botanical, of the flower. Custom alone tells us that; the flower doesn't. So in the case of works of art, there is nothing in a picture which obliges the human mind to pronounce one judgment rather than another. In fact, only a cursory knowledge is needed of the history of criticism to learn that a variety of legitimate answers has seemed proper since the Renaissance. To many critics living in the time of Vasari, the "natural" comment to make about a picture was in the context of its fidelity to its subject; in the early nineteenth century, critics began discussing pictures as if they were hieroglyphs; Freudian critics see them as evidence of their makers' repressions; Marxian critics see them as comments on the class-struggle. Such comments may indeed be foolish, but only if they are false. One cannot say that just because the critics are talking about works of art, they should not discuss them as representations of a subject-matter or as a symbolic expression of repressions or as whatever else they may actually be. There are some things which no work of art is; there are some things which only certain individuals are—in spite of Neoplatonists and Hegelians. But when a thing really stands in a context, there is no reason why human beings should not say so.

Works of art, being extremely complex, do stand in a great variety of contexts. What is more, their value depends on a variety of contexts. Sometimes incidents which do not appear in the work of art at all make it more interesting and moving. For instance, no one who does not know Christian iconography can thoroughly appreciate medieval and much renaissance painting and sculpture, just as one who does not know classical mythology cannot understand a good deal of English poetry. The keys to the symbolism are not in the works of art; they have to be possessed by the spectator before-hand and they give him information which helps determine his judgments. For example, one is standing before a picture which looks like a double portrait of two men in very elegant clothing; one of them has a thin trickle of blood oozing from his scalp and holds in his outstretched hand a book upon which is a jagged stone. One may make several interesting and indeed true judgments about this picture without any knowl-edge whatsoever about its subject-matter. One may comment on its technique, on its beautiful form, on its exquisite color, on the almost incredibly "spiritual" expression of the faces. But when one knows that the young man with the stone is Saint Stephen, surely one's comments become more rather than less intelligent. The very restraint of the picture representing so horrible a martyrdom as his is moving and gives the picture a value which it would not have otherwise. It is possible indeed that a person who does not know the meaning of the picture may value it as highly as one who does, but what sense does it make to say that one who understands its meaning is not treating it "aesthetically"?[4] One may by fiat refuse to consider such judgments as aesthetic, but a restriction of that sort eventuates in nothing but an impoverishment of interest. Moreover since the picture is as it is because of its meaning, one does not even understand the picture's nature until one understands its subject-matter.

An even more obvious case is a picture by Gauguin painted

[4] I am referring, as may not be obvious, to Jean Fouquet's *Etienne Chevalier et son Patron.*

towards the close of his life. It is a simple village landscape of cottages with pointed roofs under the snow. As a technical stunt it cannot compare with his South Sea Island subjects. It has none of the brilliance of color, none of the intensity of expression, none of the originality and exoticism of subject; it is in fact a very commonplace landscape which any one of a dozen academic painters might have painted. But when one knows its date and the fact that it was painted while Gauguin was actually in Tahiti, far from French villages and snow, it cannot but assume a new emotional force. This may be called illegitimate. But again the position of a work of art in the history of an artist's career just happens to be one of those things which give value and interest, when it is known and can be read into the work of art. If it is excluded, again by fiat, the exclusion is arbitrary and in effect obscurantistic.

I should assert then—though I make no pretense of having done more than suggest the reasonableness of my assertion—that a critic's first business is to know as much as possible about works of art and artistry. It is not his business to eliminate one by one the relationships which make art valuable and interesting to human beings, but to uncover them and to point them out to his readers. This will imply the multivalence or art, not a kind of abstract univalence. It will imply also that aesthetic value is no different from any other kind of value; that it is not eternal and supernatural, but temporal, historical, and woven intimately into the texture of human experience. Works of art have value because they have been valued, and it is the critic's task in part to say how and why they have been valued.

Second, the critic will cease to define the arts by the materials which they use, stone, words, colors, gestures, but by the human purposes which they serve. A picture is what it is not merely because it is painted, but because it is an allegory, a literal copy of reality, an abstraction, a bit of satire, a liberation of a tortured man's repressions, a commodity which he can sell, and so on. A poem, a painting, a dance, and a short story may have more in common if thus viewed, than four paintings. It is true that no painting can do what a poem does, nor can a piece of music do exactly the same thing as an essay. I am not denying that the materials used have a great influence on the results obtained. But if a man is judging a work of art, he can reasonably be expected to be sensitive to precisely these differences and to point them out if it is worth while.

Finally, the critic need not announce his judgment of the greatness or littleness of works of art, for such judgments can be made more adequately by each spectator for himself. That Mr. T. S. Eliot approves of Dante and not of Milton—or did at any rate at last reading—is of great interest; but it does not mean that we are obligated to the assumption of his taste. He happens to be a very influential poet and whatever he says about other poets is worth reading; but whereas the principles of approbation which he expresses are worth knowing, they need not be ours. Mr. Eliot is a very sensitive reader and an unparalleled prose-writer, unparalleled in the clarity of his sentences. He sees things which we do not see; he spots absurdities which we do not spot; and if we read him and enjoy discovery, we shall profit from our reading. But that does not commit us to accepting his judgments of value as our own. He, like all critics, fits into a pattern which is much bigger than his own mind; his ideas are derived from other ideas which can be deciphered within this pattern. Anyone who knew anything about the antiromanticism of such writers as Charles Maurras and, in this country, of Messrs. Babbitt and More, was able to fit Mr. Eliot's standards of value into the total philosophical movement to which he never hesitated to admit adherence. But those assumptions which led him to make certain judgments which seemed alarming to conventional readers when they were first announced, can be estimated just as any assumptions can be estimated. The reader will either accept them or reject them, just as he will accept or reject any other assumptions. But unless one believes that people who write critical essays have a kind of intuition which informs them immediately about the value of works of art and artistry, one will feel no duty to do more than try to understand their writings. And if they do operate by intuition, then essays are works of supererogation; their one task is merely to pronounce, like Heraclitus's Sibyl.

# INDEX

# INDEX

# INDEX